# Praise for *Dr. Fisher's Life on the Ark*

Les Fisher's life is one great adventure after another. . . . He's the only person I know who "speaks" gorilla, has flown pigeons for General Patton, and cashed a million dollar check from Ray Kroc. A generation grew up watching Les Fisher on TV. I know; I'm one of them. His influence on the Lincoln Park Zoo is profound, but more than a great zoo director, he's a legendary Chicago icon. His stories of catching animals flying around TV sets, or running amuck on the wrong side of the barrier on zoo grounds are mind-blowing. If only we could live a life half as exciting as his . . . well, we'd be exhausted.

**Steve Dale,**
**Host, *Pet Central* (WGN Radio) and *Animal Planet Radio***
**Author, *My Pet World***

Dr. Fisher's incredible experiences come to life in this entertaining account of his years working among the animals and the humans who cared for them.

His intimate look into the challenges of being both a veterinarian and zoo director is inspiring and at times hilarious.

Dr. Fisher has done it all—veterinary officer in General Patton's unit, TV personality, animal handler, fundraiser, and worldwide tour leader—with style, a sense of adventure and the right balance of talent, humility, and humor, to thrive in a most challenging field.

Dr. Fisher's book gives its reader the vicarious experience of the day-to-day challenges faced by a zoo director and veterinarian—demanding, rewarding, funny, sad, enlightening, and bizarre.

**Joan Embery**
**Naturalist and Animal and Conservation Ambassador**

This story of Les Fisher's life reflects a passion for all life and sets an example for people of all ages who want to work with animals and help save the natural world.

If you know Les Fisher, you know that his life has been as diverse and unique as that of the wildlife he has cared for. His knowledge of animal behavior has served him well, from handling escaped gorillas, city politicians, hungry tourists on a luxury African safari, to the millions of people who visit the zoo each year.

I found Les's stories to be fascinating, fun, unpredictable, and very rewarding. This book should be read by everyone who enjoys wildlife and remembers Marlin Perkins and *Mutual of Omaha's Wild Kingdom*.

**Jim Fowler**
**Co-host, *Mutual of Omaha's Wild Kingdom* and**
**Presenter of *Wildlife Ambassadors on Television***


Dr. Les Fisher—one of the grand gentlemen of the zoo world—shares incredible stories in *Life on the Ark*. Working with animals on a daily basis brings along its share of adventure, and after 45 years Les has experienced just about everything!

**Jack Hanna**
**Director Emeritus, Columbus Zoo and**
**Aquarium Host, *Jack Hanna's Animal Adventures***

*Dr. Fisher's Life on the Ark* takes us on a captivating voyage that challenges anything Noah faced. Not many members of the greatest generation can say they served in Patton's Third Army in charge of 2,000 pigeons—Signal Corp Unit, of course. Fisher's life didn't start out in an ark. He was dedicated to saving individual animals, but as the world population encroached on animal habitats, Dr. Fisher realized that his ship had changed. Zoos became havens and Dr. Fisher became captain of a true Ark, trying to save whole species from extinction. This book is that ship's log; a daily account of the adventure, crisis and love that occurred within every twenty-four hours of his command of the U.S.S. Lincoln Park Zoo. It's an amazing life any one of us would trade for our own. In this book, now we can.

**Bill Kurtis**
**Newsman and Television Producer**

# Dr. Fisher's Life on the Ark

*Green Alligators, Bushman, and*
*Other "Hare-Raising Tales"*
*from America's Most Popular Zoo*
*and Around the World*

## Lester E. Fisher, DVM
Foreword by Betty White

COMMUNICATIONS
Evanston, Illinois

© 2005 Lester Fisher

Published by

Racom Communications
815 Ridge Ave.
Evanston, IL 60202

Catalog-in-Publication data available from the Library of Congress.

Printed in the United States of America.
ISBN: 0-9704515-6-3

To Bushman, one of the greatest lowland gorillas
that ever lived, and the only zoo animal
I ever dreamed about.
May your spirit continue to inspire children
to care about all living creatures
and thereby assure their future.

# Contents

# Foreword by Betty White

Dr. Fisher and I met some thirty-plus years ago. It was at a trustee meeting of Morris Animal Foundation, an organization dedicated to a healthier tomorrow for companion animals and wildlife. I was, of course, impressed to meet the Director of the famous Lincoln Park Zoo in Chicago, but when I discovered this man had just done a complicated operation on the tooth of a Bengal tiger, I became an instant devotee. Our friendship, as well as our work for Morris Animal Foundation, continues to this day.

My interest in zoos started early on, tagging after my Mom and Dad who went to zoos often, not just to please their little girl, but because they enjoyed the experience—some zoos more than others—and would have gone even if they had never had me. It was from them I learned that a visit to the zoo was like traveling to a whole new country inhabited by wondrous creatures. They taught me not to rush from one exhibit to the next, but to take time watching one group until I began to really *see* the animals and their interactions. They taught me the difference between "good zoos" and those other places that displayed animals for all the wrong reasons and sent you home feeling sad.

Happily, the zoo community has changed its philosophy over the years. Good zoos are moving toward becoming protectors—better yet, conservers—rather than simply collectors of the wildlife on our shrinking planet. Good zoos today work cooperatively—sharing information, loaning animals to improve breeding situations, and working toward the concept of a zoo serving as a modern-day Ark for the perpetuation of wildlife in peril.

Among some of my happiest zoo experiences has been visiting Lincoln Park Zoo in the company of Les Fisher and going backstage to meet his magnificent gorilla group—up close and personal.

Zoos aside, it has always been such fun to hear Les and his delightful wife Wendy's accounts of their many adventures in Africa—some funny, some harrowing, but always interesting. These anecdotes make this book such a treat for those of us who travel vicariously, by armchair.

So sit back and take a cozy trip to the zoo, to Africa and beyond. Enjoy!

*Betty White*

Betty White

# Preface:
# The zoo gets in your blood

Almost 45 years to the day I began working with Chicago's Lincoln Park Zoo—first as its part-time zoo doctor, then for 30 years as the Director of the Zoo—I retired, leaving behind a great job, wonderful people, and a very large family of amazing animals.

Being the director of a big city zoo has its share of politics, fundraising responsibility, and photo opportunities, as well as the expected animal stories. There were the times I'd been called upon to pull a jaguar's tooth, slip down and crawl quickly under an elephant, or die, and chase an escaped gorilla—more than once. There were 40-plus safari adventures through India, Papua New Guinea and Africa that brought me unbelievable joy and, often, great danger, expeditions to Iceland to collect birds, and much, much more.

All of my stories start out being about animals, but in many it is the behavior of the people around them that must have left many of the animals shaking their heads. There are moments that were funny, sad, scary, and every emotion in between. Though retired, I never really left the zoo. Like the circus, once the zoo gets in your blood it stays with you forever. I am still very much a part of it and hope I always will be.

Since stepping down as the Zoo's director, I began looking back—thinking more about all the experiences I had at the zoo, my earlier career as an army veterinarian, volunteering my services at an animal shelter, starting an animal hospital, and my other adventures with animals of all kinds and sizes. The idea for this book came about as I realized how much I wanted to share the fascinating and often exciting world of which I was a part. There were good times, hard times, many *silly* and sad times that filled my days and, quite often, my nights, as well. There were famous names—some of them humans, some not—that became part of my story, as I became part of theirs. This is not my autobiography or even a memoir, but a collection of stories I want to share about some of the great friends I'll never forget—and a few people as well.

To me, the zoo was not work. It was long hours, including many seven-day weeks, yet I felt privileged to be a part of what is essentially a small city of living creatures—interacting people and animals. I was honored to be doing something that mattered in an amazing community. I went about my daily routine, though my routine was anything but that. My office was in the monkey house of a zoo, in the middle of a major park, next to Lake Michigan, three miles from the traffic, crowds, and high energy that is characteristic of downtown Chicago, one of the world's major centers of arts and commerce.

I also lived across the street from my job for many years and, like other zoo neighbors, I awoke each morning to the raucous sounds of sea lions barking and the occasional lion's roar. It was a great way to start the day and a great life to lead.

Many wonderful people made it possible and I am indebted to them. They are a part of the stories that make up this book. I will always be grateful to Marlin Perkins, the man who became America's first celebrity zoo director and a national television star. He gave me the opportunity to join the Lincoln Park Zoo family in Chicago. Initially Marlin hired me as the Zoo's part-time vet and later, when he left Chicago for St. Louis, he provided the opening that led to my being appointed the Zoo's director. In 1986 Marlin died at the age of 84, leaving behind a great legacy. I remember him best as my friend. I want to also acknowledge the people of the Chicago Park District, the parent body that employed me for so many years and provided the valuable support and funding, then stayed out of the way and let me run the zoo as I felt it should be run. People can say what they will about working for an agency of city government, but I had a great relationship with these folks—so much so that I spent 30 years as the zoo's director *working without a contract*. That would be unusual today, but I think it says something about integrity and honor.

Certainly The Lincoln Park Zoo Society and its dedicated board members, its donors, members, and staff through the years all have my sincerest thanks for paving the yellow brick road and making one of America's great zoos what it is today.

I will always have a special affection and appreciation for my staff. They brought incredible expertise and dedication to their jobs—and their animals. And for those animals, which became my extended family and brought me both joy and sorrow; without them my life would not have been nearly as rich. For them, I will always have a special place in my heart.

I am pleased that Kevin Bell, the young man I hired out of college as my Bird Curator, grew to take over as my successor. Kevin has played a supportive role in this writing endeavor, and we continue to share a special relationship. I'm proud that the Zoo's future is in good hands.

Thanks also to Joe Marconi who, after writing about a dozen or so books of his own, helped so much in the development of this one. And, to Rich Hagle and Racom Communications, who had the confidence to publish this book. My volunteer readers, Silas Mayberry, Suzanne Ridenour and Judith Tusynski, generously gave of their time to proof the final manuscript.

To the Chicago area media, my thanks for their support, their understanding, as well as their stories and photos, some of which have been included in this book.

Through the years, my family put up with all that went with my unusual job, sharing—and continuing to share—my lifetime of animal adventures and memories. I thank them for that. A very special note of appreciation to my wife Wendy, without whose encouragement, patience, and support my animal memories would have never made it to these pages.

And finally, to all the people of Chicago, who for generations provided loving and generous support of one of the oldest, most popular zoos in America, and who continue to make it for me the most exciting and enriching place in the world, thank you.

## Welcome Doc!

The young chimp was growing increasingly restless sitting on my desk. He was grabbing at the "Welcome Doc" sign to my right and at the same time going for the pens in my pocket, as the flash-bulbs threatened to blind both of us.

On my first day as Director of Chicago's Lincoln Park Zoo the media had been alerted to my arrival. The city's four major newspapers—*The Chicago American, Daily News, Sun-Times* and *Tribune*—all sent photographers who were crowded into my office which, until then, had seemed rather spacious. Either I was big news or it was a slow news day in one of America's largest cities.

Once the moment had been captured for history, the reporters and photographers left, the chimpanzee was returned to the Children's Zoo, and I was on my own. I looked around my office with its big desk, tired couch, and door to the private washroom. It was all rather average except that inside the washroom there was another door with a sign that warned, in bold, red letters: *DANGER: WILD ANIMALS!*

1

That door led directly to an area behind the cages of the monkeys and great apes, the keepers' access area or *runway*.

It wasn't as if I hadn't been in this office before. I'd been there hundreds of times in my role as part-time zoo doctor, conferring with my predecessor, Marlin Perkins. Now I was on the other side of the desk, and the entire zoo was my responsibility. It was the beginning of an animal story that would go on for many, many years.

# Childhood, dogs, and an alligator

Many people wonder if animal doctors grow up knowing that's what they'll do with their lives—if it is somehow *destiny*. I won't pretend to speak for everyone in the profession, but in my case, I don't think that was true. My life began in 1921 and I remember my Dad bringing me to the zoo as a child, a typical urban kid on a day's outing. It always seemed special. It was also *free* and therefore affordable for my Dad, who ran a butcher shop in Bridgeport, a working-class neighborhood in Chicago. As was not so unusual for shopkeepers of the time, our family lived above the store. My mom was a homemaker and helped Dad in the shop.

I attended Lindbloom Technical High School, but the classes that were to prepare me for a likely career in engineering never sparked my interest.

Though I was not especially predisposed to animals, our family did always seem to have fox terrier dogs and I once had an alligator that my older sister sent from Florida while she was on her honeymoon. I kept it for about four or five years, using my Mom's laundry tub and an adjacent yard my folks owned. Like many wild animals, it eventually grew too big and became too dangerous to be a child's pet. I did what at least hundreds of other Chicagoans did over the years—I called the zoo and gave the alligator to *them*.

At one time people could buy alligators or baby monkeys from the Sears catalog. Today selling or having such animals is illegal—not to mention dangerous. There are, however, about 52 million dogs and some 58 million cats living as pets in American homes—a clear sign that people love animals and seem to be getting by without having alligators around the house.

# The city boy goes to Iowa to learn about animals

I was not an especially great student and wasn't at all sure what I wanted to do with my life. My best friend from elementary and high school was going off to Iowa State University to study animal science so, with nothing special in mind, I followed along. I considered myself lucky to be accepted to Iowa State and luckier still to be accepted into its pre-veterinary program. It was 1938, and Illinois didn't have a veterinary college at that time.

I had to work especially hard to catch up to (and keep up with) my classmates, most of whom had grown up on farms and had spent their entire lives around animals. I was totally lost when it came to knowledge of animal husbandry, poultry science and the dairy industry, subjects that were already part of the other students' daily lives. I quickly became the butt of most of the class jokes. When it came time to estimate the laying potential of a chicken or the weight of a steer, for example, I simply guessed. I was either close or wildly off and everyone just laughed at me—the city boy who was a few hundred miles out of his element.

It was my good fortune to be accepted into Vet School, as the college didn't take many out-of-state students. Furthermore, I learned very quickly that I was not destined to be a farm practitioner. Just watching them castrate pigs cured me of any illusions I might have had in that direction. In those days, pigs were simply hung up by their back legs and *cut*—no anesthetic or other preliminaries.

I also realized that my city background would not be helpful in conversations with my future clients because conversation was a big part of a vet's job—in addition to curing the farmers' livestock.

It became clear to me that I was really interested in dog and cat medicine (small animal practice), and once again that put me at a disadvantage. Situated at the center of a major agricultural region, the college really wasn't training many vets to specialize in the care of dogs and cats. A serious veterinary school focused its attention on farm animals—livestock that people were farming to earn a living and feed the nation. Dogs and cats were very much of secondary interest to the school, and that put me in a tough spot. Fortunately, one professor, Doc Anderson, took me under his wing and had me accompany him on many of his farm calls.

While I learned what I needed to know to complete my training, he helped me understand the many aspects of veterinary medicine and how they applied to the great variety of animals in their different environments. Without his help I never could have completed school and become a vet.

## Learning some pet tricks and a few things more

Becoming a doctor, of course, is very serious business. But being a student in college isn't *all* serious business, and my years at the Veterinary College were no exception.

There was the valuable experience of learning how to perform a surgical procedure in chickens as the egg goes down the fallopian tubes. If timed just right, before the shell starts forming, it is possible to insert a tiny piece of paper with a message on it. Later, after the egg is laid and cracked open, some lucky (and surprised) egg lover gets a chicken "fortune cookie." (Kids, please don't try this at home!)

On another memorable occasion, we rigged a dead duck in the rafters before a major Iowa State basketball game. When the referee shot his gun into the air to start the second half of the game, the duck fell down from the rafters onto the gym floor right on cue—minus the rigging string we'd used to get it up there.

In spite of such high jinx, I really *was* learning to become a veterinarian and was looking forward to going into practice.

The world, however, was not standing still. World War II was heating up, and this put the future careers of thousands of young men in doubt, myself included.

## The young animal doctor goes to war . . . sort of

I was lucky enough to receive permission to apply for a reserve commission in the Army's Medical Administrative Corps. This kept me from being drafted until after graduation in 1943.

But upon graduation—four days later, to be more

specific—I was called to active duty, receiving a commission in the Veterinary Corps of the US Army.

I was stationed at Carlisle Barracks, where the Army tried to make a soldier out of me and hundreds of physicians, dentists and other medical personnel. To this very day, I have only the greatest respect for those members of the regular military who were charged with this thankless and hopeless undertaking. We, however, simply weren't interested in the "army stuff," and even now I am unable to make a bed properly.

Mostly the members of the veterinary corps are the Army's food inspectors and sanitary overseers. It is this group's primary responsibility to ensure (to the extent it is possible) that troops don't become ill from food contaminants while on duty. I began this assignment with a short stint at Heinz & Company in Pittsburgh, where I primarily oversaw the making of sausage, salami, and bologna—by the carload. I won't describe the process in detail, but suffice to say that it was years before I could eat anything that came from those large tubs of fat and meat.

From Pittsburgh, I was shipped overseas to England. My commander believed the only possible explanation for this was that I spoke Czech, my family's native tongue. I became consumed by visions of parachuting behind enemy lines, playing a major role in defending freedom and ending the war.

But when I arrived at Watford in England, my new commanding officer reviewed my credentials and asked me why I was there. I respectfully reported to him that the assignment had not been my idea. Yet, there I was and would remain for some time.

It was decided that part of my responsibility would be to help feed the 8th Air Force.

Frankly, I found it boring.

After a time, I got a bicycle and was able to go riding around the countryside on weekends, the war and weather permitting.

The Allies were taking a beating in the air, suffering heavy casualties, and were constantly bringing in fresh flight crews with navigation orientation around the British Isles. I spent a great deal of time at a place where they were breaking in the new crews in B17s. In fact, I showed up there so often that when there was an empty seat available in a plane, the pilots would take me along. I had the rare opportunity to take some wonderful and exciting rides, sometimes sitting in the bombardier's place, looking out over the beautiful English countryside.

I became friends with many of the paratroopers and came to greatly admire and envy them. They were in the thick of the war—*and* they wore dashing jumpsuits and paratrooper boots and all had a macho swagger when they walked.

I was young, single, and wanted desperately to see action—to play a meaningful role in the war, perhaps partly because my parents' homeland of Czechoslovakia had fallen to the Germans.

And it was possibly *because* I was young that I foolishly thought it would be "cool" to be a part of the paratroopers. So when an opening for a veterinary officer came up, I applied for the slot with the 82nd Airborne, which had been operating in Italy and North Africa.

I didn't get the post, and the result is that I lived to tell about it. That quartermaster unit was involved in the jump on *D-Day* and practically much of the unit was wiped out by the German army.

## Wartime, pigeons, and Patton's dog

A few weeks after *D-Day*, once the bridgehead was properly established and the troops were starting to fan out into Brittany, the peninsula on the coast at Normandy in France, I received my orders, transferred to Europe and was assigned to become a veterinary officer for the Third Army–General Patton's outfit. No sooner had I arrived, than Patton began to head towards Germany.

Students of history know General George Patton as a rare, larger-than-life figure, the man who led U.S. World War II operations in North Africa and in the Battle of the Bulge. He was "Old Blood and Guts" and was routinely described as a living legend.

Those who are *not* students of history and only know the General from actor George C. Scott's portrayal of him in the classic Hollywood screen movie *Patton* found him no less impressive.

My immediate commanding officer, Colonel Sperry, was a regular army cavalry veterinarian who had served with Patton at Fort Riley in Kansas. Sperry was a true "horse doctor" in the finest sense of the word. And he was a friend of General Patton.

The Colonel called me in one day and uttered seven fateful words: "Fisher, what do you know about pigeons?"

"Nothing, sir," I replied immediately.

It didn't matter. I was assigned to the 277th Signal Corp Unit, one of the few such units in the war. General Patton, it seemed, was the only one in the European theater who thought it made sense to have a homing pigeon unit as a communications back up. He had used them successfully in North Africa and had requested them in Europe.

So there I was, a city kid from Chicago, in a field in the middle of France (we hadn't yet left for Germany), with about 2,000 pigeons, half of which were sick with pigeon pox, various kinds of respiratory diseases, and heaven knows what else. One thing was certain: *I* didn't know.

In fact, I didn't even know how to reach into a small cage and catch a pigeon without hurting it, but when Patton was your general, it was a good idea to learn such things—and quickly—no ifs, ands, or buts, or there *would be butts* to pay!

Beyond my responsibility for the pigeon unit, and the usual food inspection details, whenever Colonel Sperry went on leave or on maneuvers, I was assigned to look after General Patton's dog, Willy, a pit bull.

This is probably a good point at which to mention that, although I was never actually in combat, I *was* shot at once or twice in Germany. My *real* fear during the war in Europe, however, was over the possibility of something happening to Willy while he was left in my care. I had not a moment's doubt that if any tragedy whatsoever were to befall Willy, Patton would take one of his pearl-handled pistols from its holster and shoot me dead on the spot.

Fortunately, Willy and I both survived. As did the Lipizzaner horses that we helped save by taking them out of Austria ahead of the advancing Russian army. I was a standby to the special unit Patton assembled to rescue and preserve the founder stock of horses that are still part of the Austrian Riding School's pride and joy in Europe. A few of those horses became part of the famed Temple Lipizzaners' stable in Chicago.

I can take no credit for winning the war, but I am proud to have served my country as an officer in the US Army. I recall my years of military service at a time when the world held its breath and nations reached out to one another for help. I think of General Patton, Willy, and the pigeons. I would remember those pigeons years later in Chicago, where the great multitude of pigeons are not used as messengers and are not generally held in high regard. I wonder what General Patton would have thought of that.

# Home, a new life, and the Lincoln Park Zoo

With the war over, I returned home to Chicago. Like many other men just out of the service, I was uncertain about what to do with my life. The mood of the country was upbeat, and so was mine.

I met with Dr. Wes Young, who had interviewed me when I applied for college in Iowa years earlier. He too was an alumnus of Iowa State University and was the Executive Director of Chicago's Anti-Cruelty Society. He recalled when the University had originally suggested he talk with the kid from Chicago who wanted to go to Iowa, noting that normally the path went in the opposite direction.

Once again, Wes was very helpful. He suggested I consider a newly created post looking after the research animals at Northwestern University Medical School. At that time the university had come under considerable criticism from anti-vivisectionists and concluded it should have a full-time veterinarian on its staff. Although I considered other offers, I accepted the job with Northwestern, which proved to be the right decision.

A short time later, again through Wes Young, I became associated with the Lincoln Park Zoo.

For many years when people heard of Lincoln Park Zoo, Marlin Perkins' name came to mind. Marlin had come from Buffalo, New York in 1946 to become the fourth Director in the history of the Lincoln Park Zoo, the second oldest zoo in America. A year later, realizing he needed veterinary help, he got to know Wes Young through The Anti-Cruelty Society.

I, in turn, had been giving Wes a hand at The Anti-Cruelty Society clinic. In my free time I helped with spaying and neutering cats and dogs, as well as administering treatment to all the animals that came through the clinic. I knew he appreciated my assistance, especially since I never submitted a bill for my services. One day Marlin called asking Wes if he could come to the zoo and Wes invited me to ride along. None of us knew of course that it was a ride that would take my life and career in a completely new direction.

Change came when Wes Young received an offer too good to refuse—an offer that would literally cause him to *go Hollywood*.

Very often, animals used in movies were treated badly. It was the middle of the 20th century, and the public demanded an end to such mistreatment. The motion picture industry responded with a policy that all movies in which animals appeared would be required to have a humane officer present during filming. Wes Young was approached and soon left Chicago for California, where he took on the position of humane officer for Hollywood productions. It was a big job, and he had his work cut out for him.

With Wes's departure, Marlin asked me to take over the part-time veterinary chores at the zoo. I had accompanied Wes to the zoo and assisted him so often that people seemed comfortable around me and satisfied that my stepping in would be an easy transition and a good fit.

I had already decided to open a small animal practice on South Harlem Avenue at Riverside Drive in Berwyn, a suburb just outside of Chicago. There were no animal hospitals in that area and, while no new business was without some risks, it seemed like a good move. I thought I had finally set my career on a path and had begun to make plans.

But Marlin Perkins was not one to take *no* for an answer.

# Marlin and me

Marlin was an interesting man, not especially tall, slight of build, but with a rather commanding way about him. Most people who knew him thought he was a bit egotistical. He usually got what he wanted. And, since my new practice did not yet have any clients, he got me. I decided to accept his offer.

We agreed I would spend a half-day at the zoo, one day a week, and cover any emergencies as they occurred. I thus became one of the few part-time—or *full-time*—zoo doctors in the United States. (Dr. Patricia O'Connor at Staten Island, New York, was another and, to my knowledge, the only woman doing what I was doing, making her something of a pioneer in the field.)

Marlin and I were totally different, in both style and personality, but we got along well and became friends. He had been a reptile curator—a *herp* man—at the St. Louis Zoo. Then he became the zoo director in Buffalo before moving on to Chicago's Lincoln Park.

He had also become a major national television star, first as the host of *Zoo Parade* and later with *Wild Kingdom,* which had an amazingly long run of 10 years, from 1963 to 1973, on the NBC-TV network. It could be seen for many additional years in syndication.

Marlin was legendary in the zoo business because, in addition to being the first celebrity zoo director, he was almost totally selftaught. He clearly liked attention and got it—something that did not always set well with his employers and colleagues. I, on the other hand, usually went about my business quietly and didn't especially enjoy the spotlight.

Maybe that was why Marlin and I got along so well for so long. I'm sure there were other reasons as well, such as the fact that Marlin never tried to tell me how to treat a sick or injured animal, and I never told him how manage the zoo.

## "Thunder"

Building a veterinary practice, like starting any business, involves long hours, hard work, and, very often, wearing many different hats. But I was satisfied that I was doing something good, even if it left me exhausted most days.

One night I had finally made it to bed, after finishing the last late evening rounds at my animal hospital and checking on the boarded dogs in the kennel. The weather outside was awful. A heavy rain had soaked the area, and I was happy to see the day end.

It was around 10:30 PM when my phone rang.

"Doc? It's Dan," the caller said, though I had immediately recognized his voice. Dan Bostrom was in charge of the hoofed animal section of the zoo. There was a sense of urgency in his voice and a grave tone I hadn't heard in him before.

"We have a problem," he began anxiously. "One of the cows can't have her calf."

There was nothing to do but head for the zoo—and *fast*, despite the torrential rainstorm. I struggled quickly into work clothes and raingear and grabbed a minimal amount of obstetric supplies. Lightning and thunder accompanied me all the way on the 45-minute drive to Lincoln Park.

I raced to the hoof stock barn at the north end of the zoo. It was an old, turn-of-the-century barn, with almost no light and a series of small stalls with very little working space. I found Dan standing next to the stall of a zebu, a small wild cattle-like animal from India.

Dan could best be described as a classic old-time keeper. He had little formal education, but a great deal of practical knowledge about animals. He was short, stocky, middle-aged and pretty much of a loner who rarely spoke with other employees. But whenever I was around him, it seemed he never stopped talking about anything and everything.

That night, however, he was quiet, just standing and watching the cow straining and pushing. She was trying hard to deliver her calf.

Dan suggested we rope her and tie her head in the corner. Together, he and I managed to wrestle her into the corner of her stall. Dan positioned himself at her head and steadied her while I slipped on an obstetrical glove and reached in.

The usual presentation at delivery is two forelimbs and the head, but in this case one front leg was tucked backwards and the calf's head was turned in such a way that it simply was not going to come out the way it was.

With a lot of effort, and fighting the cow who was pushing against my arm trying to expel the calf, I managed to replace the whole calf back inside the cow, thereby repelling it so I could get the head straightened out. It wasn't easy—particularly since I was not very experienced with large animals.

We managed to get leg ropes on the calf's two front legs and a rope and a padded hook under its lower jaw. With Dan's help, and the last ounce of energy left in the cow for a few more uterine contractions, we pulled on the calf. I had lubricated the birth canal with mineral oil and, happily, after an hour of very hard work on everyone's part, a small, healthy male finally slipped out of its mother.

Dan named him "Thunder" in honor of the stormy night he was born.

What I didn't know that night was that this experience had served as a test for the new part-time zoo doctor. Had it gone wrong, word would have spread through the zoo like a wildfire that the new doc wasn't any good. Fortunately, as the word got around and I made my usual rounds on Wednesday, several keepers said, "I heard you done well with the calf, Doc. Good luck!"

I had passed my first hurdle, thank heaven.

It did seem, however, as if I had done it the hard way. Much like my days in Iowa at vet school, when I was the joke of the class, my crash course on pigeons in France, and taking care of Willy for General Patton, learning the hard way was a pattern I seemed destined to repeat.

# Being a vet

I remember vividly a time early in my animal practice when I received a phone call in the middle of the night.

A woman, extremely anxious, said her dog was sick. She described the symptoms, and it seemed to me that the dog was not really all that ill. I gave her some suggestions and went back to sleep.

Imagine my utter horror the next morning when I opened the door to my animal hospital and found a box. Inside was the body of her dog. The attached note read simply, "This is the dog you didn't think was an emergency last night."

From that moment on, if pet owners ever called in the middle of the night, if *they* thought it was important for me to see their animals (or, of course, if I did), no matter what the hour or the weather, I would meet them at my animal hospital and give their animals my complete attention.

Another time, while helping Wes Young at The Anti-Cruelty Society clinic, I was reminded again how much animals can mean to people.

An elderly man came into the clinic with his very old, very sick dog. After examining the dog, it became clear that it was at death's door. I explained this to the man, and we agreed it was time to put the dog to sleep. He held his dog while I administered the lethal injection.

I turned to put the syringe back on the table and remove my surgical gloves. When I turned back, the man had his sleeve rolled up. He held out his arm to me.

"Doc," he said, choking back tears, "please do me next. That was the only friend I had."

We held each other for several minutes and we both cried.

I am constantly reminded of the bonds people form with their animals. To call them pets seems like such an inadequate way to describe the importance animals take on in many people's lives.

# Behind the scenes at the zoo, life and death and life

My experiences at the zoo were poignant and funny. In fact, the reason I often describe the zoo as a *small city* is that every day people are going to work there, people are coming home, animals are giving birth, and animals die. It's the cycle of life in every respect.

A "medical mystery" surfaced at the zoo's Monkey House, the original small mammal building that also housed great apes and the zoo director's office.

During my early days as a zoo doctor, while making my rounds, the keepers told me several monkeys had stopped eating and were exhibiting some minor neurological symptoms. I tried fluids and other supportive therapy, with no response. Several died.

As I performed a routine autopsy, I noticed some internal organ lesions. Lab tests showed a high level of lead. Further investigation revealed the monkeys had contracted lead poisoning from eating paint chips off the bars of their cages. The paint itself wasn't the problem but, in an effort to prevent the bars from rusting, the painters had used a primer with a high lead content. Having identified the culprit, and to prevent further illness and death, we had all the barred cages stripped and repainted with paints tested to make sure they were not toxic to the animals.

The zoo's one original building, a two-story structure, was so old it could no longer be used to house animals. Eventually, it became a commissary downstairs, where food was delivered and the horsemeat was cut and stored, awaiting distribution to the other zoo buildings.

Upstairs were some small cages and a sink. I decided to use this area as my basic animal hospital when making my weekly rounds. It was also where I performed necropsies (animal autopsies) on the animals that died during the week. This was (and remains) an important part of veterinary medicine. We knew so little about exotic animals in those days; we were continually learning all we could from the animals that died.

We became well aware that we could distinguish animals, name them, and get to know the hundreds of different species in a zoo collection, but we knew so very little about what was where *inside* the animals.

Where, for example, are a snake's heart and lungs? What is its "normal" temperature? What appeared to look normal when performing a necropsy and what did not? There was much to learn, and zoo vets were at the very beginning of the learning curve. We had a long way to go.

My normal necropsy routine included a gross anatomy look, a check of the gastrointestinal track for parasites, and a viewing of the lungs for signs of pneumonia. If I found anything unusual, I would take some snips of that particular tissue, put it in small formalin bottles and send it to the relatively new College of Veterinary Medicine at the University of Illinois in Urbana. Tissue culturing and necropsies were critical to learning all I could about all the different species of animals. In fact, through nationwide tissue sampling and sharing of results, all zoo doctors benefited, and we still do.

After a few months, I convinced Marlin to purchase a deep freeze for the animals that died. This was no small feat, as Marlin was known to be rather tight with the purse strings. But when he finally agreed, we bought a really large freezer. Other than the very big animals, every bird, mammal, and reptile that died during the week was placed in the freezer and kept there until the night before I made my Wednesday rounds. The last keeper out on Tuesday night would pull out the frozen animals and set them on the sink to defrost by Wednesday morning, when I would start my day by doing autopsies.

On a particular occasion, the zoo was experiencing one of its infrequent, but consistent major outbreaks of botulism in birds. Botulism affects the nervous system of the animal and, in the case of birds, creates a potentially major die-off, as it spreads rather quickly. During a botulism outbreak, it was not uncommon for me to arrive at the zoo and find anywhere from 5 to 25 birds in the process of thawing out, ready for autopsy.

There were so many birds one week that I returned to the zoo several times. When I examined one or two of the birds that had been in the freezer for a few hours, as they thawed, I couldn't believe my eyes. They were alive!

It took me a while to figure out what happened. My theory was that by slowing down the metabolism of the bird by putting it in the freezer, its own immune function took over and allowed the bird to recover. Many years later, in a similar die-off, I suggested actively treating birds with botulism this way. We took the dying birds, put them in the freezer for a short time, and some re-covered. Would they have recovered on their own? Who knows? We were all still learning.

# The learning continues—only bigger

Taking care of animals can be venturing into the unknown, whether dealing with birds and botulism or problems of a some-what heavier nature. I remember a situation where I actually had to "read the directions" before I could proceed. It had to do with cows—this time, *dairy cows*.

The zoo received six bred heifers for its new *Farm-in-the-Zoo*. The idea was to have the cows deliver calves to be used as a farm exhibit, then the cows could, in turn, be used to demonstrate milking.

As hoped for, the first three cows delivered fine, healthy calves, and kids flocked to the farm to see them. The accompany-ing milking demonstrations took place at 10, 12, and 2 o'clock—one or two cows each time.

The fourth and fifth cows were a little tougher. Each required some assistance because of difficult births, but I managed to get live, healthy calves from each of them. I was obviously getting quite a bit of experience by this time with cow deliveries.

Then came the sixth heifer. She went into labor, but regard-less of what I did she was simply not going to deliver the calf.

I decided I had no alternative but to perform a caesarean sec-tion on her. The problem was that I had never done a C-section on a cow—*and neither had any of my nearby colleagues*. The vets in the area were all small animal practitioners with no cattle experience, much less this type of procedure. Time was also a major factor.

Finally, one vet agreed to come to the zoo to assist me. He had no large animal experience either.

It was nighttime—which always seemed to be the case when there were problems. And, again, there was very little light, al-though at least this time we had a nice new barn.

We managed to get ropes on the cow and get her down, sedating her heavily before we injected local anesthetic around the surgical area. Then, as if adhering to a procedure followed by do-it-your-selfers for decades, I opened the manual and followed the directions.

I literally worked with a scalpel in one hand and *Sisson's Anatomy* book in my other hand, getting a slight assist in the process by propping the book up on the cow's stomach. Despite his good intentions, my colleague was not much help, though he did provide moral support.

Somehow both the cow and I survived the experience, as did the little calf, but I certainly don't recommend this as an example of good surgical procedure.

## Open wide, you're on TV

But despite these experiences—even what we would refer to as Dr. Fisher's "surgery-by-the-book procedure"—nothing qualified as an example of learning vet medicine the hard way as much as when Marlin called me to work on a jaguar with a broken tooth.

What should have been a routine procedure turned into anything but that.

First, just *getting* to the animal was extremely difficult. "Capture guns" and anesthetic darts had not yet been developed for use by vets. A big cat was captured by roping it—yes, *roping* it—with a lariat, just the way cowboys did it in those old western movies many of us grew up watching.

We had a long stick with a rope tied in a loop at one end. The trick was to get the rope loop over the cat's head, then around and under one foreleg, so we could pull the cat to the front of the cage without choking it to death. Not putting the rope under the foreleg before pulling it would be disastrous and would kill the animal.

Once we had roped the cat, we baited it with food to lure it into a special crate we had constructed. One end of the crate was clear plastic so we could watch the animal.

We began administering the anesthetic, which was itself an almost impossible task. This was still in the days when ether was the most common form of anesthetic. It had an extremely unpleasant smell, as well as being highly flammable.

We hooked-up an ether drip with cloths that ran the ether into the box and waited for the cat go to sleep. It was a very laborious process. Every time the cat looked as if it had dozed off, we would poke it just to be certain . . . and it would come up again. So we would administer more ether. And more ether. And more ether.

Before long the entire floor of the Lion House surrounding the jaguar's cage was littered with empty cans of ether, which we had secured, ten cans at a time, from nearby hospitals as we kept running out.

Finally the cat went down. Then, we had to use an ether cone over the cat's face to continue administering the anesthetic, but had to keep removing it when we were working on the tooth.

About two hours into the procedure, as if we needed to encounter more problems . . . we encountered more problems.

I had brought my dog instruments to elevate the tooth and rock it back and forth to get it out. But as the broken tooth was an upper canine, this simply wasn't working. The instruments were both too small and totally inadequate.

Also, in the rush to get the procedure underway, I had not gone first to the Field Museum, as I might normally have done, to study the anatomy of a jaguar skull. This was not an insignificant detail.

In big cats, because the canine teeth are used for ripping and carrying off prey, what can be seen outside the animal's mouth is less than one third of the tooth. The remaining *two-thirds* extends well up into the skull to allow the cat to lift huge prey and carry it off.

But in the middle of a surgical procedure, a trip to the Field Museum for research purposes was not an option.

After hours of struggling, using my dog instruments, and numerous pounds of ether, the broken and infected tooth was finally extracted.

The next time I had to perform a procedure on big cats' teeth—and every time thereafter—I would remember to bring my equine (horse) instruments, which I found worked *much* better.

Unfortunately for me, the story doesn't end there.

The final and most humiliating part of this experience is the fact that it is captured on film. The episode was recorded to be shown as an installment of Marlin Perkins' *Zoo Parade* television series for all the world—or at least a few million people in the United States—to see, while gathered around the TV with family and friends. My face, as well as my white surgical coat, was red for some time to come.

Chalk up another experience I had to learn the hard way!

Media set-up in my office—my first day as Zoo Director. Courtesy, Chicago Park District

Keo the chimp at 4 years "directing" the new Zoo Director. Courtesy, Chicago Park District

On assignment with 2,000 pigeons and General George Patton's
277th Signal Corp Unit.

IN ACTION WITH THE 277 SIG PIGEON COMPANY

Lt. Hayes

Lt. Wentz

Lt. Danskin

Capt. Fisher

Capt. Appio

Lt. Pohlman

As a Veterinary Officer for the Third Army—Patton's outfit.

Mrs. Brooks (Hope) McCormick (1980s), whose enthusiasm and support for the Zoo were legendary, with George Davis (right), LPZS Board Member. Courtesy, Lincoln Park Zoological Society

Actor Hugh O'Brian dishes it up for a baby orangutan at the Children's Zoo (1970s). Courtesy, Chicago Park District

# The sleeping tiger mystery

"When will he wake up?" Marlin asked in his third phone call to me that day.

The "he" was a magnificent Bengal tiger we had anesthetized using a new drug called Surital. The problem was that the tiger had now been sleeping for more than two days and Marlin Perkins was frantic.

The big cat had been given the drug intravenously to anesthetize him for an infected ingrown toenail. He had started limping a few days earlier, and his keeper, Bill Faedtke, a man who spoke little but was very observant, noticed that it looked like the middle claw on the tiger's left front foot had grown out far enough to curl under and grow back into the pad. This had to be very painful for the cat.

Clearly, we had to do something, and I was thrilled to be able to try out this new drug and not use ether as I'd had to do with the jaguar some time before. I continued to dislike using ether, which was difficult to administer and highly explosive.

The cat went to sleep quickly and the procedure had gone well. He was supposed to wake up within the hour. No antidote was needed, as we expected the drug to simply work itself through and out of the animal's system, which was what typically happened in smaller animals.

I had left the zoo and returned to my small animal practice. Later that day Bill's colleague, Willie Renner, a gregarious, talkative guy who was the exact opposite of Bill, was the first to call. He was concerned that the tiger was not yet awake. I told him not to worry, that I was sure the cat would be coming around soon.

Surital was considered the perfect drug for such situations. It is a relatively short-acting barbiturate that will keep a domestic cat under anesthetic for 45 minutes to an hour. I considered it the obvious choice for an ingrown claw procedure on a bigger cat.

When the tiger was still sleeping the next morning, Marlin himself called me.

No, the animal didn't seem to be in any distress.

Yes, it was breathing normally—but it was *still sleeping*.

Now I became concerned as well. But since the animal seemed to be okay, I used my most reassuring voice to tell Marlin not to worry. I suggested, however, that every two hours the keepers should roll the cat over to minimize fluid building up in its lungs, which could lead to pneumonia.

Now it was day two, and the cat was still asleep. We were all worried at this point, but there didn't seem to be anything we could do about it. The cat's vital signs were normal.

I went to the zoo and began administering intravenous fluids in an attempt to flush the drug out of the animal's system.

And still the tiger slept on.

Finally, on the third day, the cat woke up and seemed to be fine. That appeared to be the end of the story. But I still had no idea why a Bengal tiger had slept for days. It remained a total mystery for quite a while.

I never imagined it might be the new drug. I was so pleased to have an alternative to ether. It took several more incidents during the year or so that followed, when Surital was used on tigers at other zoos, for us to determine that for reasons unknown, tigers do not detoxify this anesthetic as other cat species do. Instead of it leaving their systems, it stays with them for several days, permitting the cats to snooze away much of the week. Surital works very well on other types of cats, but not tigers!

# A very good life . . . now what?

I had correctly assessed the need for an animal hospital in the community I chose to launch my vet practice and had become fairly successful. I began with a tiny office and eventually was able to buy a building that had previously been a sheet metal shop, which I converted into a small office and clinic.

I also married, and my wife and I became parents of our first child, our daughter Jane. I built a small apartment for us over the animal hospital. Since we didn't have much room, Jane's nursery was created from a space that had once been a small closet, which had a connecting air duct into the kennel area for dogs below. The situation was not unhealthy for her, but it *was* noisy. We laughed about it later, recalling how Jane actually learned to *bark* before she talked!

And there was Nikkie, a beautiful boxer, who was the family pet but, like most family pets, was much more than that to us. Nikkie had produced many show-quality pups over the years. She did, however, have a bad habit of passing prodigious amounts of gas—usually at the most inopportune times. She became embarrassing to have around the apartment and was relegated to the animal hospital, where she quickly commandeered the only couch in my little waiting area. I usually found Nikkie asleep on the couch while my clients stood waiting to have their animals examined.

Eventually we moved to a house in Riverside, and we welcomed our daughter Kate to our family. We were enjoying a comfortable life in a green and scenic suburb of Chicago. In many respects, we were living the American Dream, my practice was doing well, and our life was like a Norman Rockwell painting.

## How life began to change

Fifteen years had passed since I had agreed to become the zoo's part-time vet.

On one of my weekly visits, Marlin asked to talk with me and invited me into his office. He said he had accepted an offer from the St. Louis Zoo and was going back to where he'd started his career, this time as the zoo's top man. I was surprised that he would leave a highly visible job in as great a city as Chicago, but I was even more surprised when he said he thought I should consider being the next Director of the Lincoln Park Zoo.

I recall that all I could say at the time was "wow!" I'm sure I said it more than once. Lincoln Park Zoo was one of the best—and *best-known*—zoos in the country.

When the initial shock subsided, I began to look at the situation more realistically: I had no experience in running a zoo; I wasn't even sure I *wanted* the job.

Of course, there was my family to consider—the girls were in school, and they and my wife were enjoying our comfortable suburban life. It would be a difficult decision.

But I had to be honest. I was frustrated in my veterinary practice. It had grown to be quite large, with five full-time vets, and rather than treating animals, I found myself relegated to being a full-time administrator. I was ready for a change. Even though being the zoo director would pay a lot less, I realized I had been bitten by the zoo bug. It was something I wanted to do.

I also thought the job would be fun. Obviously, it must have never occurred to me at the time that I would be moving from one administrative job to another. I do remember Marlin asking me why

I would consider trading my successful veterinary practice to become part of the bureaucratic and political labyrinth of the Chicago Park District, the entity that owned and operated the zoo, but I think I just said something profound like, "Well, you've dealt with it, so I guess I can too."

Despite such deep thinking on my part, I was beginning to see myself in the job. Even so, I waffled for nearly two months before finally applying for the post. I continued with my regular routine of managing a full-time veterinary practice and being a part-time zoo doctor. Being the zoo director would mean considerably less money than I was earning in my practice, yet I knew this wasn't about the money.

One Wednesday morning, while I was making rounds, I was called to a zoo phone. Mr. McFetridge, President of the Chicago Park District, wanted to see me *immediately*. I cleaned up as best I could (zoo doctor work can be pretty dirty) and, wearing a work shirt and pants that suggested a man who'd spent a lot of time around animals, I headed downtown.

The Park District offices were located adjacent to Soldier Field, the city's expansive outdoor stadium on McFetridge Drive—a road named for the very man I was on my way to meet. I was somewhat anxious about being summoned in this manner, as it had never happened before.

James McFetridge was a tall, imposing and very decisive man. A high-profile labor leader, his union was Local 46, the Municipal Employees Union, and he made sure that a good number of Park District employees were among its members. He was all business. In all the years I knew him, I don't recall ever seeing him smile.

Mr. McFetridge greeted me at his office door. He wore his usual well-tailored, dark, business suit, which provided an interesting contrast to my work clothes. Without wasting time on pleasantries he boomed, "Dr. Fisher, you're the successful applicant. You are our new Zoo Director. We're holding a press conference in twenty minutes. Please stand by."

That was it. No backslapping, no champagne corks. The man was all business and I have to smile just thinking about it. I was being appointed to run an operation that was enormously important to the city of Chicago, for both residents and visitors. The man who put me in the job gave me such a simple, matter-of-fact show of confidence that his lack of "fussing" about it seemed to say there was, indeed, no need to say any more.

That was in the Spring of 1962.

A period of transition followed with Marlin remaining with the zoo until October 1. At that time I moved into what I had always known as *his* office. Now it was mine.

Alone on my first day as the director, I looked around that office and outside at the zoo grounds. What I saw fascinated me in ways that are hard to put into words. Lincoln Park Zoo is a place the people of Chicago love and treasure, where wide-eyed kids discover exotic animals that few of them would ever have the opportunity to see in the wild—or perhaps anywhere else. This was *their* place. I watched people moving about—groups, couples and families enjoying time together.

I heard people roaring with laughter and lions simply roaring. I knew I'd made the right decision to come to the zoo. It was more than a job. It would be the center of my life for many years to come.

# America's "oldest" zoo turns 94—and shows its age

Zoo colleagues joke about which American zoo is the oldest, and Central Park, Philadelphia and Lincoln Park vie for that honor. Central Park claims it was founded in 1860. The Philadelphia Zoo Society was chartered in 1859 but the Zoo actually opened in 1874. Lincoln Park was founded in 1868 with a pair of swans, so for years we disregarded Central Park's menagerie and claimed we were the *oldest* zoo while Philadelphia calls itself America's *first* zoo. It's all about marketing. When I looked around Lincoln Park in 1962, it didn't really matter which was the oldest. The zoo was 94 years old when I took over as Director. It was at a turning point. Most of the buildings on the grounds had been built at the turn of the century or in the early 1900s. The newest building was the Monkey House, where my office was located, and that had been completed in 1927.

Each time I made my weekly rounds as the zoo doctor, it was like going back in time 50 years. I had only my black bag. There were no hospital facilities, no operating area. I made do with what I had, performing surgeries in the cages of the animals and often performing necropsies wherever the animals had died.

The zoo also had no capture equipment when I took over. We still had to rope the animals and use ether to subdue them. It was a pretty primitive way to administer medical services. The worst area—at least for me—was the tunnel behind the old bear run. Every time I went in there it seemed as if I'd stepped into an Edgar Allan Poe story. The tunnel was dark, dank, and the only way to walk through it was bent over. When the bears would pound on the old metal doors from the other side of the wall, it felt as if they might come crashing through at any moment. It was a scary place to be, not to mention an almost impossible environment in which to work. Clearly, a lot needed to be done around the zoo, in terms of maintenance alone.

Many people visit the zoo to see the large, exciting animals they grow up reading about. But the big cats, the bears, and great apes in their old barred cages seemed to me as if they were in jail. Major improvements had been made in the zoo world, but Lincoln Park was years behind. Until the early 1950s, the zoo had been a completely open section of the park, with no fences or gates. The zoo was originally intended to be a 24-hour, seven-day-a-week resource to the community and had remained that way through the years.

But times were changing.

Two incidents occurred at night—incidents in which vandals killed animals. Additionally, new federal agricultural rules required more strict control of wild animals. The response to this was to install fencing around the perimeter of the zoo. There were so many sidewalks leading into the zoo, however, that 13 new entrances or gates had to be constructed. These gates were only shut at night and the zoo continued to be free to all.

Lincoln Park Zoo, despite its high profile throughout the United States, is actually quite small for a zoo in a large urban area like Chicago. The zoo property is only 29 linear acres running north and south along the edge of Lake Michigan, with an additional five acres allocated for a demonstration area—a small working Farm-in-the-Zoo—that would be separated from the main zoo at its southwest corner. The entity that had evolved into what was the Lincoln Park Zoo had actually been assembled over a century as a classic menagerie and had been placed under the care of the Chicago Park District to be used for recreation.

At the time I became its Director, the Zoo also had pony rides, a merry-go-round, and a small gauge train that went to the east of the Monkey House and circled back under a wooden tunnel. We had people selling balloons, as well as peanuts and marshmallows for the kids, though most of the snack food seemed to find their way into the stomachs of the elephants and bears. On its east-west axis, Webster Avenue ran right through the center of the zoo essentially cutting it in half. This was what I saw as I began settling into my new job. For me, a great new adventure was just beginning. It was clear, too, that I really had my work cut out for me.

# Growing the Ark

The conversation started innocently enough and soon it developed into a plan that seemed wildly exciting, as well as very important to the future of the zoo. We needed to grow our animal collection.

I was sitting in the elegantly-appointed office of Frank Schmick in downtown Chicago, when someone suggested a collecting trip to Cameroon. A collecting trip is exactly that—a trip to collect additional animals for the zoo. Frank was the Chicago Park District Commissioner for the zoo (one of the five commissioners appointed by the Mayor), as well as a board member of The Lincoln Park Zoological Society. He was an avid zoo man and he especially loved the great apes. The trip sounded like a wonderful idea—traveling to the heart of Africa with a man I greatly admired, on a serious mission to collect gorillas for the zoo. Great!

Then the reality of it began to sink in. Sitting in a comfortable office in Chicago, talking about a trip to the jungle is very different from actually *being* in the jungle.

## *In the jungle (Travels with Frank) . . .*

*As the old expression goes, it seemed like a good idea at the time.*

I knew it would get hotter when the sun came up. It had every other day we'd been in the jungle. Yet, on this particular morning it seemed like it could not *possibly* get any warmer. I felt terrible and

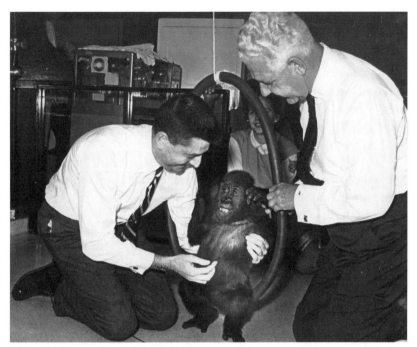

Frank Schmick (r) and one of his favorite baby gorillas. Courtesy,
Chicago Park District

knew I looked terrible. My shirt was soaking wet and sticking to
me and the day hadn't even begun.

From an air-conditioned veranda the view would have been
beautiful. We were surrounded by lush vegetation ranging in color
from dark blue-green to a pale, almost yellow hue. Sounds of
morning were all around us—monkeys calling, birds singing in a
hundred different choruses, and insects by the thousands humming a monotonous tune.

It was the insects, the heat, and the humidity that reminded
me I was *not* in an air-conditioned setting. Not that being director
of a major zoo didn't have me confronting uncomfortable, un-
clean, unpleasant situations at times, but . . .

I hadn't slept well because of the heat and humidity—and I've
*never* liked insects. I was, after all, a city kid and having them
buzzing and crawling all over me during the night was not my
idea of sweet dreams. I had cocooned myself in a sheet in the
hammock slung between two trees, but all that did was make me
sweat more.

For the fifth night in a row I had tossed, but been unable to turn, in the narrow hammock, and the coarse rope netting rubbing against my sunburned skin was not conducive to sleep either.

I awoke at 5:00 AM, before first light, and took what passed for a cold shower in our little makeshift camp. Now, forty-five minutes later, I knew I looked about the way I had last night after a long day of cutting our way through the jungle.

Not so my traveling companion and boss.

Despite all we'd been through, Frank looked as if he had just stepped off the men's best-dressed list. Here we were in the middle of the jungle in Cameroon, West Africa, in 90-degree heat and 100% humidity, and Frank looked great.

I kept thinking that since *I* was the person who was the veterinarian, the zoo director, the person familiar with animals and environments similar to the animals' natural habitat, and Frank was the elegant gentleman accustomed to sitting in an office surrounded by the all finer things life had to offer, there was something wrong with this picture. It was as if we had exchanged roles—though of course that was not the case.

But Frank definitely looked as if he were in his element here. He wasn't a big-game hunter or an explorer, or even a member of my zoo staff. Although he traveled around the world and visited the best places, staying at the best hotels and dining at the finest restaurants, out in the jungle, he looked like Stanley or Livingstone *in the heart of darkest Africa.*

Frank claimed he always slept well and upon waking donned a starched white suit that matched his shock of white hair. He never seemed to sweat and remained impeccable all day, no matter what the heat or how much mud we trekked through.

Frank wanted to take this trip with me just because of his love for gorillas. He looked like the least likely guy to be an "animal person" of anyone I knew. He was an imposing man and highly authoritative. In restaurants, he showed no mercy toward any hapless waiters or bus boys who were clumsy or indifferent. Should someone flick so much as a drop of water on him, he had been known to fly into a rage, berating that person as stupid and incompetent.

Still, I was in awe of him and how much he had accomplished. I remember dreading the first day he came to tour the zoo.

In those days, the old Monkey House had glass panels to protect visitors from the gorillas and chimps throwing things at them. Going behind the scenes—behind the glass—put visitors seriously at risk. Chimps and gorillas like to throw whatever is available and that includes handfuls of dung. They also spat and sometimes urinated on people as they passed by in the back area. More mildly, some might take a mouthful of water and wait for the ideal moment to spray a zoo visitor. It wasn't so much that they were malicious; they were just mischievous.

As the zoo doctor, I was not their favorite person, but I *was* a favorite target.

So when I took Frank, then *Mr. Schmick* to me, behind the scenes for the first time, I did so with some concern. What if he got spat upon, I wondered, *or worse*? I was sure he would have my head.

But the man who loved the gorillas and the chimps treated them like a doting grandfather. He enjoyed their antics, regardless of what they did to him. He particularly liked taking friends behind the scenes on Sunday mornings and exposing them to the great ape antics. After they were often thoroughly doused, he would take the guests back to his apartment on Chicago's Lake Shore Drive, where he would prepare a wonderful Sunday brunch. He was a self-made millionaire at a young age and had retired early so he could indulge in his hobbies, one of which was gourmet cooking.

I had come to see him as a somewhat larger-than-life figure and I can only imagine what our guides and porters in Cameroon must have thought of him. Like me, they seemed somewhat terrified, yet respectful of this man who cut a dashing "great white hunter" figure.

On our last morning in the jungle, Frank was in a jovial mood. We were at the end of our three-week journey to collect gorillas, and, at this point, had two youngsters (ages 1 or 2) in a holding area, waiting for us to catch up and head back to the States. Frank and I sat down to breakfast shortly after he arose. We were in an old trapper's hut, with open sides and a thatched roof, huddled around a tired wooden table with wobbly legs. Breakfast consisted of a thoroughly unappetizing mound of greasy eggs and questionable bacon. The toast had gone soggy from the humidity, yet looked like the only safe thing to eat.

Not feeling great to start with, I was listlessly moving the food around on my plate and thinking about the details of the days ahead—about crating and shipping our little gorillas safely home.

Frank was energetic as usual, digging into his plate of food. It amazed me that he could be so discerning about food and the quality of service at home, but eat almost anything—no matter how awful—while on safari. Before he finished his first bite of breakfast, a young male chimp dove through the opening nearest to him and grabbed his plate.

We were both so startled that we could only watch and laugh as the young animal made off with his breakfast. Frank was quick to recover his composure, however, and yelled to our trapper, who doubled as our waiter.

"I want that animal!" he roared. Immediately I could see dollar signs ringing up in the cash register as, in the trapper's mind, the chimp's value skyrocketed.

But catching a wild young chimp is not easy. We knew he was probably in the area, but corralling him was another matter.

Undaunted by the task, our trapper and his assistants began the painstaking process of trying to bait the animal with food. A trap to entangle, but not injure the animal, backed up each bait. We were using nets, so setting them up was a detailed process.

The chimp was, however, a typical chimp.

First, since it had already had breakfast—Frank's—it was not particularly hungry. Second, chimps are very intelligent animals; the closest to man in genetic composition. Only one strand of DNA separates us. Frank was not going to accept any other chimp as a substitute. He wanted *that* chimp. Clearly, we had our work cut out for us.

A day went by. Bait was taken. The nets failed. They were reset. The process was repeated. A second day passed, then a third.

We were running out of food—for both bait and for ourselves—and we still had not caught the chimp. We watched our trapper and his assistants work each day and helped where we could. It was a slow, tedious job, and our patience was running out.

The trappers seemed unconcerned. They were, after all, hired to capture animals. Sometimes it was easy; other times more difficult. Sometimes it was *impossible.* But they went about their tasks as if they had all the time in the world, particularly since they knew they would be paid for their efforts, regardless of the outcome.

In Africa, time is a relative thing. The trappers were in no hurry, but Frank and I were. We were ready to go home.

Finally, on the morning of the fourth day, the chimp took the bait, and the nets held. He was ours—and a handsome animal he was. He was nameless on that first day, but ultimately he became "Sam," and he would go on to live a long life and be a wonderful sire to many baby chimps at the zoo.

# The homecoming

Frank was exhilarated when the chimp was caught. I was tired and sweaty. But I must admit that our days spent closing in on Sam and bringing the chimp back with us, capped off a very satisfying and successful collecting trip.

The year was 1964 and bringing back gorillas from the African jungle was BIG news—even in a big news town like Chicago.

Michael Killian wrote this *Chicago Tribune* story:

### *New Celebrities Added to 'Zoo's Who'*

*Two trans-Atlantic celebrities jetted into O'Hare Field yesterday and celebrated the occasion by tweaking the nose of the pilot and bopping a doctor on the head. The pilot was Capt. John Hub of American Airlines freighter service; the doctor was Lester E. Fisher, director of the Lincoln Park Zoo; and carryings-on were all to be expected. The two celebrities are baby gorillas.*

### *Found in the Cameroon*

*Still unnamed and weighing only 30 and 15 pounds, the little boy and girl gorillas were found in the Cameroon, West Africa, last April by Franklin B. Schmick, retired investment broker and newly-named member of the park board. Schmick purchased them for donation to the zoo and arranged for their shipment Wednesday to New York, where they were picked up by Dr. Fisher and Capt. Hub yesterday.*

Dr. Fisher said the nose-tweaking and head-bopping was merely the babies' way of saying that gorillas were not meant to fly, but added that after they were on the ground a while, and placated with a few bananas, their dispositions improved.

### Put in Zoo Nursery

They were taken to the zoo's nursery, where they will live with some baby chimpanzees and orangutans a while until they are old enough to move in with the zoo's seven other gorillas in the monkey house. These of course are the mighty but aging Sinbad, Helen and Freddy, Kisoro and Mumbi, Debbie, and Frank, Sinbad's heir-apparent as the zoo's head monkey and yesterday a very disappointed gorilla.

"Originally, we were bringing the little girl gorilla over to be Frank's bride," Dr. Fisher said, "but comparing them now, the little girl is just too little. Frank will have to wait for another."

As the last howl, Frank and Dr. Fisher did not agree.

# Building a zoo and filling it

Collecting trips like the one I took with Frank were routine business trips for the Lincoln Park Zoo and other zoos in years past. Indeed, the animal collection at Lincoln Park had grown over the years in much the same way the passenger list on Noah's Ark grew, though not always two by two.

The zoo was started in 1868 with a pair of swans. And at the risk of sounding as if I am launching into *The Twelve Days of Christmas*, next came two buffalo, eight peacocks, two China geese, four guinea pigs, two prairie dogs, three foxes, one owl, two elk, twelve ducks, three wolves, two rabbits, a turtle dove, one bear, two squirrels, four eagles . . . and on it went.

Donations of animals were frequent. As previously noted, as a child I had donated my own pet alligator to the collection. The zoo's first purchase was a bear cub, acquired in 1874 for $10.

"Duchess" the elephant, who became quite famous, came to the zoo in 1889, bought from the original Barnum & Bailey Circus, along with several other exotic animals.

More often, after the turn of the century and for more than 60 years thereafter, growing the ark required the help of animal dealers.

Reproduction of most captive animals was very limited, if it happened at all, and at the time we still believed animals in the wild were in plentiful supply. When an animal died, it was a very sad affair, but it could usually be replaced rather easily. The zoo simply contacted an animal dealer or trapper who specialized in acquiring almost anything that flew, walked, crawled, slithered, or swam.

Animal dealers and trappers varied from independent one-man operations to large, highly organized companies with networks of contacts around the world.

Some of the people in the animal dealer business I dealt with frequently over the years included Fred Zeehandler, the Hunt brothers, Warren Buck, Frank Thompson, and Joe McHale—a keeper at Lincoln Park Zoo. In Europe, the Ruhe and Hagenbeck families kept the zoos supplied.

These guys—and they were all guys—were characters in a rough-and-ready business. They filled an important niche and kept visitors enthralled with a variety of amazing and exotic animals, never-before-seen in captivity.

But the process of collecting animals for a zoo was a tedious, dangerous, physically dirty and demanding job, as I quickly discovered when I traveled to Africa.

Collecting methods varied dramatically, depending on the species of animal, its habitat, country of origin and the skills of the local people used as trackers and guides. The politics of certain countries also played a role in the process of both collecting and transporting the animals. Timing could be a critical factor, as circumstances could change overnight—such as a new government taking over a country—which happened often!

# Catching animals

There were commonly accepted ways to catch different species.

Birds, for example, were caught in mist nets. These are large, open nets that stretch across an open field or in a forest area. The nets entangle birds when they fly and allow them to be released unharmed if they are not of the desired species. Nets like this are still used today by researchers in the field who study birds, count numbers in a habitat, and band birds prior to releasing them.

Reptiles can be caught in their habitat using snake sticks to bag them, but the most important part is knowing their behavior patterns and where they are likely to be during the day or night.

Until the late 1960s, larger hooved animals were pursued in vehicles, with a rider seated on the outside front fender (riding "shotgun"). The rider's weapon of choice, however, was *not* a gun but a lariat, extended on a long pole. The rider was to rope the animal at the appropriate moment. Imagine the amount of skill and experience required to rope a giraffe or a frantic zebra at just the right moment, without losing or injuring the animal—*or the rider!*

Or imagine being strapped into a little seat on the front of a vehicle lurching wildly over the African veldt or plains at 30 to 40 mph and dropping unexpectedly into an aardvark hole at the least opportune time! (I learned a few things about aardvark holes first-hand on my first safari to Africa . . . but that's later).

Unfortunately, in wild expeditions such as these, animals were sometimes hurt and, all too frequently, so were the people who were working the capture equipment. Once the capture gun, loaded with anesthetic, was invented in the early 1970s, this highly dangerous "cowboy capture" system stopped. But the old roping, used for decades, was amazingly successfully and worked extremely well in its time.

The African cowboys who roped wild animals, and their counterparts in other countries who were directly responsible for the tracking and collecting of animals, are lost to history. We don't know their names or much about them, but they were clearly a brave lot who did their jobs unstintingly and occasionally died in the course of their work. They are the unheralded heroes of the old days of animal collecting, and I imagine *their* stories could easily fill a book or two.

## Collecting animals

I found it amazing that as a zoo director in 1962, I could phone, wire, or write to dealers and trappers around the world to secure what I wanted, when I wanted it. We only had to agree on the price and date of delivery. Obviously, the more exotic the animal and likely degree of difficulty in obtaining it, the higher the price. The term "market price" had a very real meaning.

Eddie Almandarz, reptile curator, was a "natural" with this boa constrictor and every other kind of snake. (ca. 1978). Courtesy, Chicago Park District

Additionally, insurance to guarantee live delivery of an animal was expensive because, sadly, many animals that were captured did not survive long enough to be delivered to a zoo.

My 1964 trip to Cameroon, and a second trip a few years later, were among the last collecting trips of their kind for Lincoln Park Zoo. Times were changing, and so were the laws. The ethics of the zoo business were also being reexamined.

Today, a zoo's primary method of acquiring animals is through an exchange with other accredited institutions under the auspices of the Species Survival Plans of the American Zoo and Aquarium Association (AZA). There are strict rules for animal importation, whether from overseas or even across state lines.

Numerous governmental bodies regulate which animals can be exported to what countries and which can be imported. Additionally, each animal being transported comes with enough permit documentation to match the size of several city telephone directories.

Such procedures are complicated, difficult, and vitally important to ensure that animals that *shouldn't be exported* are protected in their countries of origin, and those that *are* imported can be carefully monitored for diseases and other conditions once they arrive in the United States.

The Species Survival Plan of the AZA carefully selects animals and places them with others of their species according to each animal's genetic heritage. This eliminates inbreeding among small, captive groups that represent each animal species.

But the old era hadn't quite ended at the time my predecessor Marlin Perkins was zoo director and in my early years as director as well.

Marlin, as I've noted previously, was a herp specialist—an expert on snakes—and an active collector. He and one of his keepers, Ed Almandarz, who later became Curator of Reptiles when I took charge of the zoo, went on many snake hunts over the years, capturing a number of reptiles for the zoo. In fact, long after Marlin had moved on to the St. Louis Zoo and later retired, Ed continued with annual snake hunts to Arizona, New Mexico, Louisiana, and Texas, seeking specimens for Lincoln Park.

Ed, like Marlin, was almost entirely self-taught in the zoo business. He was a wiry, small fellow with a big heart, and probably not the type of guy people thought would be comfortable handling venomous reptiles. But Ed, or Eddie as he was known to most of us, was a "natural." Although he joked that he was color-blind (and his unmatched clothing often attested to that), he was highly observant and attuned in the school of practical knowledge. He was also one of the best herp persons in the country. With his positive attitude and an incredible work ethic, all the while he worked his way up from keeper to Curator of Reptiles, I never worried about the zoo's reptile collection when it was in his care.

Ed's snake hunts took him out at night—on the road, where snakes in the southwest go to seek out heat at the end of hot, sunny days. Other locales required different knowledge of reptile habits, but mostly the process involved going where the snakes were.

His collecting equipment was pretty basic. He started with a van, specially outfitted with bins and boxes for a two-week trip, on which he would be accompanied by two keepers who were not necessarily snake people, but who could get along together and could get the job done. Their professional equipment included:

- Several snake sticks used for capture. A snake stick looks like a modified golf club with a hook or flattened end at the bottom and tongs or a spring handle at the top end;
- Cloth bags the keepers attached to their belts, to carry specimens while hiking;
- Nets for turtles, tortoises, or lizards;
- General clothing (depending upon the climate) to which was added knee high heavy leather snake boots to prevent a snake bite;
- A hat;
- Anti-venin kits;
- A miner's lamp, attached over the headgear, for nighttime collecting;
- Flashlights, penknives, and varied lengths of rope and strong string for tying bags;
- Snack food for the staff (potato chips, etc.) and of course for the reptiles (worms, crickets, small mice, chicks, and other tempting morsels);
- Record books, road maps, letters of introduction and travel money;
- Gloves were optional.

A two-week trip usually netted or *bagged* from 50 to 200 specimens for the zoo's collections, among which would be between 20 and 30 rattlesnakes, depending on the collecting locale. Rattlesnakes, and other specimens caught in quantity, would be used as collateral to trade to other zoos for specimens we didn't have.

The snake hunt was a way to collect specimens and train keepers in the handling and collecting of animals. It was also a way for me to reward keepers with time away from their regular duties while performing a productive activity for the benefit of the zoo.

# Something for the birds

Sometimes rewards can seem better than they are.

In the summer of 1981, I rewarded myself with a trip, accompanying Kevin Bell, the zoo's Bird Curator, to Iceland to collect puffins for the zoo's new Penguin-Seabird House—an experience I vowed never to repeat.

I don't know what possessed me to join Kevin, though it must have seemed like an exciting thing to do at the time. Today, when I recall being perched precipitously high above the ocean on the side of a windswept cliff, I definitely don't see it that way.

We had flown to Iceland in August, one of the warmer times of year on that weather-beaten island. We were well-prepared with the necessary permits, crates, and specially insulated boxes. Our mission was to collect puffin chicks that were old enough to travel but young enough that they would not to be overly stressed by their relocation to the new Penguin-Seabird House that would open the following fall at Lincoln Park Zoo.

Five of us, including three zookeepers, received permission from the U.S. Department of Interior, the U.S. Department of Agriculture, and the Icelandic government to collect up to 50 common puffins, 8 kittiwakes, and 8 common murres. These pelagic birds live most of their lives at sea, returning to land to nest on the most inaccessible and inhospitable cliffs imaginable. And there *I* was, competing with them for footing!

I can still remember the rain. And the cold. And wind. It was miserable.

Our slickers were muddy and only barely functional as raingear, and our arms were sore from reaching into the nests up to our armpits to collect the chicks. But this was the only way to do it if we really wanted to establish a colony of seabirds at Lincoln Park Zoo.

Once they become adults, the birds only return to their native habitat to breed, so by taking chicks, we were hoping to turn the breeding cycle in favor of Chicago.

I was the titular leader of the group, but Kevin actually headed the expedition and I remember questioning my sanity about being there, as has been noted, *perched on the side of a cliff!*

It was abundantly clear to me that the birds were much more at home there than we were.

Several times during a single afternoon, I recall seeing my life flashing before my eyes, as my slippery footing seemed ready to give way and send me plunging into the ocean crashing in on the rocks hundreds of feet below.

When I heard the words "we're done" echoing from somewhere above me, I knew it was none too soon, and I thankfully scrambled up the cliff with the others in our group, carrying our insulated boxes and precious cargo.

But at that point time became a critical factor.

Young chicks have voracious appetites and their parents would maintain a full-time fast-food service, bringing them regurgitated seafood to keep their body weights up and increasing. Since we were now their substitute parents, we had to feed them constantly, as we made our way back to the zoo in Chicago as quickly as possible.

Thanks to incredible cooperation from the Icelandic government and Iceland Air, we were safely back home in a few short days. We waited for the birds to be released from the U.S. Department of Agriculture's Quarantine Station in Newburg, New York. Thirty days later, they were en route to the Penguin-Seabird House at Lincoln Park Zoo.

An operation of this type, involving these kinds of birds, would not have been possible in the old days of collecting. With all due respect to the birds themselves, air transport made all the difference.

# Not flying quite so high

Our collecting trip to Iceland to get those cliff-perching puffins— the trip that I came to regard as a "cliff-hanger" of sorts for myself as well—became another medical mystery. Once the birds were settled in at the zoo, all seemed to be well. Then slowly, one by one, all the puffins died. It was a complete wipeout of every bird.

Each of them was necropsied and we performed dozens of laboratory tests to determine the cause of death. By the 1980s science had come a long way, and we had better access to laboratory analysis than ever before; yet the best efforts of the universities in the Chicago area, as well as the University of Illinois at Urbana, yielded nothing conclusive. We tested the paint inside the new Penguin-Seabird House, the fiberglass coating for the exhibit, and sent everything we could think of for toxicology reports. Nothing, but *nothing,* was revealed.

The only suspicious factor proved to be the freshwater fish from Lake Michigan and other Great Lakes, which we supplemented with daily vitamins and used to feed the birds. These fish showed higher than normal levels of toxic materials, including PCBs and heavy metal. After a second collecting expedition, when we brought the next collection of puffins into the zoo, we switched them to an ocean fish diet, and the problem was solved. We had no further mysterious deaths of puffins.

# Famous zoo animals I have known

## I. Judy the elephant

*"Get down! Now!"* the keeper shouted, and we both dropped to the floor. "She coulda killed ya, you know!" he added, glaring at me, suggesting that I should have known better.

I probably should have.

Judy was notorious for pulling that trick, but I was still new at the zoo.

What Judy liked to do was put a person between herself and the wall, whether it was in her inside enclosure or her outside enclosure. Then she would slowly—and almost imperceptibly—start *leaning* toward the wall. If a person wasn't aware of what was happening, she could slowly crush him or her to death. Some trick!

Being between a moving elephant and a solid wall makes the old expression about being between a rock and a hard place seem like kid stuff. Happily, when dealing with Judy, by dropping to the ground, it was possible to at least crawl out between her legs and avoid being crushed by her body.

At close to three tons, Judy was a big, Asian elephant and one of the biggest stars at the Lincoln Park Zoo. She also was very set in her ways. Not only did she use her massive bulk to keep people under control, she also used her trunk.

An elephant's trunk is like a fifth limb, and it can do wondrous things. Composed of literally tens of thousands of muscles, an elephant trunk can delicately pick up a penny, suck up gallons of water and shoot that water into its mouth, or it can tear out a tree by its roots.

During my vet days at the zoo, I saw Judy use her powerful trunk for all these things—as well as use it as a weapon. Twice during my vet career she picked up a keeper with her trunk and moved him out of her way—once tossing him completely outside the elephant enclosure. Fortunately, he wasn't hurt but he was more than a bit chagrined!

Judy was born around 1903, although some estimated she was born earlier than that—perhaps even before the turn of the century. Today we would know exactly how old she was because of our superior animal record-keeping system, but few records were kept on zoo animals back then.

Judy had made her stubborn streak known early on, most notably during her trip from Brookfield Zoo to Lincoln Park Zoo on July 2, 1943. Her story is made up of many interesting chapters, including the first one, chronicling her auspicious arrival at Lincoln Park. All Chicago knew about that!

Duchess, the great old elephant of the Lincoln Park Zoo, died in May of 1924, ostensibly from on overdose of peanuts. Because a zoo needs an elephant, Lincoln Park was anxious to have a replacement for Duchess and bought Judy from Brookfield Zoo, a sprawling zoo complex in Brookfield, Illinois, a richly landscaped suburb about 30 miles west of Chicago. All that remained was to move Judy across town to her new home.

Apparently when loading her into the truck, the springs gave way, and Judy backed out, refusing to be loaded . . . or so one version of the story goes. She probably wasn't sure of her footing, and elephants, being extremely smart, sensitive creatures, will back away from uncertain situations.

Ed Bean, then Director of Brookfield Zoo, saw a potentially great public relations opportunity and decided to walk Judy to Lincoln Park Zoo—*during the night*. By one account, he offered a keeper a new pair of shoes and $10 in cash. Another version of the story refers to a cash stipend—a reward, of sorts—from Lincoln Park.

But perhaps the most reliable account is the story told by one of the keepers who actually walked with Judy on that historic journey.

Paul J. Dittambl, a Senior Keeper, retold his version of the event in the Fall 1969 issue of the *Hoo-Zoo Newsletter*, a publication for members of The Lincoln Park Zoological Society:

> *On July 2, 1943, we set out to remedy our zoo's elephantless situation by bringing Judy, a 44-year-old Asian ex-circus performer from Brookfield Zoo.*

Heavily burdened with equipment, we teamed up with another group of keepers at Brookfield and proceeded to try to load Judy onto a specially fitted truck by backing up to the large door of her enclosure and coaxing her up onto [a] ramp of sturdy planks. But Judy then had her own ideas to the contrary. Apparently due to an unhappy memory of having, a year before, been driven to the Tribune Experimental Farm to prove an elephant could plow a field, Judy resolved it would not happen again and refused to budge.

After much coaxing, prodding and poking, we gave up, built a new ramp to the truck, this time padding it with soft, fragrant bales of hay, and again were met [with] majestic refusal.

We next attempted to walk Judy from the mall [at Brookfield Zoo] onto the truck at the same level. By then we had a spellbound audience of nearly a thousand persons. Judy stood on her rights and again refused to cooperate.

By then everyone but Judy was tired of trying to move her with gentle persuasion and we decided to pull her onto the truck bed with a 180-ton motor-driven winch. At last Judy was on the truck!

But not for long. She immediately started a kind of jig, which effected the total destruction of the stake sidings and slid off the truck on her belly, trotted over to a smaller truck and had it halfway over before we were able to divert her attention and she lumbered off, with me in hot pursuit, the red-faced butt of ribald remarks by the amused onlookers.

We finally had to compromise. At 7 PM that evening, Judy, with an escort of eight strong men, a vanguard of police on motorcycles, and two zoo staff cars, started off at her pace of 5 MPH on our 18-mile journey, followed joyously by around 50 children shooting off firecrackers and dogs yapping at Judy's heels—all ignored by her.

When we got to Maywood we 'pulled' into a gas station where Judy, to the amazement of the attendant, drank 60 gallons of water. By 10 PM we had made it to

*Garfield Park, a scheduled rest and feed stop. In grati-
tude, Judy ate two quarts of oats, a bale of hay and
drank 30 more gallons of water.*

*We left there at midnight and the kids began to be
replaced by adults. One man looked at Judy and said:
'If this was last night, I could believe it, but tonight I'm
sober and this one is alive!' By now, Judy was pretty
tired but plodded on and at 2:30 AM we finally arrived
at her new home.*

*She gave a large squeal, rolled over and went right
to sleep. Her three fellow hoofers had holes in our
shoes, blistered feet, and had lost 10 lbs each (Judy had
lost 500 lbs), but we had an elephant at last in Lincoln
Park Zoo."*

Judy received a lot of press coverage for her walk and instantly
gained celebrity status throughout Chicago.

Once at Lincoln Park Zoo, her winter quarters were at the
north end of the old Small Mammal House, which at that time
was already nearly 50 years old. In summer, from May to October, Judy was moved to her outside quarters, her summer house,
which was located on the west side of "Main Street," the long
walkway that consisted of the old bear/fox/hyena/wolf line heading up to the Lincoln Park Conservatory at the north end of the
Zoo. A sand area surrounded the house and large iron bars ringed
the outside perimeter.

To move Judy from her winter to summer quarters and back
each year, she was walked, albeit a shorter, less dramatic walk than
the one that brought her to Chicago and Lincoln Park.

However, in order to get her large bulk out and back into the
Small Mammal House every year, the large, fan-shaped windows
above the door at the west end of the building had to be removed
each time. Her keeper, a "bull-man," would then walk her home.

In those days the concept of managing elephants with a bull-
man was the accepted method. It was done that way in zoos and
circuses all over the world. Originating with the Indian concept of
a mahout—one person, full-time, throughout the elephant's life—
the bull-man concept seemed good enough, but it was difficult to
manage. When the bull-man (and again, it was always a man)

became ill, chose to take a vacation, or retired, the elephant would not accept anyone else to care for it.

Needless to say, this presented numerous problems. It was difficult to safely introduce a new person to the elephant, and, just as often, the elephant would not accept the new person.

Today, the system is much more efficient, manageable and sensible. A team of keepers (many of them women) looks after elephants in a setting more akin to a herd than to the mahout theory. It works, and is much easier to manage in terms of people. The elephants seem to like it, too.

After a dramatic entrance and a long and colorful reign at the zoo, I remember sadly the morning of May 11, 1988, when Judy's keeper stood nervously in my office.

"She isn't right, Doc," he said quietly.

I raced over to her summer quarters and found Judy, lying on her side. I knew it was important that we get her up. Quite frequently, animals that can't stand on their own can be helped to their feet and, once up, nature will take over and help them to recover. Lying down for any length of time creates unnatural pressure on the lungs and usually blocks the digestive process, which ultimately, results in the animal's death.

I was no longer the zoo doctor—Dr. Erich Maschgan held that post—and he was pacing back and forth beside Judy, trying to figure out how to get her up. Standing beside Judy, her immense girth and size were even more impressive.

I began making phone calls to various Park District offices and departments, including the riggers and ironworkers whose equipment included hoist trucks and block and tackle. Crews arrived quickly in such times of emergency and tried valiantly to improvise a system to bring Judy to her feet. Since she was inside her house, some of the block and tackle couldn't even get to her.

We were able to rig-up something, but try as we might, we could not get her to her feet. It was becoming clear that Judy's time had come, and the end for her was approaching quickly.

The death note we placed in her records read simply, "Animal down at 9:30 AM. Unable to get her to stand. Death at 5:30 PM."

Like many Asian elephants brought into this country at that time, Judy was probably caught in the wild for the express purpose of performing in a circus. And quite a circus performer she was for many years, until she was sold to Brookfield Zoo. Perhaps she was sold because she was stubborn and ornery, qualities that were not all that uncommon in elephants. Certainly Judy's personality fell into that category.

At the time of her death, we believed Judy was the oldest elephant in captivity at any zoo. If the estimated birth date of 1903 was correct, she was more than 85 years old, so we concluded that she died of natural causes.

But death, even when it is attributed to old age, is still a death and an occasion of great sorrow in the zoo community. The animals we care for are not simply animals to us; they are members of our family. We all mourned Judy that day.

Working in a zoo requires us to accept the natural life cycle of the animals in our care. So as much as we mourn the ones we lose, we celebrate the births and every new animal that becomes part of our zoo family. Stubborn, ornery Judy is gone, but not forgotten among those who knew her and truly miss her.

# Famous zoo animals I have known

## II. Mike the polar bear

A great addition to the Lincoln Park Zoo family was Mike, the polar bear, whom I knew from the time he was a young cub.

When Mike arrived in 1956—a gift from the Alaska Territory Elks Association—he weighed barely 15 pounds and resembled an adorable white fluff ball.

Mike grew up to become a truly magnificent animal. He was about 8 feet tall when standing upright and, in his prime, weighed around 900 pounds. Mike lived at the end of the old Bear Line on Main Street, and it seemed as if everyone wanted to see him, no matter what other animals they visited at the zoo.

He had so many fans and admirers that some people even cooked special meals for him and would surreptitiously toss them over the barrier for him to devour. We never actually caught anyone doing this, but it was common knowledge around the zoo that it happened.

Some of the zoo "regulars" who visited every day acknowledged that they'd prepared various baked goods for Mike, as well as an occasional beef casserole. Although his regular diet consisted of whole fish, as well as a prepared bear diet that was similar to dog food, Mike's favorite food was marshmallows—the kind that were sold by the bagful at the nearby concession stand and would be vigorously tossed to him by his many visitors.

Mike would stand on his hind legs, with his front paws up to his mouth, wave to visitors, open his mouth wide, and catch the marshmallows being hurled over the iron railing of the bear cage.

Of course marshmallows aren't normally in a polar bear's diet—especially thousands of marshmallows over a lifetime. So in addition to providing him with way too much sugar, they created a sticky mess, both inside the animal cage and on the walkways. Much to the chagrin of Mike and his many visitors, we had to stop selling marshmallows at the concession stand, which was too bad, as they were a very popular item.

But by the time we stopped selling marshmallows, the damage to Mike's teeth was already done—or at least so we thought.

As Mike got older, he had more and more problems with his teeth. Dental problems occur in the animal's natural habitat too, but not from marshmallows. In the wild, the animal has to suffer. In Mike's case, when he opened his mouth wide, you could see some broken canines and clearly one in particular that caused him trouble when eating. He would paw at his mouth with his forefoot and try to bite his food on the other side, away from the problem tooth.

We decided we had to subdue Mike long enough to take a look at the tooth and determine the extent of the problem. As he was already a favorite of local media, we thought it only appropriate to alert the press that we were going to take Mike to the dentist (though in reality, the dentist would be coming to Mike). We asked if some of the reporters and photographers wanted to be on hand at the zoo to observe the procedure.

I had already contacted our dental advisory group (a number of *people doctors* interested in animal medicine that we had assembled as an advisory group over the years) and asked them to work with us as I expected we would need their help.

The weather in Chicago was beautiful, and it was obviously a slow news day. *All* the media seemed to be on hand, along with the dental advisory group, our staff, and the regular bear keepers. It was quite a crowd.

We chose to use a newer tranquilizing drug we had not tried on bears before, which had proved superior to other chemical tranquilizers when used on other animals. Phencyclidine is a fairly safe drug under normal circumstances, and it places the animal in an anesthetic state. What's good about it is that the difference between the animal being asleep and waking is more than a few minutes.

Using phencyclidine created a wider margin of safety than we'd had with the other drugs, where we sometimes had only seconds between the animal being fully out and then, suddenly, fully awake.

What we didn't know about phencyclidine (and many drugs in the beginning) was how much to use on an animal. Eventually dosages were determined over time by sharing our experiences with those of other vets, but in the early days using a new drug meant guessing and administering a dosage based upon the approximate weight of an animal.

Having moved Mike to an adjacent cage, we emptied his small swimming pool as best we could but, with our old plumbing, there was still some water at the bottom of the pool. Next, Dr. Maschgan, our zoo doctor, darted Mike with the tranquilizer gun. *Finally,* we were finished with ropes, thank heaven.

Mike went down after one injection of phencyclidine in the rump.

Using an eight-foot pole and reaching carefully between the iron bars, I gently nudged his behind to see if he was really asleep. Getting no apparent response except some reflex movement from his muscles, we felt it was safe to go in with him.

However, just to make sure he was really out, and to minimize any pain from the procedure, I suggested administering an additional drug to really knock him out cold. I'd already learned from my experience with the jaguar. I was concerned that removing the broken teeth would be difficult because, canine teeth are as embedded into the jaw in bears much as they are in the big cats. They extend way up into the upper and way down into the lower, jawbone. This allows bears to catch large seals in their mouths and with one paw literally lift them out of the water.

At this point I felt it was safe for everyone else to enter the enclosure—all the better for everyone to have a good view of the procedure, rather than standing at a distance outside the cage.

Getting everyone in, however, wasn't easy. Access to the front of Mike's cage was through a tiny door about four feet high and three feet wide. People had to sort of ease their way in very carefully, so it took a while to get the press and their camera gear inside, along with the dental advisory group and the members of my staff.

About the time that our dentist veterinarian started his examination of Mike's mouth, particularly the broken and infected teeth, Mike began to stir. He wasn't fully awake, but his legs started moving, as if he were running in place and his head began moving up and down.

Everyone assumed Mike was waking up and none of us wanted to be in there with him when he did.

I shouted at the press people to get out as quickly as possible, and they tried to do just that. If the scene hadn't been so scary it would have been comical. Here were about a dozen adults with a lot of camera equipment, all trying frantically to get through one tiny little door at the same time. There was a lot of fussing, as I recall, over who had priority to get out first.

I, on the other hand, felt that as "captain of the ship" I had to be the last to go. So everyone, including my staff, left ahead of me. It was a long few minutes as I considered how at any moment Mike would come back to life and leap on top of me.

I believe bears, especially polar bears, are the most dangerous animals in any zoo. They strike without giving any apparent visual warning (unlike the big cats), and I kept thinking about that as I looked over at Mike, twitching and shaking.

Minutes passed, the twitching and shaking stopped, and Mike settled back into a quiet sleep. Once again, we opened the cage door, nudged him with the long stick, and I invited my staff, the media, and the dentist advisory group back into cage.

This time, however, their enthusiasm was somewhat tempered, but after a while they must have concluded that if I was in there, it must be safe for them too. Slowly, one by one, the group reassembled.

The procedure took quite some time and was difficult, but we eventually managed to extract two of Mike's broken teeth.

Two years later, we had to repeat this procedure and extract more of Mike's teeth. By then, however, we had learned through sharing our "tremor" experience with our colleagues that with bears, certain dosages of phencyclidine would produce convulsions during anesthesia.

We also learned that Mike's dental problems were most likely not the result of a steady diet of marshmallows, but rather his habit of biting off chunks of rock at the back of his cage. This broke his teeth, which would then ultimately become infected. I doubt, however, that the marshmallows helped the situation.

Mike lived to a good age—21 years—more than average for a polar bear. He was a favorite among zoo visitors and one of our more popular zoo animals. When Mike died, my staff knew that I would want to personally perform the necropsy, and I did.

# Famous zoo animals I have known

## III. Bushman, the legendary lowland gorilla

During my early years at the zoo there were actually three "most popular" animals. One of them was certainly Bushman, the lowland gorilla who became a legend at Lincoln Park Zoo and is still remembered with affection after three-quarters of a century.

Bushman was a wild-caught young gorilla from Cameroon, West Africa who came to Lincoln Park Zoo at a time when gorillas rarely survived being captured. Years ago, standard procedure was to kill the mother gorilla and, often, others in the troop who would try to protect the youngster.

If baby gorillas survived that ordeal, they rarely survived the next few days because no one knew what to feed them. Then the poor creatures had to endure a journey by sea of several weeks, all the while stuffed into a small crate in a dark, damp, usually cold *hold* of a ship. It was at this point that many developed pneumonia and died. But if they survived the voyage, they didn't survive life at a zoo. Little was known about what they ate or what they needed. For every little gorilla that made it to a zoo alive, many others died. It was a very sad part of the history of the animal world and certainly a sad episode in the history of zoos.

Bushman was special right from the beginning—whatever the story of where he came from or how he was caught, and that story had many versions.

One was that his mother was killed by African hunters in Mbalmayo, about 50 miles south of Yaounde, Cameroon, and he was found shortly thereafter nearby and brought to a missionary camp in Elat, Cameroon in 1928.

Another version said J.L. Buck of Camden, New Jersey

captured him and that he was a nursing baby. No mention of his mother was made.

Yet a third account has Bushman as a mere babe when a village chieftain wounded his mother and drove her away into the forest, following which the chief took the baby home and hired a wet nurse to care for him. Thereafter, he became the chief's pet and was treated as a prince.

What we *do* know is that somewhere in French Cameroon in 1928, Bushman was orphaned. We believe he was taken in by an African chieftain and was named Nigi Batwi, meaning "Wild Man of the Forest." We also know that he was well cared for and was a healthy baby.

In 1929, a Presbyterian missionary named Dr. W.C. Johnson arrived at the tribal camp and immediately took a shine to the young gorilla. He convinced the chief to part with the animal for $200. We also know that James Blaine and Annie Mary Allen, other missionaries from Chicago, helped care for him and seemed to know what he needed to survive.

That appears to be about the time animal dealer Julius Buck entered the picture. Buck saw the animal in Cameroon and recognized its moneymaking potential.

But the gorilla was not for sale.

Finally, Buck was able to strike a deal. He learned that the missionaries wanted stained glass windows for the new Yaounde Church they were building. He agreed to pay for the windows with the proceeds from the sale of the little gorilla in the United States.

I had heard the story about the stained glass windows when I first came to Lincoln Park, but never gave it much credence. There were many stories going around about Bushman by the time I began caring for him in 1947. I thought this was just one more.

Apparently, Bushman came to the United States with Buck and was offered to several zoos. Given the track record of keeping a gorilla alive at that time, no one was willing to pay Buck's asking price, knowing the animal would likely die shortly thereafter.

No one, that is, but Alfred E. Parker, the third Director of Lincoln Park Zoo. Parker immediately liked what he saw and bought Nigi Batwi for $3,500. This was considered an incredible sum of money in 1931, when the country was in the middle of the Great Depression.

The young 37-pound gorilla was immediately renamed "Bushman" and made his Chicago debut to a frenzied media crowd. Thousands of people came to the zoo to see the incredible ape for themselves and during the 1933 Chicago World's Fair he made friends with visitors from around the world. Bushman quickly became an international celebrity.

Early in his zoo career, while still a youngster, Bushman was given free rein. He was little, he was cute, and he was *reasonably* under control. His lifelong keeper, Eddie Robinson, could take him on a leash around the zoo. Bushman was featured in numerous zoo publicity photos. He was treated more like a pet than a wild animal.

But, eventually, Bushman's increasing strength proved too much for Robinson, who reluctantly had to keep him in his cage after a terrifying walk one day—a day Robinson spent on the wrong end of Bushman's leash when Robinson could not coax Bushman back into his cage.

Bushman was indeed magnificent, growing to a height of 6'2" and a weight of 550 pounds. His arm span was 12 feet and he was the largest gorilla in captivity at the time. Ringling Brothers' *Gargantua*, the other famous gorilla of that decade, was slightly smaller.

In mid-summer, 1950 Bushman had a coronary that partially paralyzed his right arm and leg. He was already showing some signs of arthritis and heart disease prior to that incident, but when the coronary occurred, I became extremely concerned. Not only was he "Chicago's darling," but all of us at the zoo had a special place in our hearts for Bushman. He was so popular with visitors that when word got out that he was sick, more than 120,000 people came to visit him in a single day.

The end for Bushman came on New Year's Day, 1951.

I was at home when I got the call, and I rushed to the zoo, but it was too late. Bushman had apparently died in his sleep. We were beside ourselves. It just seemed as if he would go on forever, even though we knew that was impossible. We are professionals and had witnessed the passing of countless animals about which we cared very deeply, but we just couldn't imagine the zoo without him.

At the time of his death Bushman was 23 years old, the oldest gorilla in captivity.

Marlin Perkins was Zoo Director at the time and he had a

life-size portrait of Bushman placed in the cage that had been his home.

In the weeks following his death, something extraordinary occurred. Thousands of mourners filed past Bushman's empty cage in respectful, silent tribute. It was amazing to see how he seemed to have touched so many lives so deeply, the deep affection people continued to have for him, and the great sadness that showed on their faces when they passed his empty cage. I still get misty thinking about him and that time.

In the early 1960s, when I was in Cameroon on a collecting trip for more gorillas, I visited the little chapel in Yaounde and asked about the stained glass windows. The minister pointed and said proudly, "There, those are *the Bushman windows*."

I stopped to admire the beautiful windows and bowed my head in memory of that wonderful animal. I left the church and Africa shortly after that, knowing that at least that part of the story of Bushman's early life was true.

Bushman had touched the hearts of so many people and to me he was one of the greatest, if not *the greatest* animal that ever lived. Voted "the most outstanding single animal in any zoo in the world" by the American Zoo Directors in 1946, he certainly got my vote. He also sparked my lifelong love of gorillas, the world's gentle giants.

One final note: More than a half-century later, Bushman lives on at The Field Museum, where he was taken after his death (and where many of Lincoln Park Zoo's animals go for further study after they die). More than 750,000 people a year still come to see Bushman, who taxidermists mounted in his classic gorilla stance. He is still one of the most popular exhibits at the museum.

I will never forget him.

## Gorilla gorilla gorilla

On July 22, 1970 my guests did not expect to be rousted from the table midway through an excellent dinner of leg of lamb—yes, not all veterinarians are vegetarians—but, there they now sat, quietly reassembled on chairs arranged in a circle behind me, in the old primate house at the zoo.

"Push!" someone couldn't resist murmuring.

My family and I had moved into a comfortable apartment

across the street from the zoo. I had made the decision that there would be no more frantic cross-town dashes when emergency calls came, and such a call had come on what was planned to be a relaxing evening with friends. It had begun calmly enough, before turning into an evening capped by an extraordinary and historic event.

The phone call that interrupted dinner was my night keeper at the zoo, alerting me that Mumbi, our female lowland gorilla (scientific name: *Gorilla gorilla gorilla*), was showing early signs of labor.

This came as no surprise, as the keepers had observed breeding between Mumbi and Kisoro, her mate, many months back and had been monitoring her ever since. A urine sample sent to the lab of a local hospital confirmed her pregnancy at the three-month mark, and we knew that around this time she was nearing her 8-1/2 months term. We'd established a 24-hour watch on Mumbi for the past few days and were looking forward to the first birth of a gorilla at Lincoln Park Zoo.

Few such captive births had occurred around the country—or *around the world*—although the Columbus Zoo had produced Colo, the first gorilla born in captivity, in 1956.

I had consulted with both veterinary colleagues and human OB/GYN specialists in Chicago, including Dr. Mel Bailey of our medical advisory committee. Mumbi was such an unusually good-tempered animal that I had been able to go in the cage with her, accompanied by Dr. Bailey, for a simple hands-on examination. He had confirmed her pregnancy early on and examined her once or twice more during the subsequent months to determine the position of the fetus.

When the call came about Mumbi, my guests all wanted to know what was happening, so I suggested they skip dinner and come with me to the zoo. I promised that, if they were very quiet, they could stay and be witnesses to what I hoped would be an important and historic moment for the zoo.

I also called everyone on my staff to come watch Mumbi give birth. And I called Dr. Bailey, who was on his way to a nearby hospital to deliver a human baby, but promised he would come to the zoo as soon as possible.

Mumbi paced about her cage, clearly very restless. Most gorilla births occur rather quickly, but Mumbi was both a small gorilla and a first-time mother, so this delivery was taking longer. She would go to the back of the cage for treats we provided for her, which allowed me to handle her just enough to check that the fetus was properly positioned. I advised everyone to be patient, we simply had to let nature take its course.

Eventually, the amniotic sac ruptured and a tiny head was visible. Despite strong labor contractions, the birth was slow and took about an hour. Happily, it was uneventful (for Mumbi). A live, normal baby gorilla appeared, and she scooped it up in her big hand and held it in her arms.

We were all very emotional, deeply overcome—and exhausted—just watching Mumbi. Saul Kitchener, my assistant director (and one of the burliest, gruffest people I knew, with a voice that could boom across the zoo and a temper to match), stood watching as tears ran down his face. It was a miracle moment, as well as a "first" for our little Chicago zoo.

Dr. Bailey arrived after the fact and declared mother and baby were fine. My staff remained to monitor them, and my guests and I returned to my apartment, where the conversation remained lively, but the rest of dinner seemed rather mundane after what we'd just witnessed.

The next issue of the Zoo Society's newsletter carried a story that began:

> *By now, news has spread worldwide that Mumbi and Kisoro [her mate] have produced the first baby gorilla ever to be born in the 102 years of Lincoln Park Zoo's existence.*

# A promise kept

Mumbi's baby, named Kumba, was the result of a commitment I had made to myself when I first began caring for Bushman, and later for his successor Sinbad, and all the other gorillas that followed them. I wanted our gorillas to become gorillas—*real gorillas*, not the mythical, ferocious beasts of *King Kong* and other Hollywood fictions.

Western lowland gorillas are the only type of gorillas in captivity. The mountain gorillas studied by George Schaller, and later by Dian Fossey, are another type and the third species of gorilla is the eastern lowland gorilla, which researchers are only now learning more about.

All gorillas are wonderful, smart, sensitive, and very gentle creatures. Their genetic composition is very close to humans, though not quite as close to us as chimps. They are *sharing* animals that live in close-knit family groups in the wild and the males, or *silverbacks*, so called because their backs turn gray/white as they age, are highly protective of their group. If necessary, they will defend their families even at the cost of their own lives.

When I joined the zoo, we knew little about a gorilla's needs—nutritionally, medically, and socially. We kept Bushman alone and isolated all his life in a sterile cage, exactly the opposite of how gorillas live in the wild. We didn't give him anything to stimulate his curious mind. We learned only after his death that he had a B1 thiamine deficiency because we erroneously believed gorillas ate only vegetation, rather than a mix of grubs, vegetation and, sometimes, small animals and birds.

## More gorillas

One thing we *did* know was that gorillas fascinated people in ways that almost no other zoo animals did. Even before Bushman died, Marlin Perkins sought a replacement for this great animal. In 1948 he brought in four young gorillas—Rajah, Lotus, Irving B. Young, and Sinbad. He had gone to Cameroon himself to collect them.

Rajah, a male gorilla, was shipped to Germany to pair up with a lone female. But when "he" arrived in Hanover, it turned out that Rajah was a *she*. (Marlin had a hard time living *that* down.) Rajah lived only another year after going to Europe at the young age of seven or eight.

Lotus had serious health problems. During one medical procedure, the gorilla never woke up from the anesthetic.

Irving B. Young, who had been named for a Chicago businessman, died at only about five years of age. None of the gorillas lived to be as old as Bushman—except Sinbad.

Sinbad turned out to be as impressive an animal as Bushman, at least in size. When I first examined him in 1948 he weighed only 28 pounds. Ultimately, he would grow to more than *500 pounds*!

As Sinbad matured, he was paired with Lotus in an early

attempt to produce babies. Everyone in the zoo world wanted to be the first to have a baby gorilla.

But Sinbad bit and hurt Lotus badly when they were put together. I'm convinced it was not because he was mean, but because of the small cages and our lack of knowledge in preparing gorillas to be paired up.

As I had to administer medical care to Lotus after that incident, which was pretty bad, I had to agree with Marlin that another attempt at pairing might not be worth it. So Sinbad lived out his life in solitary confinement in the old primate house. When the other great apes moved to the new Great Ape House in 1976, Sinbad was deemed too old to go with them. He remained alone in the Primate House. We were concerned that just putting him under anesthesia might kill him.

Sinbad was the second oldest gorilla in captivity at the time, when he suffered what appeared to be a stroke or heart attack. He died on March 18, 1985 at the age of 38. His 6-foot frame was wracked with arthritis, and he had been on an aspirin regimen for some time. Although he appeared healthy and alert only moments before, when his time came he simply slumped over and died.

The death of Sinbad was a tremendous personal loss for me. It signaled the end of the old gorilla era at Lincoln Park Zoo, but his passing also signaled new beginnings for a time when gorillas were together in troops and provided with a day full of activities to replicate their time in the wild.

In 1951 Marlin told the press, "Bushman is irreplaceable. Money cannot buy another Bushman." I felt that way about Sinbad as well.

One animal does not *replace* another animal. Each has his or her own personality, and stands on his or her own merits.

Sinbad was never replaced, but he did have some great successors in the long line of magnificent male gorillas at Lincoln Park Zoo. Frank and I brought back some of these animals ourselves from Africa. Others came to us through the years and, as our understanding grew and our experience expanded, many of the gorillas were born right at Lincoln Park Zoo.

Examining a newborn llama. Courtesy, Chicago Park District

Bengal tiger cubs were given their own nursery in the old Lion House (1950s). Courtesy, Chicago Park District

By 1964 our Bengal tiger cubs had a new Zoo Nursery and incubator to enjoy at the Children's Zoo. Courtesy, Chicago Park District

Christmas at the Children's Zoo Nursery. (c. 1968) Courtesy, Chicago Park District

Restraining a big jaguar with ropes was the only way to safely treat its infected eye in 1964. Courtesy, Chicago Park District

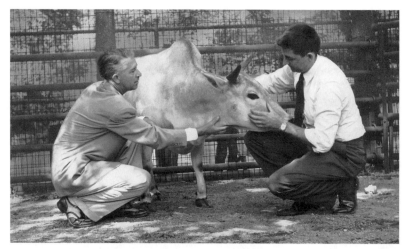

*Zoo Parade,* 1952, with Marlin Perkins and a zebu cow. Courtesy, Chicago Park District

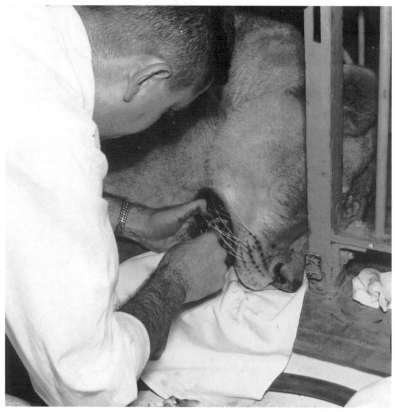

Dental surgery in the 1950s on an African lion. Courtesy, Chicago Park District

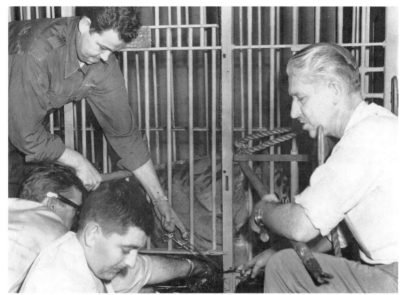

*Zoo Parade* captured this surgical procedure in the early 1950s. Marlin Perkins (r) supervises. Courtesy, Chicago Park District

In the 1960s I joined Mayor Richard J. Daley (center), Walter Erman, Founding Chair of The Lincoln Park Zoo Society, and Peter Bensinger, President of the Society (at right) to break ground for the initial rebuilding of the Zoo. Courtesy, Chicago Park District

Lincoln Park Zoo ca. 1900 with a keeper in front of the old Small Mammal House. Courtesy, Chicago Historical Society

Dr. Marlin Perkins, Zoo Director, uncrates Sinbad the gorilla in 1948 after his long journey from Cameroon. Courtesy, Chicago Park District

Frank Schmick at the daily Chimpanzee Tea Party with Pat Sammarco (l) and Pat Sass (r), "Zoo leaders" at our Children's Zoo (ca. 1966).

Sinbad as an adult. Courtesy, Chicago Park District

Debbie, an outstanding foster mom to Kivu and many other baby gorillas that needed to be reintroduced to the gorilla group after being hand-reared for medical reasons. Courtesy, Chicago Park District

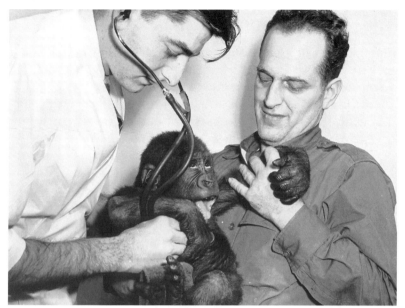

Examining Sinbad the gorilla when he arrived at the Zoo in 1948.
Roy Hoff (r) became Sinbad's lifetime keeper. Courtesy, Chicago
Park District

Mrs. Patrick G. (Shirley) Ryan helped forge the Zoo's partnership
with The Junior League of Chicago in the 1970s to raise awareness
for endangered species. Courtesy, Chicago Park District

# And STILL more gorillas

Among the gorillas that came to Lincoln Park Zoo were Freddie and Helen, whom I named after C.L. Frederick and his wife Helen, two of our long-time supporters, and founders of The Lincoln Park Zoological Society. It was my prerogative to name animals so I used that as an occasion to honor those who were supportive of the zoo and its work through the years.

There were Frank and Lenore, named for the Schmicks who, like the Fredericks, were nutty about gorillas. I also named Mary, Debbie and Otto—Mary for a daughter of the Schmicks, Debbie for their granddaughter, and Otto for Otto Kerner, the late Governor of Illinois, who during his life had been another friend of the zoo.

Kisoro, who had also come from Cameroon, was named for the area he came from, a practice we have continued through the years. Today, most of our gorillas have the names of places in Africa or their names mean something special in African languages, such as Swahili, Rwandese, or Bantu.

The nine gorillas brought into the zoo's collection in the 1960s made up what we now call "founder" stock. These are animals that were caught in the wild. Over the years it has become virtually impossible to collect a gorilla from the wild so those who were acquired in that way were—and still are—considered exceptionally valuable to the captive gorilla gene pool.

But, unlike Sinbad, who died celibate and alone as Bushman had, all of these gorillas got the benefit of a new way of looking at gorillas—as the gentle, inquisitive, smart animals they really are.

Kisoro was not as large as Bushman or Sinbad, but he made history as the first adult gorilla to go back east on his voyage across the Atlantic. Having sired Kumba with Mumbi, he was just too big for the other females and was badly needed in Britain where he was put with females at the late John Aspinall's private Howlett's Zoo Park. There he sired many babies before coming back to the States to live out his life at the Denver Zoo.

At 400 pounds and about 5'4", Otto was significantly smaller than either Sinbad or Bushman, but he was a formidable animal and had the personality of a rock star. With his characteristic "Mohawk" on his large head (an exaggerated look because of his particularly large sagital crest, as well as his habit of plucking the side hairs out), he was media-star material.

Otto had his day when the young filmmaker Dugan Rosalini

captured us moving the great apes to their new home at Lincoln Park Zoo in 1976. Otto was the film's star and with this nation-wide exposure, thanks to PBS broadcasting, *Otto: Zoo Gorilla*, he became a household word in Chicago and around the country.

Still, Otto didn't inherit the mantle of top zoo gorilla until Sinbad's death in 1985. He did, however, sire 11 babies, helping Lincoln Park Zoo earn its designation as "Gorilla Capital of the World."

Otto was another of the zoo's gorillas to die of a stroke or massive heart attack at the age of 24, in 1988. Was there a pattern developing for male gorillas? Were heart problems fairly common? We wondered about that as history repeated itself. An on-going scientific study of cardiac problems of gorillas has yet to provide the answer.

While Otto was rambunctious and playful, Freddie was calm and laid back—so much so that we called him "Uncle Freddie." He didn't seem very interested in breeding, but was particularly good with the babies that were offspring of other gorillas. It was not uncommon for Freddie to have two or three youngsters climbing all over him while he simply sat there, looking nonplussed. Eventually, he did father a few babies, but his best role was just that of a very tolerant and easy-going gorilla.

And, he was reportedly our first ambassador. As our gorilla collection grew thanks to our tremendous success at breeding, Lincoln Park was experiencing over-crowding in its new Great Ape House. Other zoos were desperate to get gorillas for their collections so we started our "ambassador program."

It was almost unheard of for one zoo to send a good gorilla to another zoo. They were valuable and, in most instances, they were the zoos' most popular animals, as well as being media stars, natural magnets for photo opportunities and publicity. News of our generous loan of Kisoro brought a barrage of calls from zoos asking if I would be willing to give up any other gorillas.

While historically zoos (and their directors) were quite territorial and not very cooperative in such matters, I always felt differently. Perhaps it had something to do with my being a vet, but I asked where would we be if we had not shared medical information with each other?—information I so desperately needed to move wild animal care to the next level. And where would we be as the laws began to tighten on how and where we could collect animals?

In my mind, zoos needed to cooperate seriously with one another if we were to create and maintain a true haven for endangered animals. I didn't see how any zoo could—or *should*—go it alone any longer.

So when the St. Louis Zoo was opening its new great ape facility, I made a decision to send it not just one gorilla, but a whole family of gorillas—Freddie's family of five. My colleagues, some of whom were convinced I'd gone mad, regarded this as a pretty bold move. But I thought it could be the beginning of a new era of cooperation and, after all, Lincoln Park Zoo already had *so many gorillas!*

# The trouble with gorillas

Part of our breeding success was luck.

We had more females born than males when, statistically, the ratio should have been about 50/50. Such an imbalance in favor of girls allowed us to leave them together in the group. If there had been more males, it would have been necessary to separate them when the males got to be teenagers, as they would have competed with the older males for breeding privileges. With so many girls, our gorilla families just grew bigger and bigger and bigger.

Our gorillas also raised their babies in the group. I started this system when Kumba was born. I left her with Mumbi, even though it was not considered prudent by many zoo professionals. Because a gorilla's hand is so big, it is impossible to see if a baby is on the breast or nursing when that hand is holding a baby to its chest. Some zoos still pull babies routinely to be hand-reared, but I was encouraged to leave the baby with its mother and once again let nature take its course.

I got the nerve to do this after consulting with the pediatrician who had cared for my daughters—and who happened to live across the street from the zoo, in the same building where I lived. Dr. Martin Hardy was a no-nonsense practitioner with the proverbial heart of gold. He told me to leave the baby with its mother; that it was not uncommon for a human baby to go three to four days without nursing and still be healthy. He urged me to wait and see how Mumbi would respond.

She *did* nurse the baby, and all was well. From that moment on I left the baby gorillas with their mothers every time. Only when I felt an infant was in imminent danger, would we act. We did pull a few babies whose mothers simply wouldn't or couldn't nurse them, but very few. The vast majority of babies were raised by their mothers in the gorilla troop, which helped all the other members of the troop, especially the young female gorillas, to learn how it was done.

Our new Great Ape House probably also contributed to our breeding success. It was built in-the-round, with several core areas, so it was like a multi-layered donut. Not only did it provide the animals with much more space, it allowed the males to hear, smell, and see each other from one habitat to the next. In retrospect, this was a brilliant idea. The close proximity to other males stimulated their breeding, as they believed they were competing with each other. Of course I can't prove it, but we think it helped.

We did have our sad experiences over the years with some of our founder gorillas.

Mary developed a chronic digestive disease that prevented her absorption of food. Treating her was a challenge. No matter what we did, she simply wasn't getting enough nutrition from her food, and we lost her.

Debbie bred many times with different males, but never conceived. For many years we considered her a failure, but her real legacy turned out to be far more valuable than giving birth. When babies had to be pulled from their mothers or the group due to an injury or some other problem, we had to hand-raise them. But we wanted them to follow the examples of gorillas, not be like little people. We wanted to reintroduce them to become gorillas again as soon as possible. That's very tricky because in the wild, the males can practice infanticide on infants that they have not sired. This sounds cruel but it is a way to promote genetic diversity.

A male takes over a group of females and kills the nursing babies. That immediately puts the females back into estrus, so he can breed with them and promote his own bloodline, introducing new genes into the gene pool. We used to think there was something wrong with male monkeys that did this, but we eventually learned that it was part of their normal life cycle, not aberrant behavior.

But even if the male is not a problem for an introduced youngster, a female can be. She may not accept a youngster into the group if she has not bonded with it.

Debbie proved to be the solution. Although she had not had babies of her own, she was a great aunt. We were able to repeatedly introduce hand-reared youngsters to her, and she bonded with them. When we introduced them both back into the group she was there to protect them.

Today it is not so easy and takes a long time, but with each successful reintroduction, we credit a great measure of our success to Debbie. Many people may well regard her as the most valuable gorilla ever at Lincoln Park Zoo. By 2003 when Debbie died, she had helped reintroduce 10 gorilla babies back into their groups.

Lenore was a tough case. She came to us in 1969 and was quite a bit older than the typical two to three year-old gorillas we usually brought back from the wild. Sinbad had been the youngest at about eight months and Lenore was the oldest at six years. She gave birth to four babies during her lifetime, but her claim to fame was to become the first gorilla great-grandmother in any zoo in the world. Additionally, she spent the last few years of her life as a partial amputee, learning to swing her "club" arm (amputated at the elbow) around to put any gorilla she wanted in his or her place.

In 1988, when a bone infection in her wrist wouldn't heal, we had two options: euthanasia or amputation. I was encouraged again by a colleague, the former director at the Basel Zoo in Switzerland, who exhibited a female gorilla with only one leg—also an amputee case. The animal thrived and gave birth successfully and hardly anyone noticed that she only had one leg. Lenore was much the same. She was a healthy animal at the time we decided to amputate and was able to live out her years more happily than she had begun.

During a routine exam late in her life, we saw what could have been the cause of Lenore's cranky personality. The area around her stomach was filled with buckshot, which had been there for years. We surmised that it was probably the result of being hit while clinging to her mother who was likely killed in order for someone to take Lenore when she was a tiny baby. I am glad *that* era of collecting is over!

Lenore had indeed been testy from the start, with a dour expression to match. She created quite a stir in the media when she arrived at the zoo, as *Chicago Tribune* writer Maria Donato reported on September 10, 1999, in an obituary to Lenore when she died at the age of 36:

> *Even before she arrived in Chicago from Cameroon in 1969, this 6-year-old gorilla made news by missing her flight—and zoo officials went to the airport to greet a gorilla-less plane. A miscommunication prompted a panic about a gorilla presumably loose on an airplane from Africa.*
>
> *All the while, Lenore had been calmly sitting in a crate in New York's Kennedy Airport watching airport workers lure another gorilla, which had slipped out of his crate, back inside with a banana.*

Great apes accounted for some of our most fun times, as well as some of the most difficult medical mysteries over the years. One of the most vexing cases was Mary, the lowland gorilla who was wild-caught and one of the group named for a member of Frank Schmick's family, his daughter Mary.

Mary had come from West Africa when she was about two years old. She seemed to be growing into a fine, healthy animal until she was about 12 years old. At that time she became a very fussy eater. Then she developed ongoing diarrhea, which resulted in her losing weight. A variety of standard blood, parasite, and stool tests were performed, but nothing showed up.

Finally, we called in gastroenterologist, Dr. Marshall Sparberg, a specialist with Passavant Hospital in Chicago, now Northwestern Memorial Hospital. Dr. Sparberg felt that a serial barium x-ray would be essential to determine what was wrong with Mary.

The problem was that this test would have to be done in the hospital since we did not have the proper equipment to conduct such tests at the zoo. Dr. Sparberg did not think the available portable equipment would provide an accurate reading. So Mary was scheduled for the procedure at Passavant Hospital, at night.

We brought her in on a stretcher without attracting much

attention. After all, she was anesthetized and was mostly under a sheet anyway. However, once she had been given the barium, the problems started. In order for it to go through her system sufficiently for the x-ray to be accurate, she had to be "walked" upright and she couldn't walk up and down the halls by herself.

I took one side and Mark Rosenthal, our Mammal Curator, took the other. With Mary heavily sedated, we looped one of her arms around each of our shoulders and walked her up and down the hall in the basement of the hospital. A few harried hospital staff people and exhausted interns did double takes as they passed us, but amazingly not a single person stopped to ask the identity of the strange patient.

Her sojourn at the hospital was otherwise fairly uneventful, and Mary returned to the zoo. When she woke up, she was back in her cage.

The test results showed a severely inflamed bowel. It was clear that Mary was unable to digest much of her food. Her condition was similar to Crohn's Disease, but in Mary's case, we could do little for her.

After some months, she succumbed to the disease, having wasted away from a robust gorilla to a shadow of her former self. It was a sad day for us all when she died. I still think of Mary and smile, remembering how we walked up and down the hospital halls with her that night, perhaps one of that facility's most unusual patients.

I hope that what we started at Lincoln Park Zoo will go on forever. We brought along several dozen babies and several multigenerational families of gorillas at Lincoln Park Zoo. We've also been able to send animals all over the country and the world, sharing Lincoln Park's gorilla gorilla gorillas with others.

I promised Bushman and Sinbad that we would do better for their species, and I believe we have.

# Famous zoo animals I have known

## IV. Gino the Dutch lowland gorilla

One of the greatest accolades a colleague ever paid me is related to the gorillas and our success at Lincoln Park. One day I received a call from Dick van Dam, then the director of the Rotterdam Zoo in The Netherlands.

"Les, we have just had a baby gorilla born, and we will have to hand-raise him," he said. "But when he's old enough, I want to send him to you so he can learn to become a gorilla. You've been able to do this better than anyone, and even though this baby is very important to us, I feel it is more important he come to you so he can grow up properly."

A year later, I proudly welcomed Gino (named for a movie star in Holland) into our zoo family, but not without some embarrassment.

Gino arrived via KLM, accompanied by the keeper who had hand-raised him. He clung fiercely to her, but looked around in-quiringly with his big, brown eyes as they exited the first class section of the plane. (No crate for this kid!)

His Dutch "mom" was to spend a week or two with Gino and our Great Ape House keepers to ease Gino's transition from her to his new caretakers.

From the first encounter we were captivated. Gino's fur was very black and shiny, and he had a truly winsome expression.

It amazes me how each gorilla baby can look so different, but still so much like its mother or father. The genetic lines of both Frank and Helen have always been particularly strong and once the babies grew up, it was easy to see which ones had Frank or Helen as parents, grandparents, or even great-grandparents.

It was clear that Gino was going to be a very handsome animal, and, if an animal can display indications of vanity at an early age, he seemed to know it.

Gino also had a very gentle nature. While not quite as laid back as Uncle Freddie, he was clearly a good animal, with no signs of a mean streak. As he grew up, he was as much fun and as playful as Otto had been. When he twirled and somersaulted about the cage, he seemed to virtually "smile" with delight.

After Gino had been at Lincoln Park for a few days we invited the Dutch Consul General to come to the zoo for a publicity photo. We arranged for the press to be on hand and took the Consul General behind the wire mesh on the keeper side of the habitats.

It became evident quite early that the diplomat was not an animal man.

He was clearly uncomfortable just being at the zoo, much less going behind the scenes with me, but he agreed (albeit reluctantly) that it would be good press for The Netherlands and a nice photo could be taken of us with Gino and his Dutch "mom."

Members of the media remained behind the glass in the public area and would photograph the event from there. We then took Gino and his entourage out into the public area so the press could get better pictures.

Before we left the back area, however, I offered to show the Consul General around to the various habitats to see our other gorillas, orangutans and chimpanzees. I would later come to regard this gesture as a well-intentioned, but big mistake.

Perhaps what happened next was inevitable. I probably should have known better.

As I've mentioned, in the areas behind the scenes at the old Monkey House, the apes would throw what they wanted at anyone who passed within range and, unfortunately, we had not completely eliminated this problem in our new Great Ape House.

The difference in the new habitat was that often when the animals sat up on their concrete shelves, they gleefully scooped off everything that had collected on the shelf and threw it down on their unsuspecting visitors.

"Everything" usually meant a mixture of water, urine, discarded food, feces, and straw. Those of us working at the zoo were used to this, kept our guard up, and took it in stride. But when the Dutch Consul General rounded the corner of one of the chimp habitats, a youngster let loose a great armful of stuff and, of course, managed to soak (and decorate) the poor man quite magnificently.

The Consul General was not amused.

In fact, he was *totally disgusted*. Nothing I said would placate him, except perhaps my limp comment, "Well, at least you'll have a good story and your picture in the paper with Gino for all your trouble."

He couldn't get out of there fast enough. Once outside in the public area, a few more pictures were taken and we all went our separate ways.

The next morning, I looked eagerly in the *Chicago Tribune* and *Chicago Sun-Times* for the picture I was sure would help ease the Consul General's terrible memories of his experience at the zoo.

To my horror, the photos each newspaper had published

showed Gino, his Dutch "mom," and me. Both newspapers had carefully cropped out the Consul General.

He wasn't anywhere in any photo!

Nor was his name mentioned anywhere in the accompanying story!

So much for my great idea of a publicity shot. I must admit, though, Gino did look awfully cute.

Gino's "mom" went home two weeks later after tearfully bidding Gino farewell. He adapted to our keepers, but it would be a long time before he would graduate to being introduced to any gorillas. We kept him in the Great Ape House rather than the Zoo Nursery because part of the process of getting him to become a gorilla was to hear other gorillas and to smell them nearby.

Finally, Gino took the next step and spent a great deal of time in a cage next to "Aunt" Debbie. Then they were separated only by mesh so they could see and touch each other. Many months later, a few more female gorillas were introduced, and, at last, the process concluded with an introduction to Frank. Gino became a part of Frank's group.

Ultimately, he grew into a strapping teenager and began to challenge Frank. It was clearly time to give Gino his own troop. As predicted, he had matured into a handsome silverback and became the father of many babies at Lincoln Park Zoo. Gino was a good breeder and was also very gentle with his babies.

One strange thing about each of Gino's babies was that they lacked pigment on either a digit (toe or finger) or around their mouths. Gino also has a rather pink lower lip and this must be a strong genetic trait as each of his offspring can be clearly identified by one pink finger, toe, or part of their lip, rather than the classic black gorilla skin all over their bodies. It's not obvious to most people, but if a person were to look carefully, they would see it.

Gino, probably more than any other gorilla at Lincoln Park Zoo, became the greatest gorilla ambassador of them all. More people have probably come to see him than any other gorilla in the world.

After much deliberation, we agreed to send Gino and his family to be featured attractions at Disney's new *Animal Kingdom* when it opened in Orlando, Florida in 1997. There, he would continue to delight people from all over the United States and around the world.

But he never forgot his roots.

Two years after he settled in at *Animal Kingdom*, we attended a conference there and, of course, we wanted to see Gino and his troop, which had added several babies since he'd arrived in Florida.

When we arrived, Gino was sleeping soundly against the glass window of the exhibit. Hundreds of people were watching him and enjoying the antics of his large family in the spacious, natural habitat behind him.

He opened one eye to sort of check out the crowd and spotted my wife, Wendy, and me at the back of the group. He looked, looked again, then sat up and stared at us. He then got up slowly, keeping one eye on us and ran back and forth slamming the glass. When he was young, he loved to play (through the mesh) with Wendy and as he grew up, she continued to interact with him through the glass. He was clearly delighted to see her and other friends he identified from the zoo.

A Disney staff person immediately came out and said loudly, "Someone from Lincoln Park is here! Gino recognizes them."

We admitted it was Wendy and me and went around the exhibit to the other side. Gino walked across the large outdoor habitat, all the while keeping us in view. He sat looking at us as we eventually walked down the path leading to the exit, but he wouldn't stare at us. He gave us the classic sideways glance that adult male gorillas give when they want to see what's happening but don't want to admit they really want a good look at you.

I came away thrilled that I had not only fulfilled my Dutch colleague's request to help Gino become a real gorilla, but that Gino was now in his element—as close to a natural habitat as anyone could build and a lot safer than he would be in the wild.

He was a magnificent, full-grown silverback, surrounded by his wonderful family and lots of youngsters, and serving as an ambassador for the families and youngsters who visit Disney's *Animal Kingdom* and want to learn about gorillas.

The Disney people say that Gino is *the* star at *Animal Kingdom*.

# Medical mysteries, mishaps, marvels, and other zoo phenomena

One of the biggest medical mysteries of my early career came to my attention when we captured animals for medical treatment. That's when I learned about the invisible kille—stress.

Capturing animals for treatment in the late 1940s was an experience I compared to my urban boyhood images of what the Wild West must have been like. That was a time of roping big cats, cornering and grabbing antelope, hurling nets over primates, and a variety of other ingenious, adventurous methods of capture.

Practicing medicine at the zoo meant plenty of manpower, skill, excellent timing, and a large dose of luck were needed to catch an animal—even one confined to a cage or an outdoor enclosure. Usually, it took several attempts to catch an animal. By the time it was "in hand," the animal was totally stressed out, and we were lucky if a keeper wasn't injured in the process.

Catching antelope, for example, required cornering them in a smaller portion of their enclosure. Two men moved in slowly toward the animal with a large, flat table or board, while five others waited for their "signal." When we were reasonably close—perhaps a few feet away—the head keeper or I would yell, *Now,* and each person would make a grab at the poor creature, one keeper assigned to each leg and usually one at the head to grab the horns.

Occasionally, we all missed, and the animal simply leaped over our heads, neatly clearing the group and the large board we had used to corner him or her. So the process was repeated and sometimes it took more than an hour before we got the animal to where we could administer medical treatment.

Monkeys posed other challenges. They usually had to be netted, which required entering the cage with a large net and throwing it over the animal—or *trying* to throw it over the animal.

As monkeys are very adept with their hands and feet, no matter how fast we moved, trying to get the net over them, they would be busy working to extricate themselves. It was usually a dreadfully frustrating and time-consuming experience. I could easily lose a morning or afternoon just trying to get to a monkey to treat it.

We also netted birds—especially large ones, but more often I simply reached into the cage and grabbed them. Again, I usually came up empty-handed on the first few tries, but eventually I got the bird.

The worst part of these ordeals was that the animal was totally bonkers by the time we got to it. I worry about the effects of stress on wild animals through these experiences because, sadly, I've watched antelope die in chutes, monkeys die in nets, and birds simply expire while I held them in my hand.

Often necropsies showed nothing wrong with these animals (except the wound or problem I was trying to catch them to treat). I believe they simply died of stress.

Speed is also an extremely important consideration when working on wild animals. Once the animal was captured, I tried to perform whatever medical procedure or surgery was required as rapidly as possible and still handle the animal with care. My motto was "in and out" when it came to surgeries. Even after our better anesthetics were introduced, along with capture guns, I still held that this was the best course to follow.

The range of medical procedures a zoo doctor needs to master is extraordinary, from performing a caesarean section on a pregnant wild cat to eye surgery on a gorilla. In recent years, veterinarians have begun to limit their practices, just as physicians do. One of the first such specialists was Dr. Sam Vainisi, who began his veterinary career as an intern in my animal hospital. Sam's specialty was the treatment of eyes, and he helped us on several occasions at the zoo.

Sam was one of the nicest men I ever met and a brilliant surgeon with an easy-going manner that wore well during tough procedures. He performed surgery on a tiger that had a cataract in one eye and on baby cheetahs that developed cataracts due to a virus the mother carried but did not exhibit herself. He also operated on Erich, a baby orangutan affected with juvenile cataracts in both eyes. We weren't sure if the cataracts were a result of poor nutrition, viruses, such as we saw in the cheetah, or other factors. In almost all cases the cataracts were in young animals, and, in all cases, the cataract surgery was successful, making it possible for each animal to have fully restored sight.

One of the funnier "medical marvels" developed after Erich, the baby orangutan, had eye surgery. He grew to be a healthy, normal male orangutan in every way—though Stan, our older, much larger orangutan, seemed to have a rather unnatural sexual interest in Erich. Everyone just chalked it up to the poor old guy being confined alone for so many years.

That is until the first day of a three-day conference I was hosting at Lincoln Park Zoo for the Gorilla and Orangutan Species Survival Plan groups. These men and women were very knowledgeable about great apes, and they had come to meet at Lincoln

Park because our success with gorilla groups was well known. I was chair of the Gorilla Species Survival Plan, and some of the most noted authorities on great apes were in my office when I got a call from Jimmy Higgins, senior keeper in our Great Ape House.

Jimmy sure knew about gorillas, orangutans, and chimps—especially his own. He considered himself *the* authority on great apes at Lincoln Park Zoo. When he called me on this particular day, Jimmy was clearly excited, but he was also somewhat subdued. The words tumbled quickly out of his mouth, "Doc, Erich just had a baby," he said, and quickly hung up.

I put down the phone and attempted to conceal my astonishment from my colleagues. But I decided I had to tell them, as they'd know soon enough anyway.

One can only imagine the ribbing I took for the remaining days of the conference—and for some time thereafter—and from around the globe. Word spread quickly that Les Fisher, head of the zoo with perhaps the most successful gorilla-breeding program around, couldn't tell a male orangutan from a female. One of my peers even sent me a detailed drawing showing the difference between boys and girls.

I had to admit it *was* pretty extraordinary. Here was an animal that had been examined closely as a youngster when he (actually *she*) had had eye surgery, but apparently everyone thought that someone else had done a complete exam. Of course our big male, orangutan, Stan, knew all along what eventually became obvious to the rest of us. Erich, who had originally been named for Lincoln Park Zoo's first chief veterinarian, my colleague Erich Maschgan, was hastily renamed *Ericha*.

And a fine mother she was.

# Help is on the way

The zoo staff was—and still is—dedicated, committed, and very skilled. But sometimes even that's not enough. Through the years a number of my veterinarian colleagues would come to help, as have other doctors and medical personnel. Many fine specialists in human medicine have worked to treat our gorillas, including specialists in orthopedics. The chief doctor for the Chicago Bulls basketball team, Dr. John Hefferson, and Dr. Steven Stern, volunteered their services to do arthroscopic surgery on Frank's knee.

Frank, at the time our oldest male gorilla, had been favoring one knee. Based on our x-rays, he clearly had arthritis and had probably been in pain, on and off, for several years. He responded only slightly to anti-inflammatory medicine, including aspirin, but over time his condition grew worse. It was Dr. Hefferon who suggested doing the arthroscopic surgery to give Frank some relief.

The surgery was not such an issue, but the follow-up care after surgery was a big concern. Frank needed physical therapy, which was clearly out of the question. So, without the rehab, Frank developed a stiff joint from the surgery; however he was out of pain. His stiff, but essentially much improved, leg allowed him to lead a better life. By all accounts, the surgery was a great success, and Frank was able to continue siring a number of babies, once he was out of pain, and, quite literally, back on his feet.

Age-related health issues in zoo animals are fairly recent concerns. Historically, most zoo animals didn't live to old age. More typical concerns of a zoo doctor are about youngsters who developed injuries or diseases.

One such situation involved a young male gorilla being mother raised in the Great Ape House. He was riding on his mother's back one moment and screaming in pain a moment later. The keepers rushed out to see what happened and saw his tiny gorilla hand, with three fingers, one of which was his thumb, hanging by strips of skin. They had been torn right off, only the skin kept them attached.

The keepers surmised that the mother had been near the wire mesh at the back of the habitat, and the infant had been hanging on to the mesh. When she moved suddenly away, having been chased by another gorilla, the baby's hand must have been entangled in the mesh, and he couldn't release his fingers fast enough.

The mother and her infant were separated, though not without some difficulty, so that Dr. Tom Meehan, the zoo vet, could examine the infant's hand. It was a mess. And because the thumb was involved, the injury would clearly affect the baby's climbing ability in the future.

We called nearby Children's Memorial Hospital, requesting assistance from a pediatric hand surgeon as quickly as possible. Fortunately, over the years the zoo staff and I had established a wonderful rapport with the hospital and its doctors. They were always willing to help us, particularly with the great apes, whose infants are so close to human babies.

A pediatric surgeon arrived quickly with his entire surgical team and specialized equipment. Delicate hand surgery on a tiny infant requires a well-coordinated team effort, and this was a matter of many hands working hard to save one.

Reattachment wasn't possible on the thumb, but it *was* on the first and index fingers; however the doctors worried a great deal about infection. Normally, with a child, a shunt would be put in place to drain the wound, but for an active infant gorilla, that was impossible. The doctor was not optimistic about the risk of infection.

I, however, was much less concerned. I had seen wild animals with terrible wounds, both in the wild and at the zoo, and I know that wild animals have tremendous natural healing abilities. Call it a survival mechanism. So I told the doctors I didn't think it would be a problem—and they thought I was nuts.

But as the weeks passed, they were amazed that infection did not set in, and the wound started to heal well. After some months the baby was reintroduced to the gorilla troop, using Debbie once again as the "auntie" to aid in the reintroduction process. It worked, and the infant began to tentatively grasp things. The concern remained, however, as to whether or not he could lead a normal life without his thumb.

The answer is, *he has*. Over time the other three fingers became enlarged, and the two reattached fingers moved over slightly to take the place of the non-existent thumb. Today it would be difficult to distinguish which hand among our active young gorillas was the damaged one, particularly with regard to the animal's climbing ability!

Calling upon human medical teams for help has become almost standard operating procedure at Lincoln Park Zoo, but, in the early years, it was pretty revolutionary. Imagine the neonatal unit arriving to help perform a caesarean section on a pregnant Afghan leopard. The species is so rare that every live birth is critically important to the zoo, so every precaution is taken.

I called the neonatal unit at Children's Memorial Hospital when the time was near, and a complete team came ready to take over the minute the C-section was completed. It is truly remarkable to watch a dozen people take a tiny infant—human or animal—and work as one, performing a seamless operation to give the newborn every possible chance to live.

I've been privileged to work with many doctors and nurses over the years, fine and dedicated professionals who have spent hours of their time, as volunteers, helping save and heal our most endangered animals.

# Thor, the zoo's only green polar bear

My tales of medical mysteries would not, however, be complete without two of the strangest ones I ever encountered. One was merely odd, but the other was a tragedy that seemed impossible to comprehend.

Thor was the Lincoln Park Zoo's successor adult polar bear to Mike. At more than 1,000 pounds, he was a truly magnificent animal. Having come to Lincoln Park from another zoo while he was still a "youngster" Thor delighted youngsters each day, swimming by the underwater viewing area and pushing off from one window so visitors could see his furry feet up against the glass.

Unlike most other polar bears on exhibit at the zoo, Thor's antics let observers actually see the fur on the soles of his feet, helping people understand that polar bears have a natural "non-skid surface" for walking on ice in their native Arctic habitat.

Every summer Thor looked beautifully white and fluffy, but, quite gradually every fall and winter, his color turned black, and one year he actually turned green.

We couldn't figure out what was causing this phenomenon until we realized Thor had green algae growing in his hair. Not *on* his hair, but *in* his hair.

Polar bear hairs are in fact hollow and transparent, and it is refractive light that makes them appear white. When the bears lose a large amount of fur, they begin to appear black, the natural color of their skin. When Thor started turning green, we realized that the algae was actually growing inside his hollow hair follicles, creating *a green haired bear.*

So Thor went from white to black each fall due to a skin problem, and the loss of his hair. Then, over a period of months, he turned green because he spent so much of his time in the water, the remaining hair filled with algae growth.

It took a while to solve this mystery, but, once we did, we hung a sign to let visitors know Thor had a skin disease but felt fine, and his green coloring was due to green algae in his fur.

Members of the public seemed to accept this explanation (which was the best we could do), and Thor lived out his life either black or green every winter. More than once, we thought about having him march in the city's St. Patrick's Day parade!

# The mystery of Pearl the elephant

Pearl was a young Asian elephant that came to Lincoln Park Zoo from the Houston Zoo, which had cared for her mother during her pregnancy. She was lively, fun, inquisitive, and just plain adorable—everything we could want her to be at four years old. And she was a real crowd-pleaser.

Then, during the fall season, her first at Lincoln Park, Pearl suddenly stopped eating. Three days later, she was dead. We were stunned, shocked, and dumbstruck.

What happened? How could such a lively, young, full-of-beans elephant die so suddenly? Theories ran through the zoo like water.

Because the elephant yard had a number of big, old oak trees, some people thought she might have eaten too many acorns and been poisoned—something that actually can and *does* happen to cattle that eat acorns.

Others thought she'd eaten some type of foreign object. A few keepers thought that the zoo's two older female elephants might have mistreated Pearl. It seemed everyone had an opinion or theory, but a necropsy showed nothing definitive.

We all mourned the death of this wonderful animal, but were at a loss to explain what had happened to her.

I had immediately called the Director of the Houston Zoo, where the staff was also devastated upon learning of Pearl's death. I am sure some of them blamed the care—or *lack* of care—she'd received from our zoo for whatever happened to her.

However, a few years later there was another sudden, unexplainable death of a young Asian elephant, this time at the National Zoo in Washington, DC. Then a third such incident occurred at another zoo. In each case the autopsies provided no conclusive information.

But the pathologist who had reviewed Pearl's slides sent them to National Zoo for comparison and, slowly, the pieces of the puzzle began coming together.

Adult *African* elephants carry a virus that doesn't affect baby African elephants, but can prove deadly to baby *Asian* elephants. Sadly, it took years for us to become aware of this. Once we knew, we re-examined the zoo's philosophy and policy regarding the mixing of African and Asian elephants in a single exhibit. Many zoos, particularly those with baby elephants, began separating African and Asian elephants to prevent a recurrence of such tragedies.

Even with the best medicine, the assistance and support of teams of doctors and medical personnel, and new drugs and capture techniques, we don't win them all. We are still learning every day.

Handling large animals, particularly when they are injured or sick, can be challenging under the best of conditions. The capture gun was truly a breakthrough for zoos and field biologists. It was developed in Georgia to safely capture white-tailed deer for a field research study. We used the same technique as that developed in the wild—a Crosman's air rifle with a loaded syringe at the end. I would fill the syringe with the "appropriate" dose and stand outside the cage to fire at the animal's rump. The syringe stayed in long enough to quickly anesthetize the animal. Then when we went in to administer treatment, we would recover the syringe.

Note my reference to the "appropriate" dose. In fact, we could only guess at what that dosage should be. The dosage of most immobilizing drugs was based on the weight of the animal, and we didn't have exact weights for most of our animals. We would eyeball the animal, guess at its weight, and then approximate the dosage. It was hardly an exact science, but it did work pretty well as a crude level of measurement.

Although the air rifle was a significant improvement over our previous capture methods, it was still not a perfect solution. The impact of the syringe from the force of the air rifle often damaged the area of the animal where it struck, causing bruising and trauma upon impact.

The ultimate solution, which is still used today, is the blow-gun or dart, developed by South American tribes in their native jungle habitat. It is typically used for hunting with poison darts. We adapted their technique to use a syringe loaded into the end of the blow dart, then by blowing gently into the tube we could "shoot" the syringe into the animal with much less impact and trauma. It is ironic that what has been called one of the most "primitive" technologies is now the best in our modern, high-tech era.

# The zoo goes on a diet

Every day around noon an elderly lady stepped off the bus at the corner of Stockton Drive and Webster Avenue and walked slowly to the old bear line at the north end of Lincoln Park Zoo.

She carried an old brown shopping bag, practically dragging it, as the bag appeared to weigh as much as she herself. In summer she wore an old flowered housecoat and thin shoes that could have passed for bedroom slippers. In winter, a bedraggled wool coat that seemed several sizes too large, covered her and a gray scarf was wrapped around her head. Big leather work gloves wrapped her hands, regardless of the weather or temperature.

The woman appeared undaunted by the big *DO NOT FEED THE ANIMALS* signs that hung on every cage along the length of the bear run. Nor did the high iron bars that separated her from the polar bears, grizzly bears, black bears, sloth bears, and sun bears discourage her.

Standing as close as she could get to the railing, she would reach down into her bag, removing a loaf of bread for one bear, a container of frozen beef stew for another, and some old meat for a third. She wound up her throwing arm and deftly pitched the food into the appropriate cage. The bears all seemed to know her well and welcomed her daily visits. They greeted her by standing on their hind legs, seemingly reaching to the top of the iron bars, sometimes even catching the food she threw to them.

She didn't play favorites. Every bear got something. If a particular bear got bread one day, it got something better, like beef stew, the next day.

Walking slowly along the row of cages, throwing food until the large bag was empty, she'd then turn and slowly make her way back to the bus stop, and wait patiently for the southbound bus.

The woman was "a regular" when I became Director at the zoo, and it was only when we tore down the old Bear Line to make way for the new Regenstein Large Mammal Habitat that she stopped coming to see her bears. She had never missed a day to feed them, the keepers told me. When they asked her why she cooked for the bears and came to feed them every day, she said simply, "Because they like it."

And I'm sure they did.

Her feeding the bears was entirely against zoo policy, of course, and not at all providing the kind of good nutrition we needed to ensure. But through the early years, as she maintained her ritual feeding and added variety to their diet, the woman probably helped the bears more than she hurt them.

When I began working at the zoo, as a young vet, we knew so little about what to feed many of the animals that it's amazing any of them survived, much less lived to a decent age.

Bears traditionally got day-old bread; big cats got horse-meat; hoofed stock received hay and bread; monkeys were given fruits and vegetables; and so it went. There were no prepared diets, no cat or dog chow. People simply used what was cheap and easy to obtain. It was not until the early 1950s that zoo managers began thinking about what the animals ate in the wild and what would be appropriate for them to eat in captivity. In those days, here certainly were no nutritionists on staff at any zoo.

# Horsemeat, vitamins, cats, and birds

In the early days of the zoo, keeping animals alive and maintaining proper nutrition was not considered that important. If an animal sadly died, the zoo could always get another. It was not until the 1970s that we became seriously interested in making certain our animals received better, more appropriate kinds of food.

We discovered around the 1960s that big cats fed exclusively horsemeat were not getting the balanced diet we had once believed.

The zoo would receive a frozen half slab of a horse that would arrive cut in quarters, delivered to the old commissary area at the north end of the zoo. We used band saws to cut these large frozen masses of horsemeat into more manageable pieces of two to fifteen pounds each, and this would be fed to the big cats six days a week. One day each week the cats fasted, our theory being that animals in nature have sort of a feast and famine syndrome, and don't eat every day as people tend to do.

The animals did reasonably well on this diet, but they didn't live long and when they had babies, their offspring weren't always normal. Newborn lions and some of the other big cat cubs developed rickets and did not do well overall. A researcher looked at the calcium/phosphorous ratio and lab tests showed horsemeat was 20-parts phosphorous to one-part calcium, rather than the required ratio of one-to-one or one-to-one-and-a-half.

To address the problem we would thaw the meat, cut a pocket in one side of the chunk and add some calcium gluconate powder. We'd compress the pocket enough that powder stuck to the fresh meat, increasing calcium sufficiently to provide a balanced diet.

We also learned that cats are not exclusively meat eaters. Field researchers in the wild reported many big cats eat the internal organs of their prey first, thereby getting a quantity of grain and grass from the stomach, along with viscera and blood, before going on to eat the meat.

With this in mind, we began feeding big cats whole chickens, and we switched to vitamin supplements. Eventually, as with domestic animals, prepared diets were developed that provided nutritional balance, and this subsequently became the main source of food for the big cats. The result of these improvements was that we immediately saw more babies being produced and healthier adult and baby animals, which lived much longer.

Longevity is not the only criterion for determining the health of an animal, but it is the one we went by in the early years. Just as there is certainty to life, there is certainty to death. Many small animals and specialized amphibians, small birds, and some of the snakes live very short lives—sometimes only a few months to a few years. Zoos having butterfly exhibits—something we wouldn't have even considered in my early zoo years—report that some specimens live as little as a week, while others live just a day. In fact, some butterflies hatch without the ability to feed, as they have no mouths. Their sole purpose is to hatch, fly, mate, and die. They are not designed to eat or live longer than the time required to reproduce.

At the other extreme of longevity are the big mammals. Although Duchess the elephant was reported to have lived to 85 years, I suspect no one really knew her age. When Judy the elephant died during my watch at Lincoln Park Zoo she was also perhaps 85 years old and was the oldest Asiatic elephant living in North America at that time.

Big cats can—and *do*—live 15–20 years in captivity, while bears live 20–25 years. It depends on the individual animal as well as on nutrition and general health issues. Now that we understand what most of these exotic animals need, they live much longer in the captive state than in the wild.

In the wild, a relatively small injury can become infected and end up costing an animal its life. In nature, when elephants last set of teeth erupt, are ground down, then fall out, the animal starves to death. Nature is not as caring as a zoo environment; the sick and the old become prey to other animals, so geriatric animals are rarely found in the wild.

Stories about the longevity of birds in the parrot family have taken on mythic proportions through the years. Indeed, some people believe parrots can live to be 100 years old. But a long life would be 60–75 years, which is still a very long time for a small animal, and it is why having a parrot can be a lifelong commitment.

## Longevity

Animals that are supposed to live the longest, both in the wild and in captivity, are the giant tortoises—specifically, the Galapagos and Aldabra tortoises. These relics from another era are remarkable, and even more so when you see them in the wild. Riding horseback through farmers, fields in the Galapagos, where all the tortoises are protected and allowed to roam where they choose, I was taken by our guide's comment when we found our first tortoise. He said, "Look at him! He was alive and living right here before your constitution was signed!"

Of course, there are no records going back that far for that particular animal, which is part of the problem of determining age. Today, records on captive animals—and some of those in captivity such as younger giant tortoises—are meticulously kept so in the future we *will* know the exact lifespan of many animals and age ranges for different species.

Permanent markings are now made on every captive animal in the zoo. Birds are banded when they're hatched, and their permanent numbers are recorded both in printed form and in computer files. The band may be adjusted for growth, but it stays with the animal forever.

Small animals are tattooed on their inside thighs or along a limb, while some hoofed animals have plastic buttons put into their ears, following the same procedure we use for domestic cattle and sheep.

This system has dramatically improved recordkeeping and animal husbandry techniques as animals also are shifted from one zoo to another, sometimes several times over their lifetimes.

For some of the older individuals, born long before this system was put in place some two decades ago, we still must guesstimate, as we did in the old days, just as we did regarding the cause of death.

On May 4, 1924 when Duchess the elephant died at the reported age of 85, she was first reported to have succumbed to an overdose of peanuts provided by an unusually large and enthusiastic crowd of Sunday visitors. Already being treated for a bout of acute indigestion, Duchess was thought to have been in recovery until she ingested such large quantities of peanuts.

Then-Zoo Director Parker's explanation to the media as to her cause of death was, "Duchess had enough experience to know that a lady of her age should be careful not to eat peanuts during convalescence."

What was actually the cause of death, or her true age, no one ever really knew.

# Go fish

In an earlier era we learned the hard way, by losing valuable animals or seeing disease that didn't make sense. Such was the case with our furry marine mammals. Sea lions and seals were always fed fish. What *type* of fish they were fed depended on what was available at the lowest cost and that policy also proved to be a poor one as many animals developed neurological diseases. Finally we realized many had severe deficiencies of vitamin B.

While it is true that vitamin B is indeed present in raw fish, when fish are frozen as part of a large shipment, a thiaminase factor destroys the vitamin B complex during thawing. The solution to this was relatively easy; we pushed vitamin B complex supplements into the mouths of the thawed fish before feeding them to the seals and sea lions. It worked well, and is a procedure that is still used today.

We also learned that fish are not fish, so to speak, in that when we used Great Lakes fish to feed our puffins, we had a complete wipeout—*all the birds died.* After exhaustive testing, all that could be found was a higher than normal heavy metal and PCB content in the birds. With that in mind, we switched to *ocean* fish, which certainly also suffer from effects of pollution, but apparently to a much lesser degree, as the puffins thrived on an ocean fish diet.

Some time later, our public health service recommended that humans limit their intake of Great Lakes fish, mainly due to the high levels of PCBs and other toxins in those fish. By that time we had already concluded there was a problem with Great Lakes fish. Our puffins had become the "canaries in the mine," alerting us early on to the existence of poisons.

Keeping other types of birds alive and healthy has always been a complex issue when it came to diets. After already noting the differences in types of fish, I must now explain that, for purposes of diet, birds are not simply *birds.* They eat a wide variety of foods and are classified by types, such as *seed eaters, fruit eaters, fish eaters, insect eaters,* and of course *raptors,* including *birds of prey*—some of which eat live prey, but some of which are scavengers.

In addition to meeting these specialized food requirements, we had to be aware that, as in reptiles, light can be a significant issue.

We knew about ultraviolet light, and we knew that wild animals are exposed to natural sunshine, but what we *didn't* know was how complex a factor this played in health and reproduction. Adding the right amount of ultraviolet light ultimately proved to have an enormous effect on a variety of health and reproductive issues that we had been dealing with for years in birds, reptiles, and even some primates.

# Mostly monkeys

Monkeys and great apes posed other challenges. They are close to humans, but they certainly don't eat like humans! So, what *do* they eat?

When Bushman was alive, we studied him and concluded that gorillas ate mostly vegetative material, so we presumed great apes were true vegetarians. But when Bushman died, an autopsy indicated he had suffered from some vitamin B complex deficiencies, among other factors.

We immediately starting giving our great apes reconstituted powdered milk, to which we would add various vitamin supplements we knew were important for the well-being of these animals. We also began adding small pieces of raw meat to their food, replacing the bugs and grubs they would normally catch in the wild as they foraged for their greenery.

We learned of a special diet that had been developed for laboratory monkeys—specifically *rhesus monkeys*—because lab animals have to be in good health and live long lives. Nutrition is always an essential part of any experiment's success. Research had produced a pellet called the "monkey biscuit." A forerunner to this pellet had been developed by Dr. Herbert Ratcliffe, of the Philadelphia Zoo, a pioneer in the field of nutritional care for wild animals. He prepared nutritious *cakes* for great apes. This was followed by the commercial development of wild animal diets. Purina stood out among major companies involved in the early research of monkey pellets. *Their* biscuit was called Monkey Chow®, part of the company's inventory of branded products that included Cat Chow® and Dog Chow®.

Whenever I think of Monkey Chow®, however, I have to smile, recalling an incident at a cocktail party some 30 years ago in an elegant apartment on Chicago's prestigious Lake Shore Drive.

I was appearing regularly on television at the time and was often recognized around town and greeted by people I didn't know. A well-dressed older woman approached me and said, "Dr. Fisher, I've watched your show for years, but you never seem to age. How is it that you don't have any gray hair?"

I smiled at her and answered, *"Monkey Chow."*

She looked at me strangely, and, before I could offer a more appropriate reply, she wandered off into the crowd. I never did catch up with her again and wondered how many people she told of my secret for a more youthful appearance.

Monkeys and apes now get Monkey Chow® first thing every morning when they are hungry. This takes care of almost all their nutritional needs since all their vitamins, minerals, protein, carbohydrates, and fat are included in the biscuit. They could survive on nothing else but water. But just as humans could also be sustained on a similar diet, who would want to eat only one food? Zoo animals today are fed a variety of fruits and vegetables including oranges, celery, lettuce, grapes, apples, nuts, seeds, raisins, and much, much more. They are also fed more frequently and their cages are no longer tidy. They're generally a mess—but the animals seem to like it that way!

Straw is put down as a bedding option, and the zoo staff sprinkles food (and sometimes Cheerios) in the straw and around the cage. And we occasionally add a tasty cardboard carton. This provides foraging opportunities and activities to keep the monkeys and apes active all day, which is essential to good mental, as well as physical, health. Although the cardboard box is not found in nature, the glue holding it together is an edible favorite of the apes and dismantling the box is an activity they love.

We extended the foraging concept to our hoofstock and other animals, as few of them sit down once a day and eat until they are full. Most animals "move and nibble" in their daily activity. The exceptions are most of the cats and raptors, that catch and eat small prey all at one time.

However, lions with a large kill will return to it over several days and leopards will drag a carcass up a tree and come back to eat it over a period of time. Modern zoos try to simulate how a wild animal typically spends its waking time and recreate that environment for their captive animals.

This philosophy was reinforced for me several years ago when I visited a European colleague at his zoo. As we walked around, I noticed his keepers were throwing some old bread to the zebras, antelope, and other hoofed animals, much as we used to do 30–40 years ago.

I asked my colleague why he continued to do that now that we knew better. He replied that, of course, the animals didn't live on that alone, but the act was purely psychological. The animals could nibble on things during the day and keep active, both to keep up the interest of visitors and for the sake of the animal.

Back home at Lincoln Park Zoo, we continued the practice of using bagels and bread. It should be noted that many of the zoo's Bactrian camels can be very discriminating with regard to their preferences for specific types of bagels!

# A few words about food

Zoo nutrition at Lincoln Park received a huge boost when the Dr. Scholl Foundation funded a pioneering Nutrition Conference at the zoo in 1980. The first conference covered such topics as *Nutritional Cataracts in Timber Wolves; Milk Composition and Formula Selection for Hand-Rearing Young Mammals; Digestibility Tests for Evaluating the Nutritive Value of Feeds;* and *Hydroponic Crops: A Valuable Alternative For Feeding Zoo Animals*, among many others.

The 1980 conference was the first of its kind for zoos in the United States, but it was certainly not the last. Thanks to continuing support from the Dr. Scholl Foundation, seven subsequent conferences were held, in what became a pioneering effort to reach thousands of zoo colleagues and provide opportunities to meet and share nutritional successes and failures.

The published proceedings were distributed to zoo vets, curators, keepers, and university faculty members, further leveraging the Foundation's initial support.

I will be forever grateful to the Foundation for making possible what I believe were a series of programs that advanced the ability of zoo professionals to adequately care for captive animals.

Today, Lincoln Park Zoo employs a full-time nutritionist who helps formulate the animal diets to assure each species nutritional needs are met.

Feeding the animals has come a long way during my years in the zoo business. Today, it's a science, and even the cage signage has changed. The *DO NOT FEED* signs of old have been replaced in many cases with more positive messages, such as, "Thank you, but we've already eaten" or "Animals are on a scientific diet. Please do not feed."

Of course, some people still can't resist feeding the animals anyway. Food and the occasional foreign objects still make their way into animal enclosures, but thankfully the days of a Duchess dying from an overdose of peanuts, fed to her by overenthusiastic zoo visitors, is a thing of the past.

# The gourmet koalas

Of all the animals that have challenged zoo personnel when it comes to diet, none beats the koala, that seemingly endearing creature from the land down under.

Koalas are beloved—thanks in part to years of excellent TV advertising by an airline that adopted the little marsupial as its mascot.

But koalas are *not* really cuddly, adorable creatures—nor are they bears. They are, in fact, quite feisty and very stubborn, and they have a unique dietary adaptation developed over thousands of years—they eat only fresh eucalyptus, and only specific types of fresh eucalyptus at that.

When our first koalas arrived at Lincoln Park Zoo, we had a problem. We couldn't exactly just phone the local market and ask that it send over an order of eucalyptus, nor could we grow it in Chicago year round. The only cost-effective solution was to lease five acres of land in southern Florida and contract with a local horticulture expert to plant and grow eucalyptus for us. Then we contracted with a local airline to arrange for it to deliver the plants twice each week from Florida.

But the situation became even more complicated and costly.

Koalas are truly persnickety eaters. One day they might want one kind of eucalyptus, and the next day another. There's no point in growing just one type of eucalyptus. Living in the wild, they would simply climb into their tree-of-choice on any given day to satisfy their taste buds. We, on the other hand, had to cater to their every whim.

So we grew five different kinds of eucalyptus that fell within the koalas' dietary range and had all five flown up to Chicago from Florida twice a week. They ate only the choicest little leaves, though not always even that, so feeding them proved to be both costly and wasteful. When the koalas wouldn't eat, the eucalyptus went to waste.

Why don't all zoos have koalas?

The short answer is that they simply cannot afford to indulge them. In fact, for years only the San Diego and Los Angeles zoos had koalas, mainly because their locations' climate afforded them the opportunity to grow eucalyptus on their own zoo grounds.

Today, when one of those TV spots with the cute, cuddly koalas appears on the screen, I know it prompts people to smile.

I, on the other hand, smell five types of eucalyptus and visualize air transport invoices. That's when I change the channel.

# Buildings, budgets, and food

Having a zoo commissary—a central distribution point for zoo food—was a luxury that the Lincoln Park Zoo simply couldn't afford in the early days. Originally, we had an old two-story structure that was used to accept food deliveries. The basement had a band saw, a cooler, and several old six-foot tables.

From there we distributed the food to the zoo buildings, each of which had a home refrigerator. Deliveries included frozen horsemeat, day-old bread, cast-off produce no longer fit for human consumption, from the city's produce market as well as fish from local Chicago and coastal purveyors. Other deliveries were of straw, hay, seeds, nuts, mice, chicks, crickets, and mealworms, the latter primarily acquired for birds and lizards.

Each building was responsible for its own food preparation every day. For a few years we tried to grow our own grass with a hydroponic unit, but found it wasn't very cost effective.

Then, one fall day in 1974, I was invited to join Reuben Thorson, a zoo Board member, for an impromptu lunch with some friends of his, Joan and Ray Kroc. At the last minute Reuben called to ask me to bring along the recently completed architectural drawings for our proposed new Great Ape House and Hospital.

During lunch, Reuben urged me to show Ray and Joan our plans, which seemed so ambitious to me at the time—more like a dream than reality. I was almost too embarrassed to show them. Almost, but not quite.

I laid out our plans for the proposed $7 million capital campaign. To me, the price tag might as well as have been a billion. I had no idea how we were going to raise that kind of money. I knew that I was a zoo director, not a fundraiser. Nervously, I tried to refocus my attention on lunch.

"What about food?" Ray asked. I told him about how things worked at the zoo. "A restaurant without a good kitchen isn't successful," he said.

As we talked a bit more, suddenly the hospital plan became transformed into a Commissary/Hospital Building.

An hour later Ray Kroc, the man who re-engineered the fast

food industry, wrote out a personal check for $1 million and handed it to me.

I don't remember saying goodbye. I have no memory of where we ate lunch or what we ate. I only recall floating back to the zoo. Ray's check was the lead gift in a campaign that would eventually top off at $9 million and provide Lincoln Park Zoo with a new Commissary/Hospital and Great Ape House in 1976, and subsequently launched the entire rebuilding of the zoo.

The food budget for the zoo was more than $300,000 a year, and most deliveries of fresh items are made twice a week. Without adequate freezer and cooler space, before the commissary was built, deliveries of perishable items had to be made every day. With the capacity of the huge new walk-in freezer and refrigerator, we were able to cut costs by buying in bulk.

The zoo commissary allows for a centralized food operation that is equipped to handle everything from crickets to eucalyptus. The only exception is hay, which is so bulky it is better delivered directly to the buildings that use it, such as the zebra/antelope barn and the Farm-in-the-Zoo. The zoo uses about 250 tons of the best-quality hay each year, most of it alfalfa or timothy hay, depending upon the commissary's requirements.

The people who work in the commissary are animal specialists and know the vagaries of their restaurant clientele. They prepare food in accordance with hundreds of diets for the many different species of animals—clearly, an expansive and *expensive* operation. Ray Kroc was right about the kitchen. The zoo's food service became far more successful once it had a good kitchen.

# Counting crickets

I've never been one to micro-manage, but one of the things that always bothered me during my years as Zoo Director was that I had to sign off on the deliveries of food made to the commissary. This seemed such a mindless and bureaucratic task since we had a highly competent staff that was responsible for making certain we got what we ordered when we needed it.

Still, every time I faced the delivery bill for "crickets," I always hesitated, just for an instant, before signing it. It went back to my earliest days as Director when I was trying to be very conscientious about everything, even the smallest details.

To me, crickets were a conundrum. We received 10,000 crickets per order from Flucker's Cricket Ranch. They were used to feed small mammals, primates, birds, and lizards. The label indicated that each box contained 5,000 crickets, yet I always wondered, "How can I be sure about that?"

I certainly wasn't going to count them myself, or ask anyone else to do it, but I was never really certain that someone wasn't shorting us! The delivery of crickets always bothered me.

Then, there was the matter of taste.

At an early conference held for the zoo, Flucker's, our source for crickets, had a bowl full of chocolates at their booth. Being a *chocaholic*, I grabbed a handful and tossed them into my mouth, savoring the sweetness. It was only after I had swallowed a goodly number that I learned they were chocolate-covered crickets—a clever, if questionably tasty, promotion by Flucker's.

Unwittingly ingesting chocolate-covered crickets did nothing to instill confidence in me about Flucker's as a supplier or the company's ability to count to 5,000 without making a mistake at our expense, but I did have to admit their product didn't taste bad, though it would not be my first choice for chocolates!

Of course, Flucker's did have a method of counting—they simply weighed the box. And that was close enough for me.

# Hatari's story—
# a young elephant goes west

"Doc, I'm coming back" was all the man said. Then the phone went dead.

It had been about seven hours since he arrived at the zoo and five hours since he left to take Hatari, our young African elephant, from Chicago to the Phoenix Zoo in Arizona.

Hatari had been given to the Lincoln Park Zoo at a ceremony held in the Zoo Rookery just a few years earlier. That had been an exciting day for the zoo. John Wayne and other Hollywood actors who had appeared in the hit film *Hatari* were on hand to formally present the baby elephant to the zoo at the annual meeting of our newly formed Zoo Society.

But now, three years later, the "baby" had grown up and we no longer had room for her. A colleague of mine at the new

Phoenix Zoo agreed to take her, so I arranged for transport through a recognized animal dealer in Florida.

When moving day arrived four weeks later, the driver contracted for the transport pulled up in a regular rental van, in tow behind the cab. I questioned how he planned to move an elephant in such a vehicle.

"Don't worry, Doc," he boomed. "I've moved lots of animals. She doesn't need to be chained down."

I tried to persuade him otherwise, suggesting he at least place a restraining chain on one leg. Hatari had grown into an obstreperous four-year-old pre-teen—and she knew, quite literally, how to throw her weight around.

But the driver wouldn't listen. He told me again how experienced he was and assured me he'd handle it his way. I reminded him that once the animal left the zoo she was his responsibility, but he would not be deterred.

After loading her into the little aluminum box with the small cab in front, he drove off, jauntily waving goodbye as he passed through the gate.

I told my staff I was not at all sure the driver could make the trip safely with the elephant in that truck. In fact, I was confident we hadn't seen the last of the driver, but I kept that last thought to myself.

And now he was on his way back to the zoo. But it wasn't until he drove through the gate once again that the extent of his problem was known.

The top of the truck had been peeled back like a sardine can and the cab of the truck was completely crushed where the elephant had leaned over it with considerable force. Hatari's head, trunk and small tusks were peering out of the top of the truck while the driver was scrunched over in the cab, barely able to control the vehicle.

As I approached the truck and waited for the driver, with considerable time and effort, to extricate himself from the cab, I could barely contain my laughter. It was a truly ridiculous scene.

I could see that the elephant wasn't hurt, except for some minor lacerations around her tusks and mouth when she had "peeled back" the aluminum top of the truck before forcefully scrunching the cab.

"I know, Doc," the driver said, holding up a hand before anyone could speak. "I know, we'll do it your way now."

He left to get another rental truck. I have no idea who paid for the damage to the first one. This time we drilled holes in the floor of the truck, attached a chain and, once the elephant was loaded into the truck, secured her left front leg. This helped prevent further mischief as well as her possibly falling down and hurting herself if the truck made a quick turn. This time the driver waived goodbye to us and made it safely to Phoenix.

It would be nice to say the story of Hatari's trip to Phoenix ends there on a high note and with a smile. But that was not to be.

There were repercussions from the move that went beyond the wreckage of a rented truck. I soon received a letter from lawyers representing Paramount Pictures, informing me that I had no right to move *their animal,* as it had been a gift to the Lincoln Park Zoo.

I tried to explain my reasoning, but the lawyers insisted I had broken the contract and had needed their permission to move Hatari. Since the elephant was already in its new home, I was finally able to persuade Paramount to go along with the relocation, avoiding what in my mind was already turning into a front-page story of the zoo being sued by one of Hollywood's most powerful movie studios!

# The sometimes-friendly skies

Moving wild and exotic animals is almost never easy, and such moves always leave us with some interesting stories to tell. But the process is considerably easier now than it was 40 years ago.

Before air transport, the only way to bring an animal to the United States from overseas was by ship. And a long journey it was, starting with transporting a crate by truck to the nearest port. The trucking aspect of the trip alone was often a logistics nightmare as roads in and out of remote areas were, in many cases, non-existent.

Sometimes small roads had to be built to create access to larger roads. In many instances, roads were not paved beyond major urban areas. There were arrangements to be made to provide water and food for the animals during transport, as well as to assure they were cared for when keepers were not accompanying them on their journey.

Permits to cross borders were a hassle to obtain and, eventually, as in the case of Africa, animals would end up at a quarantine station within a port while awaiting the ship for the long ocean journey. Quarantining of animals is routine both inbound and outbound. At the other end of the trip waited another truck to carry the animal to another quarantine location before being permitted to go on to its final destination. The whole process took months.

We marvel that so many animals we acquired in the old days actually survived these long trips, but they did. Most of them arrived safely despite the long journey, stress, and the hundreds of obstacles along the way.

Just as capturing animals with the aid of a capture gun is so much more humane than netting or roping them, shipping animals by air minimizes the time an animal needs to be in a holding cage or crate.

But strict requirements by different carriers still dictate which carrier can take an elephant, for example, and *when* they can take it. Some cargo planes are configured in such a way that they cannot handle large crates, making it vital that we know these planes and any unique requirements they might have. Which planes have cargo holds that have ambient temperatures is also essential information, as anyone knows who has shipped a dog or cat in the luggage compartment.

# The short travel story of the elephant in the middle seat

Knowing the rules of the road, so to speak, about what transport companies accept what types of cargo—and at what times—came in handy when I went to Sri Lanka for our Asian baby elephant, Bozie. Well, it *sort of* came in handy—along with a large dose of good luck.

In November of 1976, I became aware that several Asian baby elephants were available for adoption at an animal orphanage run by the government of Sri Lanka. The facility where the elephants were being kept was just outside the capital city of Columbo.

The cost for a baby elephant was $2,000, payable to the government of Sri Lanka. This was to cover the cost of the animal's care during its time in the orphanage. Pat and Art Bowes, members of our Zoo Society—and staunch zoo supporters—agreed to put up the money if I could secure the necessary import permits from Washington.

Rather suddenly, with almost no advance notice, the permits went through, but I had to be in Caracas, Venezuela for an international zoo conference. I had only 120 hours—that's *five days*—to go to Sri Lanka, get the elephant, and bring it back to the United States before going on to Caracas the next day. Pretty much everyone I spoke with assured me it could not be done. There was no way I would be able to work through the bureaucracy in less than two weeks. Still, I felt obligated to try.

As promised, everything that could go wrong on the trip did.

With my head crowded with the details of what I had been told I would encounter in Asia, I didn't immediately notice my cab driver's wrong turn en route to Chicago's O'Hare Airport and I almost missed my flight to London.

I did make the flight, however, and arrived in London to learn my scheduled flight to Sri Lanka was cancelled. I stood standby, catching a flight from London to Zurich, then Zurich to Bombay and on to Columbo on Air India, arriving there with the hours quickly ticking away. I called the local colleague who'd agreed to help me in Sri Lanka, but he had already left for the meeting in Caracas. I was on my own.

After about two hours of rest at a nearby hotel, a Columbo Zoo staff member helped me get to the orphanage where I chose what I decided was the best baby elephant of the bunch. But I was told I couldn't have that particular elephant, as it was designated to be a gift to the United States for the National Zoo in Washington.

Beginning the selection process again, I selected the one I believed was *the next best baby*—an adorable little female.

My next stop was British Airways to book a flight to London and on to Chicago. I first had to get my export permits stamped, an ordeal that took hours—rather than the twenty minutes I had allowed for this process. Rubber stamps were flying on what seemed to be thousands of pieces of paper. Everyone was most courteous, but what should have been just a formality took on a life of its own!

I had to have a crate built for the elephant, which I managed to do—just in time for the rains to begin.

The roads from the animal orphanage were nearly impassable, especially for a large truck hauling even a small elephant. We did make it to Colombo, however, only to have the truck carrying the elephant get into a "fender-bender" with a passing motorist, something that would not have surprised me in crowded Chicago . . . *but Sri Lanka?*

In Colombo an automobile accident, no matter how minor the damage, is *not* a minor incident. We settled the matter and got back on the road.

With less than an hour to spare, we reached the airport where the agent told me my crate would not fit into the hold of that particular aircraft. So much for knowing my cargo statistics, I thought. It was by sheer good luck, that KLM had a plane coming through hours later that could handle a crate of that size, so I changed my reservation to KLM.

Once we relocated to the KLM freight area, the agent there told me my crate had to be wrapped in plastic to insure that the elephant's "leave-behinds" would be kept out of the cargo hold.

So we wrapped the crate in plastic . . . , which lasted about five seconds. The baby elephant started poking its little trunk out of the slates, stripping off the plastic—which it then tried to eat. I took the plastic down.

The agent returned and the plastic went back up.

Down.

Up.

Down.

Up, until finally I talked the agent into forgetting the plastic, and we agreed to put a large amount of absorbent straw under the baby!

Finally, the plane—zoo director and baby elephant on board—was airborne!

With three stops en route to London.

The flight was, quite literally, the milk run, as each time the plane landed, under the supervision of the co-pilot I warmed up milk and entered the freight compartment to bottle-feed the baby (using a large bucket with a nipple on it—the standard bottle technique for a calf or baby elephant). I can't remember where we landed between Colombo and Amsterdam, but I do remember in the middle of the night on one airstrip the plane was surrounded by dozens of men with heavy-duty rifles. Perhaps the other passengers didn't notice—they were probably asleep anyway, but I was out there on the ground with the men with the guns trying to bottle feed my baby elephant!

When the plane finally landed in Amsterdam, we off-loaded the baby elephant for a few hours so it could move around. Amsterdam was—and still is—one of the few airports that actually had an animal hospital set up for such emergencies, and I took full use of it. Then it was back on board and on to Chicago.

The flight to Chicago was a split freighter—passengers and freight separated by a connecting door. I warmed up milk in the passenger's galley, much to the flight attendant's dismay, but after my third or fourth trip back to feed the animal it seemed everyone on board got into the spirit of the adventure and both passengers and crew all wanted a look at the baby elephant that was sharing their flight—a baby elephant that greeted us with high-pitched squeals every time we arrived with her warm milk. I jokingly thought about bringing her up to the front section of the plane—perhaps putting her in a middle seat. But I didn't.

I had sent a telex in advance, so a zoo truck was waiting to meet me, and staff was ready to take the elephant to its new home at Lincoln Park Zoo.

This was the fifth day, and I felt as if I'd had about two hours sleep since I'd left Chicago, which was probably close to accurate. I achieved what I had been assured was the impossible—*and I had done it all legally and by the book!*

I boarded the flight that would take me to the conference in Venezuela and collapsed into my seat. My colleagues couldn't understand why I almost fell asleep so often through most of the conference!

As the year went on, the National Zoo kept calling me to talk about the baby elephant it had been given by the Government of Sri Lanka. The elephant had been sick for the first eight months following its arrival and nearly died. I recall getting these calls at least three or four times a month.

That elephant, of course, was the one I had selected first but was told I could not have. As time went by, I could not have been happier with my second choice. Bozie (named in honor of her sponsors, Pat and Art Bowes) was very healthy and ultimately, about 20 years later, became the first elephant in Illinois to give birth!

*That* story also became a "travel adventure" of sorts, as Bozie was first taken to Springfield, Missouri to breed with that zoo's male elephant, Onyx. She was then returned home so she could give birth back at Lincoln Park Zoo, the first pregnant elephant to be successfully moved in a later stage of pregnancy. Fortunately, this time her delivery was not on such a tight schedule.

## Gorilla moving day(s)

Transporting animals is a big assignment in virtually every respect. In addition to the many animals I have brought back from safari, expeditions, collecting trips, and times I went to claim gifts, there have been those we sent *out* to new homes.

**Jane**, a young female orangutan that Lincoln Park Zoo shipped to San Diego, calmly arrived waving her arm out the side of her crate, ready to greet the world—while also trying to open her crate! She had methodically eaten off most of one side of her wooden crate during the airplane ride.

**Freddie** was the docile male gorilla we sent with his family to the St. Louis Zoo to start a gorilla group in its new great ape facility; our four **"gorilla bachelor boys"** went to Cleveland for longer than a "boys night out" since they are still there years later, as Cleveland had room for them, and Lincoln Park did not; and of course **Gino**, our young male superstar and his family went to Disney's Animal Kingdom to start their gorilla troop and remain major attractions.

Later, we sent all our remaining gorillas to Louisville, Kentucky while Lincoln Park Zoo's new home for great apes was under construction. That adds up to quite a few apes on the move.

Gorilla moving day is always of interest to the media, assuming all goes well. The moves make great headlines, as noted . . .

*Zoo Gorillas head south: Six apes from Lincoln Park Zoo are headed for a warmer, roomier home near Orlando, Florida*

Chicago Sun-Times, 6/11/97

*Four Swinging Bachelors Arrive From Chicago*
            —Cleveland MetroParks publication, 1994

Beyond the headlines, gorilla moving offers great promotional opportunities.

When Lincoln Park Zoo moved Koundu, a big silverback male—and son of Kisoro, the adult gorilla we sent to England—and his family to set up house in the Denver Zoo's new Primate Panorama habitat, they got an unexpected bonus! One of the young females unexpectedly gave birth just days before the move was to take place.

Since the process of moving animals between zoos takes months to plan, and securing the necessary permits and coordinating logistics are considerable, we decided we had to go ahead with the move. The baby was too little to go in a crate with its mother when she was shipped, so Eric Meyers, one of our great ape keepers, hand-carried the baby to Denver.

United Airlines offered us a first class ticket for Eric and his tiny traveling companion. Most other passengers were unaware of the special newborn primate in the first class cabin—especially since "the baby" was dressed in a baby snuggly and wrapped warmly in a blanket. Eric himself played the role of devoted father well, as his wife had given birth to their third child only weeks before.

The pilot, however, could not contain himself. Once the plane was airborne he announced that there was a VIP passenger in the first class cabin—a baby gorilla—and that every passenger would receive a free banana to commemorate the trip!

# A big move, a new house, some important work, and a great film

Moving animals from one zoo to another can happen for a variety of reasons, such as to relocate an animal to a facility with more space or for an opportunity to breed, for husbandry reasons, or to bring new animals into an existing collection.

Sometimes the move occurs within a zoo's own institution.

The greatest great ape move of all time happened right within Lincoln Park Zoo.

In 1973 I had reached a major decision that Lincoln Park Zoo could simply no longer house great apes—gorillas, chimpanzees, and orangutans—adequately in cages. It simply wasn't right to confine so many in such tight quarters, yet I had no alternative. I had already looked around the United States, thinking about where I could place these wonderful, thoughtful, sensitive creatures.

We then began exploring the possibility of raising enough money to construct a new great ape house at Lincoln Park Zoo. We came up with a focus, a plan, and superb architectural drawings that showed what was possible. And we asked for help. Our efforts were rewarded by an outpouring of substantial capital gifts from many of Chicago's leading citizens and foundations, as noted by the Krocs' generous lead gift.

In June 1976 we prepared for the opening of the zoo's new Great Ape House with a special preview event for donors, members, visitors—and for the great apes.

Moving 25 big great apes (gorillas, chimpanzees and orangutans) to a new home all at one time—all in two days—required incredible coordination by the entire Lincoln Park Zoo staff, along with a large team of volunteer doctors, nurses, and technicians. I decided this also offered a unique opportunity to get accurate baseline statistics on every animal—height, weight, heart rate, etc.,—and to thoroughly x-ray and examine every aspect of each animal.

The old Monkey House where the animals lived was converted into a very crowded M.A.S.H.-type environment with each physician-specialist and his or her team operating in an incredibly small space. We developed a punch list and virtual assembly line for examining and testing each animal to minimize the time the animal would be under anesthesia, while at the same time maximizing the amount of information we could get during the process.

I also decided it was important to document such a move, as no one had attempted a move of this magnitude anywhere in the zoo world.

An old contact of mine led me to a young filmmaker named Dugan Rosalini, who when all was said and done, produced a brilliant documentary of the move, focusing on our big adult male gorilla, Otto.

*Otto: Zoo Gorilla* was the result of weeks of filming before,

We named our first baby male Baringo giraffe "Billy B" in honor of Bill Bartholomay, President of the Chicago Park District and long-time friend of the zoo. Courtesy, Chicago Park District

South American spectacled bear and cub (ca. 1986). Courtesy,
Chicago Park District

Ring-tailed lemur from Madagascar. Courtesy, Chicago Park
District

Kevin Bell (far right), bird curator and later my successor as zoo director, spearheaded our 1981 collecting trip to Iceland in search of puffins.

Judy the elephant and her keeper, Paul Dittambl (ca. 1950). Courtesy, Chicago Park District

Making rounds at the old bear run, I would trick Mike the polar bear into a visual dental exam by offering him some food. Courtesy, Chicago Park District

Bushman as a youngster with Alfred E. Parker, Zoo Director, who paid a considerable amount of money to bring him to Lincoln Park in the early 1930s. Courtesy, Chicago Park District

By 1940 Bushman was one of the two most famous gorillas in the world; the other was the circus star, Gargantua. Courtesy, Chicago Park District

In 1970 Mumbi made headlines with the birth of Kumba, the first gorilla born at Lincoln Park Zoo. Courtesy, Chicago Park District

Kumba celebrates her first birthday (1971, her parents: Kisoro and Mumbi). Courtesy, Chicago Tribune

Despite our best efforts to leave baby gorillas with their mothers, these two needed hand-rearing (1979). Courtesy, Chicago Park District

during and after the big move, and subsequent additional months of editing. It is still shown on PBS television stations nationwide. The film truly captured the moment, not just of our momentous move, but of the personality of Otto, who became almost as famous as Bushman.

As for the big project itself, we managed to move every animal successfully and without incident. And the body of knowledge that resulted from our examinations and tests proved invaluable to other zoos working with gorillas, chimpanzees, and orangutans.

# An important film with a sad scene

Not every move is successful and sometimes recording them for posterity can be disastrous. Such was the case when TV newsman Bill Kurtis came to Lincoln Park Zoo to film a documentary on endangered species for CBS. He had traveled to all parts of the world where trafficking in endangered species and their body parts—such as tiger penises and rhino horns—was accepted as just business. At the zoo, he wanted to film some work we were doing involving one of our rare snow leopards, as Lincoln Park has been a leader in the breeding of this highly endangered and beautiful big cat, found primarily in the Himalayan Mountains.

We regarded the scheduled move of an older female snow leopard to another cage for management purposes, while undergoing a routine series of tests and examinations, as nothing special. Still, we thought it would present an interesting visual story, and Bill thought it would be the perfect segment to end his documentary.

With everyone assembled in the old Lion House, and the camera rolling, we anesthetized the animal and moved her to the next cage. The vets began their routine examination. Blood was drawn from the jugular vein, in the neck area, for this standard procedure. But in this instance, the animal began bleeding profusely and in spite of the heroic efforts of the vets and two assistants, it bled to death—on camera.

We were devastated by the loss of this valuable animal that had been a part of our collection for 14 years. We were also very concerned about how the story—captured on film—would be presented and how the public might react upon seeing it. And as many times as the media had done wonderful stories at or about the zoo, we always knew we never had any control over what would be said or how the finished piece would look. So we waited and waited.

The resulting CBS program showed how so many people worldwide were working hard to push animals to extinction. Bill Kurtis then used the zoo footage at the end of the story, vividly capturing the intensely personal feelings and devastated expressions on the faces of our group as they valiantly tried to save the snow leopard. As the visual image was one of tragedy, Kurtis' voiceover told of the many people intent on helping animals toward extinction, while a few were trying desperately to save endangered species— and the film footage spoke for itself.

Perhaps the snow leopard's death served an important purpose, dramatically making a statement we could not make ourselves.

We learned from the necropsy that the animal had complete cirrhosis of the liver. Her blood could no longer clot normally and any injury, even a pinprick, would have killed her. We didn't know it at the time, but her fate was already sealed.

## Sex and the single zoo animal

I happened to be in Marlin's office when he took the transatlantic call. All I could hear at my end was Marlin's soft, "Oh," and see a look of disbelief on his face. "Are you sure?" he asked.

Apparently, whoever was on the other end of the call was sure. He put down the phone and looked at me.

"That was Amsterdam," he said finally. "They want to know why we sent them a female gorilla."

Now it was my turn to pause, then let the look of confusion and disbelief cross my face, before having it dissolve into one of extreme embarrassment. It was I, after all, as the zoo vet, who should have known.

Rajah, a young gorilla Marlin brought to Lincoln Park in 1947, was now a subadult. Because he was (supposedly) male, we chose him to be sent to the Amsterdam Zoo to be paired with a young female gorilla about the same age. We spent months negotiating the transfer; weeks having a special crate built, and invested additional time making air transport arrangements and getting all the permit papers in order. This was the first time a gorilla was being shipped across the Atlantic—*the other way*—to Europe, and the story made headlines in Chicago's newspapers.

I was so pleased that Rajah had gone into the crate and settled down without a fuss, and happy we had been able to send a keeper with him on his long journey that, on the day of the move, I had forgotten to *sex* Rajah—to examine and categorize him. I presumed Marlin had *sexed* Rajah as a youngster and, as the Zoo Director, knew what he had in his collection.

Well, Marlin *had* sexed Rajah, but in young gorillas it is not as easy as one might think to tell a male from a female. The testicles and penis of a male gorilla are not so visually evident as a human and, in youngsters, often recede up into the body cavity making it sometimes difficult to see.

But Marlin, proud as ever, was not one to take responsibility for the mistake. It was clearly going to be *my* mistake and I would have to live with it.

Rajah never returned to Lincoln Park, living out the rest of her life in Europe.

*Sexing* many species of exotic animals was very difficult in my early days at the zoo, and I wasn't alone in that regard. We just did not know as much as we know now, and even modern technology cannot overcome the occasional human error.

In some species, there are clear visual differences in males and females. With lions, for example, size can be an indicator as, in many species, males are substantially larger. But this is not true for *all* species, such as snowy owls and some other birds of prey where the female is always quite a bit larger.

Birds present particular problems as their sexual organs are concealed inside the abdomen. If they don't present a color or size differential, it is virtually impossible to distinguish between a male and female.

Laparoscopy changed all that. We can now insert a thin tube into the area near the stomach of a bird and, using a tiny bright light on the end, we can tell whether it is male or female. With the advent of laproscopy and the discovery in most zoo collections that we didn't even have the right sexes together, it was amazing how the number of hatchings increased once we shuffled our birds around so we were clearly putting males and females together!

# Gorillas in love (or something like it)

Sometimes the pairing of animals is not only dangerous, but can be deadly. Many larger mammals have very distinct preferences in terms of individual animals, which makes introducing them a dicey proposition.

Keo, our old male chimpanzee, was a magnificent young animal and had grown up in our Children's Zoo. He'd been a media star as a youngster as he was easy to handle. We referred to him as "Mr. Personality" at numerous events. Keo played with a female chimp, which was also at the Children's Zoo, but she had never become a zoo star. Eventually it was time to move them both to the Primate House. We had great hopes that some baby chimps would result.

However, when they matured both physically and sexually, instead of making love, they declared war.

The female was no match for Keo who physically abused her and sent her cowering into a corner screaming. This match was not only *not* made in heaven, it clearly wasn't going to work.

I managed to locate another female chimp, one that had been born at the Staten Island Zoo and was a few years older than Keo. She was named Patsy in honor of Dr. Patricia O'Connor, the first woman zoo vet, who was the director of the zoo.

Patsy was, quite frankly, a very homely chimp. When she arrived, I was rather dismayed, but what did I know? After a few efforts by Keo to dominate her—to which she responded with bites and blows to his body and ego—the couple settled down and, over the years, produced many babies. Every one of those babies was simply beautiful, which perhaps proves the old adage that love is strange.

Tara was a female gorilla with some strong preferences when it came to pairing. Having been with her mate, the famous Samson, in Milwaukee for more than 24 years, her reproductive years were almost over when AZA's Species Survival Plan for gorillas suggested she be moved to Lincoln Park.

The plan was for Tara to hopefully be stimulated and mate with Otto, our prime silverback male. It was a last-ditch effort to have her produce a baby as she was wild caught and had what is called founder stock genes not yet represented in the captive gorilla population. As we can no longer bring wild-caught babies into the national or international captive gorilla breeding pool, getting as much founder-stock DNA into the mix as possible is critical to our long-term success in breeding gorillas.

So Tara came to Lincoln Park, a cranky, older lady with a real attitude. When the long introductions were over (putting Tara near Otto in a separate cage, then eventually still separated but able to touch each other, then finally together in the same cage), Tara would not let Otto mate with her.

After several unsuccessful attempts at pairing, in which Tara would get severe bites from Otto, she was recuperating in a back cage. It was then that keepers noticed she was making eye contact with our other, smaller male gorilla, Frank. He was almost as old as Otto and a proven breeder, but not the one chosen by the SSP committee.

After observing Tara for some weeks and watching Frank's response, we received permission from the committee to try Tara with Frank. A formal introduction process was begun.

Eventually, Frank and Tara were put together. Although the scowl never left Tara's face, she accepted Frank's advances and, over time, became pregnant. Everyone was thrilled!

But after the baby was born, Tara simply didn't know what to do with it. She wouldn't pick it up when it cried, and she carried it upside down at other times. We weren't sure she was nursing the baby—or that she even knew that she was supposed to.

After a few days of giving her a chance to raise the baby, we reluctantly pulled it while it still was strong enough to survive. Mother-reared infants are the goal and we're willing to wait several days, trying to make it work, but these babies are so precious that we simply cannot wait *too long* or they won't have the strength to survive on their own. The baby, named Mandara, was taken to our zoo nursery for hand-rearing.

After a few months, the director of the Milwaukee Zoo paid me a visit to retrieve the infant. He wanted to raise her in Milwaukee so he could use her to promote the fundraising campaign for a badly needed new primate building.

Mandara became known as the "million dollar baby," because she ultimately helped the Milwaukee Zoo raise enough money for a magnificent new facility for great apes.

From Milwaukee she went on to the National Zoo in Washington, DC where she had several babies and even took over the nursing and care of a gorilla that belonged to another female who had abandoned it. Mandara was already caring for her own baby, so she probably figured "what's one more?" This was a first for a gorilla in captivity.

Sadly, Tara did not produce another baby but remained at Lincoln Park Zoo until her death a few years later.

Females accepting males is very important for breeding. If that seems obvious, it's not. In nature, the male pursues and the female chooses. She often will reject a suitor she doesn't think is worthy of her. Her choice is usually the animal she feels is the strongest and has the best genes. She will reject inferior males.

But in the zoo world, we make the selections for the animals, and we are not always right. Only *they* will determine that.

## Tough love, animal style

When our huge polar bear, Mike, grew up and matured it was time to pair him with a potential mate. I consider adult male polar bears to be the most dangerous animal in the zoo so introducing a female to Mike was something I approached with great trepidation. I ordered a young female from an animal dealer in Europe and Szaska arrived, a beautiful snow-white ball of fluff. I waited three years to introduce her to Mike, but she was still less than half his size. I was concerned.

My staff went through the usual pre-introduction steps and, finally, after months of preparation, the day came. We opened the door between their two cages. We were ready with hoses and fire extinguishers—standard-issue introduction deterrents in case Mike tried to hurt or kill her. I held my breath as I watched the two bears.

Mike ran at Skaska, but retreated to his own cage when she growled at him.

Ten minutes later, he was back and lunged toward her again. A simple swipe of his big front paw would have killed her. But instead, she hit him in the face with one of her front paws and proceeded to chase him back into his own cage.

That was it. They settled down and lived many quiet years together, but no babies resulted from this pair.

Lincoln Park's first baby elephant was a result of our Asian female, Bozie, and Springfield, Missouri's male, Onyx. There has not been much success with artificial insemination for elephants, so getting an animal to breed requires sending a female to a male.

Males don't usually travel, as the host zoo would not have the strong restraints required to keep a male, so it is always the female that goes to the male.

After three years of planning, Bozie went to Missouri. Finally, she was cycling and ready to breed. Despite what appeared as a successful mating, it was many months before Bozie returned to Lincoln Park, her pregnancy confirmed and well along. With a 22-month pregnancy, there is a lot of waiting.

In 1990 our collective efforts paid off and Illinois had its first baby elephant born in the state—a 190-pound bouncing baby girl, Shanti. We all cried when the baby was delivered without difficulty and were overwhelmed—*as was Bozie*. She was the orphaned baby elephant I had traveled to Sri Lanka to claim 14 years earlier and she had never seen a newborn elephant! But she became an exemplary mother and took it all in stride.

When we moved Kisoro, our breeding silverback male to England's Howlett's Zoo Park, it was a first on many counts. Kisoro was the first adult gorilla to make the transatlantic crossing eastbound (Rajah was the first gorilla of any age) and one of the first breeding loans we had arranged for internationally. It came about when my eccentric gambling friend John Aspinall badly needed a proven breeding male for his mature females: 13 year-old Mouila and 12 year-old Jiyu. Because we already had Otto, Frank, and Fred becoming silverbacks at Lincoln Park, I agreed to send Kisoro, with the understanding that we would share in any babies born. This is a standard breeding agreement with various species.

At the time, however, it was a breakthrough agreement. Kisoro was shipped to England amid much fanfare.

Kisoro sired a number of babies and virtually ensured the success of John's gorilla collection. For a long time, John and I had more successful gorilla births between us than anyone in the world.

One of Kisoro's progeny, Koundu, eventually started his own troop first at Lincoln Park, then in Denver where we sent his family many years later. It was a win-win situation for John, for me, and especially for the future of lowland gorillas.

Not all matches end successfully. Our saddest story involved a female that took years to arrange for our rare and highly endangered male Afghanistan leopard, Christian. The keepers knicknamed him "Killer" because his habit is killing what he can grab and pulling it through the wire mesh of his outside cage in the

Lion House. Prey have included rabbits, squirrels, and a variety of sparrows and songbirds. He is indiscriminate—and lethal.

Finally, after our staff searched the world, we located a suitable female Afghanistan leopard at the Bristol Zoo, England. Arrangements were made to have her shipped to the U.S. to begin the lengthy introduction process as soon as she was out of quarantine.

We followed the long, standard procedure and, after weeks of what seemed like a successful introduction, opened the door between their two cages. They appeared fine, and settled down for the night.

The next day, a warm summer morning, my wife, Wendy, and I planned to ride our bikes along the lakefront, stopping at the zoo to see how the leopards were doing. It was early—before the zoo was officially open—but all we could see was Christian in the outside cage.

Wendy joked that, "He probably killed and ate her!"

"Don't even think that after all we've gone through to get this lovely female," I said.

But when we checked back with staff later in the morning, the truth was too painful to believe. He had, indeed, killed the female, dragging her into his cage, and had begun to eat her.

Wendy was joking, but had been way too right this time around.

Christian, meanwhile, remains a solitary animal. We would like to try to breed this valuable animal again, but cannot risk losing another female. The story might be one of sex and the single animal, but in this case, it definitely was not a love story.

# That's entertainment!

"Doc, you gotta do *something*. We *have* to use that studio."

The NBC-TV producer was calling me—again—as he had every day for four days. Each day he sounded more frustrated than the one before. Now he was screaming.

I held the phone away from my ear as I tried to think again if there was *anything* I could do. Nothing came to mind.

Marlin Perkins had opened the door, so maybe indirectly, this was all *his* fault. Not really, of course. People loved animals and Marlin's successful TV programs *Zoo Parade* and *Wild Kingdom* were very appealing. Now, with his having left Chicago for St. Louis, there was a void and producers called frequently, inviting me to appear on programs with unusual, exotic, or even just interesting animals.

The NBC program Monday had been one of many and not at all out of the ordinary, but now it was Thursday, and the situation was not ordinary at all.

I had taken a small, yellow-headed Amazon parrot to the show. It was a cute, rather talkative bird that I thought would be perfect. All had gone well at first. The bird had come out of the carrying crate easily and climbed up my arm to my shoulder where it sat happily chattering away while I talked about parrots in general, parrots as pets, their talking ability, how smart they were, and answered questions from the host. We were near the end of the show and the director had given the signal that it was a wrap, when suddenly the bird took off, flying up to the rafters of the studio.

With birds of prey, jesses (light leather thongs) are attached to one leg and can be held to keep a bird from taking off. Parrots, however, don't require jesses as they typically stay on the perch where they are placed, such as on my shoulder.

But not this time. The tape was still rolling as we looked up at the parrot, now perched atop a pipe overhead that ran the length of the studio. NBC in Chicago was then located in the Merchandise Mart, one of the city's most famous commercial buildings, and some of its ceilings were *very high*—perhaps 25 feet or more.

We wrapped up the taping session, and I asked for the cameraman's hoist, which had a lift on it. We maneuvered it into position so I could climb up and get the parrot. But the bird seemed to like the studio and obviously had no intention of going back to the zoo—at least not just yet.

Each time we moved the hoist into position and I climbed up, as soon as I reached out to take the parrot, it moved just out of reach. We repeated the procedure at least six or seven times. Finally, I decided the bird would have to stay there. It was very quiet so I couldn't see the harm. The producers also said they were running out of time and needed the studio to tape another program. I said I would be back for the parrot at the end of the day, confident that after a few hours it would come down.

But by afternoon, I received the first call from the producer.

"Come and get your parrot out of here!" he demanded. " I can't use the studio. Every time we start to tape, the damn parrot starts to talk! He's ruining my tapings!"

So down I went and repeated the exercise we'd attempted that morning.

No luck.

I left again, and they closed the studio for the night. I told the producer that the parrot would be down by morning because it would get hungry.

When the next morning arrived, they again tried to tape a program in the studio, and, again, the parrot began screeching after being stone silent until the TV crew started to work.

And so it went for four days.

I shuttled back and forth between the zoo and the Merchandise Mart. NBC had to move all its equipment to another studio, and the producers and station management were becoming increasingly upset. A television studio not available for use means lost money, and this one had not been available for days.

At last, on the fifth day, the parrot was hungry enough that when I showed up and took the hoist up to get it, the bird climbed into my hand, then onto my shoulder as if nothing had happened. Everyone seemed quite ready to wring its neck, but of course that's not advisable when dealing with a TV star!

That was the first time such a thing had happened to me in my TV career. Unfortunately, it would not be the last.

# The doctor on *Zoo Parade*

Being part of the entertainment world had never been my ambition. But from the time, early on, that Marlin recruited me as the doctor on his *Zoo Parade* shows, which were produced at Lincoln Park Zoo, my television career blossomed.

Chicago was the center for television production during the medium's early years in the 1940s. Shows were filmed or recorded live—there was no such thing as a retake. I got to meet and work with many of TV's legendary actors and be part of some interesting entertainment adventures.

*Zoo Parade* came about in 1945 when Marlin was asked to bring some live zoo animals to the WBKB television studio at State and Lake Streets. The animal segments would be used as "filler."

Although very few homes had television sets at that time, the viewer response to the animal shows was so great that by 1947, *Zoo Parade* made history in Chicago, joining other live shows, such as *Kukla, Fran and Ollie; Mr. Wizard;* and *Ding Dong School.*

NBC began producing the zoo shows in a small space in the basement of the old Reptile House—its on location zoo studio. Kennel Ration was a sponsor, and Jim Hurlbut acted as the side-kick, as well as doing the commercials live. He played foil to Marlin's "great bwana" image. After several seasons on Chicago TV, the show went national, and Lincoln Park Zoo was seen every Sunday afternoon throughout the United States.

In those early days I had no idea how to handle a television show, and, frankly, not many other people did either. Television was like the Wild West. There were limited scripts, and the programs were pretty much "take it as it comes," which was fun, but also led to some very interesting situations.

*Everything* was shown as it happened—roping lions, wrestling alligators into restraints, catching monkeys in nets, five men handling 12-foot pythons, putting antelopes in chutes, and every other procedure, including performing surgery on a snake's jaw!

And we only got one chance to do it right!

There were also little things that made live television, well, "live."

I remember Jim Hurlburt doing a television commercial in the Lion House on a very hot summer day. Flies kept landing on his face. As he talked about the virtues of Kennel Ration dog food, he was swatting at the flies. It didn't seem funny at the time, but watching the recorded footage today, it is truly hysterical! TV was like that much of the time.

Once, when the TV station was experiencing union problems, we actually did a "remote" from my animal hospital in Berwyn, just outside Chicago. I certainly appeared as the straight man to Marlin's magnificent theatrical persona.

The programs continued until Marlin left the zoo in 1962. By that time it had evolved into Mutual of Omaha's *Wild Kingdom*, and Marlin's career in entertainment took him around the world. That left me to handle Chicago.

# The Ark in the Park:
# Ray, TV, and me

The second career of Marlin Perkins had become a sore point with his employers at the Chicago Park District. So when I became the zoo's director, I made it clear that I had no ambition to follow in Marlin's famous footsteps. In fact, I wanted to lie low so I could please my new bosses. After all, they had hired me to be a zoo director, not an entertainer.

But after several years at the zoo, WGN-TV, the large independent local TV station, approached me about doing a Chicago zoo show. There was an open slot on Saturday mornings. The timing seemed right and my employers thought it would be good public relations for the zoo, so I agreed to do it. For several years I brought animals to the studio each week, starting with a Farm Show, then covering many of the other animals in the zoo—at least those that could travel to the studio.

Compared to Marlin's track record, that experience was relatively short lived.

I got a call from the TV station informing me that the Saturday morning time slot would be filled with reruns of old movie serials with Flash Gordon!

But soon WGN wanted me back, this time to join a popular show that aired every morning, Monday through Friday with TV veteran Ray Rayner. I didn't know Ray, but I thought it would be good exposure for the zoo, so I agreed to try it.

My experience on *The Ray Rayner Show* was among the highlights of my years spent working with animals. Ray was one of the nicest people I'd met and worked with, and certainly one of the most talented. Twice each week, we presented an 8–10-minute zoo segment that was inserted into his program. We called it *The Ark in the Park*.

The Irish Rovers had a song that included the verse, *"There were green alligators and long-necked geese . . . "* and we used it to introduce the segments, which were taped at the studio as well as on location at the zoo. The show was a huge success, and our animal segment was so popular it continued for at least a dozen years. Often, when I was walking through the zoo on rounds, I would hear visitors humming or singing as I walked by, . . . *green alligators and long-necked geese . . .* That always put a smile on my face.

Ray's success was due, at least in part, to the fact that he was supposedly doing a children's show, but it really appealed to families and people of all ages. Although the animal segments had a strong educational element, they were always presented in a light manner with frequent comic moments that made it fun to watch.

Interestingly, Ray was not at all comfortable around animals. When we agreed to work together I brought my dog, a beautiful collie named Heather, to the first show. Ray eventually agreed to hold her lead. Over the years he was converted and became a real animal lover.

When Ray decided to retire, I was saddened as we'd become close friends and I truly enjoyed working with him. I had no intention of continuing in "the entertainment business." But once again, WGN-TV management called and asked me to fill a slot on one of its most popular programs, *Bozo's Circus*. I had heard a lot about the show and how the waiting list for tickets stretched years into the future. (Rumor was that parents wrote in for tickets to *Bozo* on the day their child was born in hopes that the tickets would arrive by the time the child was four or five years old—it was *that* popular.)

I'd never seen the program, and the first day I reported to the WGN studio to tape my animal segment, I'm embarrassed to say I didn't know which clown was the famous Bozo and which was Cookie, his clown sidekick. I learned which was which fairly quickly, and both men became good friends over the years. The five-minute segments on *Bozo* continued to generate excellent publicity for the zoo as we filmed both in the studio and occasionally at the zoo, with throngs of people watching and cheering us on.

Under the greasepaint and red wig, time continues to pass— even for the most beloved of clowns. When the second "Bozo" retired and the program went off the air, WGN did not call again. By that time I had retired, too, so it was time to bring the entertainment phase of my career to a close.

But years later, in places far from home, I would be walking along and hear someone begin to sing . . . *green alligators and long-necked geese* . . . and someone would ask me if I am *really* Dr. Fisher—the zoo doctor from TV. WGN television cast a wide net and gave Lincoln Park Zoo a big boost over many, many years.

My time with the zoo included a major "entertainment" component that spanned 45 years, during which I met some wonderful people.

Lee Phillip was a popular TV host with a long-running midday program. I brought a penguin to her show on one memorable occasion. It should be noted that penguins—much like koalas— are not as nice or charming as they appear. Lee had asked for a penguin to complement her doll series—that year a penguin doll was featured.

I explained to Lee that penguins are unpredictable, but she was not deterred—that is, until I put the penguin on the floor next to her. It proceeded immediately to lunge at her and tried to bite her. She kept backing away until she finally walked off the stage. I was left alone on the set—to finish *her show* without her!

Top-rated Chicago newsman Fahey Flynn invited me to be a guest on his show several times with animals in tow, and I also paid some visits to one of radio's longest-running programs, *Extension 720* with Milt Rosenberg of the University of Chicago. Other TV shows included NBC's *Kidding Around* with Steve Smith, a great entertainer and clown who went on to run Ringling Brother's circus clown school. Steve always had a young girl as his co-host and, over the years, I appeared so many times that I got to know three girls who came and went as each grew too old for the format.

*Kidding Around* had us involved in all kinds of bits, including showing the slowest and fastest animal. We usually filmed on Saturday mornings so my wife, Wendy, would go with me, sometimes just to come along, other times to help with the animals.

One Saturday, we were running late. I had called ahead to the Children's Zoo and asked them to have a tortoise and a small bird of prey, a kestrel, ready for me to take to the TV studio. I'd chosen them to represent the "slowest" and "fastest" animals, respectively on the program.

We dashed into the zoo, picked up the cages and drove downtown to the NBC studios. With the tape rolling, I showed the tortoise and handed it to the program's host. I reached into the carrying case to bring out the kestral and, before I could grab hold of the leather jesses, the bird took off right past me and up to the rafters of the TV studio. I couldn't help but think of the parrot incident years earlier. At least, I thought, this little guy can't talk!

The cameraman was quick and followed the bird's flight. There it sat. I felt ridiculous as I talked about how really fast these small birds of prey are! What I had not known was that the jesses were too short on this kestral, and zoo staff people had planned to tell me that and ask that I wait until they put longer ones on—just to be safe. But they had taken a coffee break when I zoomed in to collect the carrying cases, so no one ever had a chance to warn me!

I waited until the show ended, and the producer told me I could get the bird down. It was perched on a pipe high above the studio, but next to it a ceiling tile was missing. Wendy asked one of the cameramen where that hole led. His answer, unbeknownst to me, was not encouraging.

"That hole leads to the air duct and vent system for the whole Merchandise Mart," he said. "He goes in there, you'll never see him again."

Since I didn't know this, I confidently climbed the cameraman's hoist and reached out to grab the bird. On my second attempt, I grabbed hold of the birds jesses and brought him down. That's when Wendy told me how lucky I was.

The studio folks never even blinked. This crew didn't know the parrot story!

# Lights! Camera! Animals!

I was asked to bring some animals for a Halloween TV show and decided on a bat, a tarantula, and our own black cat. The cat was actually a sweetie pie, but I thought I'd pass her off as a rare Scottish wild cat (kidding of course). We put her in a carrying case for the trip to the TV studio, along with the glass box for the tarantula, and another for the bat. Though they couldn't be let out of their cages, the camera could film through the glass.

When we arrived at the studio, Wendy took our cat Billiken out of the carrier, and the cat went berserk. She clawed at Wendy and tried to bite her. The taping was about to begin, and Wendy handed off the cat to me. We decided we'd better go with the cat first.

Not only did Billiken not calm down, she went from bad to worse—turning my hands into a bloody mess while I chattered on about how she was a Scottish wild cat. By the time I handed her back to Wendy who quickly dropped her in the carrying case, I went on to the bat and tarantula and forgot to mention the cat was really a domestic black house cat! She had acted her part so well that she should have earned the "best dramatic performance by a cat" award that year.

But when we got home, she returned to being a sweetie pie.

Our cat was either a great actress or just not cut out for show business!

We also appeared on TV programs at Easter, typically with bunnies and chicks from the Farm-in-the-Zoo. One year, however, we decided to take a piglet as the sow at the Farm had just farrowed.

It was a cold day with a biting North wind, and the little piglet was only a few days old. The keeper at the Farm-in-the-Zoo wrapped the piglet in a wool blanket and told Wendy to put it under her coat—something she was used to doing with snakes in bags and other animals that needed to be kept warm.

Neither of us gave the matter much thought at the time. We would tape the segment for *Kidding Around* at NBC, return the animal to the zoo, then go on to meet some relatives of mine at a nice restaurant for Saturday lunch.

All went well at the studio, we returned the piglet to the Farm-in-the-Zoo and left for our lunch date. These particular relatives, cousins from California, were rather wealthy and might be called "highbrow." Wendy and I had not been married long and they had never met her. She wore a lovely outfit and good jewelry and wanted to look her best. At first, everything was fine, but as we reached our table, we began to warm up from a morning of having been out in the extreme Chicago cold. It was at that point that Wendy started to emit a very "earthy" pig smell. She was aware of it, I was aware of it, and my cousins were very clearly aware of it.

We tried to explain to this sophisticated Los Angeles couple (who didn't care for animals) why Wendy was so fragrant—taking a piglet to a TV taping and keeping it under her coat because it was so cold outside, but it didn't matter. I don't think they ever understood, and Wendy and I were convinced they thought I had married someone who stunk to high heaven!

## TV never smelled like this!

Through the years, Wendy has demonstrated many exceptional qualities, one of them being she is a really good sport. As if her piglet incident involving my relatives had not been enough, she signed on for *another* pig episode involving the TV show *Kidding Around* some time later.

Once again, we were planning to use a newborn piglet for a

Saturday morning taping. But it turned out that the sow had not given birth until that very morning. In fact, it was still birthing the litter when we arrived at the Farm-in-the-Zoo. Clearly, we couldn't take one of the newborns, which was barely out of the amniotic sack.

The keeper suggested instead that we take a three-month old piglet that was still at our Farm, but scheduled to return to its farm in about a week. We agreed that was probably our best alternative.

This time, Wendy was dressed in jeans and her winter parka. She easily climbed the fence to grab the frightened 20 plus-pound lump of squirming, squealing pig. He was so startled at her scooping him up into her arms that he promptly defecated—all down the front of her jacket, down her pants legs, and on to her shoes.

We were already late for the TV taping so all we could do was wipe her down with paper towels and head for the studio. We arrived at NBC with Wendy smelling to high heaven and the piglet screaming bloody murder.

Entering Chicago's Merchandise Mart building via the main lobby, we walked passed the front desk and the security guard—who never even looked up, as if pigs came through the lobby of one of the city's most famous buildings every day—but when we arrived at the studio everyone noticed Wendy immediately.

I took the piglet from her for the program taping, and the production team very politely asked Wendy if she would please stand at the farthest possible end of the hallway away from everybody and everything!

I'll admit, she smelled awful!

With the taping over and the pig safely returned to the Farm, we headed home. Fortunately our dry cleaner is a good sport who performed above and beyond the call of duty. In fact, our dry cleaner has learned from experience over the years not to ask us what the stains are on our clothes. Too many times, he heard more than he wanted to know.

# More about TV, radio, and special events

Not all of our appearances on the NBC show *Kidding Around* ended in on-air disasters—only enough of them to make it seem that way. Once Wendy and I got on the elevator in the Merchandise Mart in Chicago, on our way to a taping of the program. Another couple followed us onto the elevator and looked surprised. Wendy was holding an adorable baby chimpanzee in her arms.

The keeper at the Zoo Nursery had dressed the chimp in cute pink baby clothes and wrapped it in a pink blanket to keep it warm. All that could be seen was its black, hairy little chimp face peering out of the blanket. The couple stared at us, then at our "baby." Their faces were fixed with the same expression—an interesting blend of shock, horror, surprise, amusement, and curiosity. They quickly straightened up, did an about-face to stare at the closed elevator doors, not quite sure what they had actually seen, seemingly afraid to speak. As they stepped off the elevator, we burst out laughing. They must have thought we had the ugliest baby in the world!

But at least we had an animal with us that day.

Over the years I appeared on *Kidding Around* and other TV programs, so my calendar was often very full. I would call keepers or other staffers in different sections of the zoo and have them choose a small animal and get it ready for me to quickly pick up and take to the television tapings. I would look in, grab the handling gloves if they had been put on the top of a carrier (which usually meant I had an iguana, bird of prey, or a hedgehog), and dash off to the studio.

On one particularly busy day, I had called the Zoo Nursery and asked that a baby animal be put in a carrying case. I often relied on the discretion of the keeper to choose an animal that was healthy, easy to handle, etc. I think that day I had planned to take a kinkajou.

When I arrived, the keeper was away on a break. I was running late again, so I rushed in and grabbed the case. I could see there was a pink blanket inside so everything appeared to be ready for me.

A short time later I was on the air. I carefully opened the case and began describing the animal I was going to show to the TV audience. I reached in and felt about for the little creature. Then I reached in again. Nothing. The carrier was empty, except for the blanket. There *was* no animal in the case!

I was left to explain the story, but had no animal to show. The blanket was pink, but my face was very, very red!

Over the years, I brought animals to places other than television studios. Zoo animals were sometimes guests at special parties and media events, and, as one might imagine, they didn't always behave according to the script.

Though I never handled venomous reptiles during any events or shows, I was bitten and scratched by a variety of animals— both on and off TV. It's just a hazard of the trade, but it's not easy to keep smiling and talking, pretending not to notice the blood flowing while the animal struggles. Even more troublesome, however, is when someone else gets bitten!

When Paul Hecker, our zoo concessionaire was honored at a retirement party at Café Brauer, now a fine Chicago establishment for banquets and other events, I was asked to bring a bird for a photo opportunity. I was happy to oblige and brought a colorful macaw, the largest of the parrot family.

The bird sat on my shoulder while I stood next to Paul for the picture. Everyone seemed to be having a great time until the macaw moved over to Paul's shoulder and quickly lunged at his eyeglasses, missing the glasses, and biting Paul on the bridge of his nose. Parrots— especially large, macaws—have incredibly powerful beaks and it is not practical to try to pry the beak open. So I watched in horror, with my bosses shouting at me to do something, while blood streamed down Paul's nose, and the bird clamped down with its full strength. I was extremely experienced with animals but could think of nothing I could do under the circumstances.

The only saving grace was that the event was an evening party with plenty of refreshments served by that time and Paul was feeling very little pain. I finally managed to get the bird off him, but my bosses were none too happy with my animal show that day.

I recalled that Marlin Perkins himself, an expert reptile handler, had been bitten twice by poisonous snakes while on his *Zoo Parade* TV show. As noted, such occurrences are unfortunately hazards of the trade.

On another occasion, The Lincoln Park Zoo Society arranged a photo session for its Women's Board members to announce the opening of the new Penguin-Seabird House. I was being photographed with Mrs. Brooks (Hope) McCormick, President of the Women's Board. To provide some visual interest, I held a penguin between us. The penguin became extremely rambunctious, and the next thing I knew, just as the photographers asked us to move in closer, the penguin lunged toward Hope and poked at her cheek, just below her eye. Fortunately, it only nicked her cheek and missed her eye, but once again, I was chagrined.

Such incidents only reinforce my belief that *it is not possible to predict animal behavior 100%—even for people who handle the animals regularly.*

At the zoo, the animals meet the press quite frequently because, simply put, animals make a good story even better.

Each year, for example, Lincoln Park Zoo participated in the Blessing of the Animals at St. Chrysostom's Church in Chicago. To mark Rogation Sunday, we took animals from the zoo to join with pets brought from all over the city, plus the canine corps of the Chicago Police Department. It made a nice story and good pictures.

The zoo also staged two annual events in Spring that attracted the media. The first was February 2nd, *Ground Hog Day*, which the press covered no matter what the day's important news might include. Each year our poor ground hog had to be unceremoniously turned out of his log home, while onlookers observed intently whether or not he saw his shadow and, as such, would provide an omen as to what the weather would be for the next several weeks. Our guy never quite achieved the celebrity-performer-weather forecaster status of Pennsylvania's Punxsutawney Phil, but he gave it his best.

The second staged event was April Fool's Day. We received thousands of calls throughout the day, as did every other zoo across the country, from people who have been duped into "returning calls" placed by a Mr. Lion, Mr. Wolf, Mr. Bear, etc. The zoo switchboard became overloaded in the early days. Later, our receptionist simply went a little nuts.

So each year we invited the media to observe how our staff handled the phones on that day. We would put a baby chimp or a baby orangutan, with a phone in its hand, behind the desk. Sometimes we put honey or soft bananas on the phone so the animal would put it in its mouth. The stunt never failed to result in a funny photograph and story on the evening news or in the next day's paper.

We celebrated special animal's birthdays occasionally, especially when Shanti, the baby elephant had her day. Our staff would set up a huge "cake" made of vegetables that she and her mother Bozie could demolish and eat. We also called the press when the temperature hit 100 degrees in summer and threw a huge block of ice in with Mike, the polar bear. After the new polar bear habitat was constructed, we switched to throwing in bags of ice cubes. A huge block of ice manipulated by a large polar bear could have broken the underwater viewing glass in the new exhibit.

As the zoo became more popular over the years we created a number of special events and fundraisers, such as WLS' *Run for the Zoo*. I particularly remember my first Run for two reasons.

For publicity purposes I had brought out a number of animals, but on that morning I was short on animal handlers. I pressed Wendy into service with a huge boa constrictor. I remember her asking how to handle it and, as I ran off to the starting line, I shouted, "Just don't let it get near crowds . . . and if it bites, don't pull your hand away or you'll break its teeth." She didn't find this briefing especially comforting, she would tell me later, as she had never handled a snake before—a fact I hadn't realized—and the crowd of runners and supporters that day was more than 5,000 people.

I was asked to stand in the front row of the crowd of runners at the start of the event and beginning running with them as the cameras captured the moment. This should not have been a problem since I was in good shape, it was a fun run, and a family event. I would simply run off to the side down the block a bit.

But once that starting gun was fired, I realized I was running for my life! We'd gone at least three *long* blocks before I was able to break away from my spot at the front of the pack and make it to the sidelines . . . where I collapsed. I hadn't realized that the front line runners are not only in excellent shape, but are serious about running. Compared to them, I was in no shape at all.

In subsequent years, I knew to stand off to the side when the starter's gun was fired!

Probably my most anxiety-producing public relations event came in April 1986, when I was asked to perform with the magnificent Chicago Symphony Orchestra, under the direction of Henry Mazer.

I was thrilled to be chosen to read *Adventures in a Zoo* and *Peter and the Wolf*, accompanied by members of the orchestra at a special afternoon concert for children.

But there were some problems. I met with Maestro Mazer the first afternoon and for some reason I had trouble pronouncing his name. After mispronouncing it several times, he looked at me, shrugged and said simply, "Just call me Henry."

Then he tried to send me home with just the musical score, to study the music and learn where my lines came in. I had to tell him that, although I'd taken violin as a child, I didn't read music and was, in fact, not very musical at all. He looked dismayed but was generous enough not to say anything. Finally, he gave me the score and a tape, which I listened to for hours. Somehow I got through the concert without missing any cues, but it was a very stressful experience.

Handling wild animals was one thing, but performing with the Chicago Symphony Orchestra, as much as I enjoy music, was quite another!

I think back to the television shows I've been a part of over the years and all the media-related activities at the zoo, such as *Caroling to the Animals* at the holidays; *Magic Day; Press Day; Dad's Day; Spooky Zoo Spectacular* at Halloween, the community concerts, and so much more—virtually all of which drew huge crowds and enormous press coverage.

But with all my media appearances, as well as the countless still photo set-ups for the newspapers and the personal appearances at events, I realize how fleeting fame is. That truth was brought home to me one day several years ago.

It was the holiday season and we were in Marshall Field's department store in Chicago. My wife Wendy was helping me pick out two sweaters for my now-adult daughters. I became tired, waiting while she shopped, so I sat down on the edge of a mannequin display near the store escalators.

By the time Wendy finished shopping and found where I was sitting, I was laughing. Two teenagers had just gone up the nearby escalator, looked down and saw me sitting there.

"Look!" one of them shouted, "there's Dr. Whatchamacallit!"

I wonder if they knew the song about *green alligators and long-necked geese.*

# Great escapes!
# (and some not so great ones)

The keeper was breathless by the time he reached my office.

"Doc," he blurted, "How much is a flamingo worth?"

"About $100," I said. "Why?"

"Well, there's $100 worth flying out over Lake Michigan right now."

One of our flamingos had flown away! Well, maybe not exactly, but that was the net result. For the next several days we received reports of sightings in Gary, Indiana or on Michigan's south shore, near Benton Harbor. Then, the calls stopped. We never did find out what happened to the bird.

We *do* know how it escaped however.

This was at a time that we clipped birds' flight feathers to keep them from flying off. But if they stretched their wings while standing in an outdoor enclosure and caught just the right updraft of air, they could indeed lift off and glide right out of their enclosure. Usually they didn't get far—perhaps 50 yards or so, but in this case the flamingo was not clipped properly and had caught a really good updraft and flew out over the lake.

We learned finally to "pinion" the birds. The last segment of one wing is surgically removed in what is a much more effective method of keeping birds from "flying" out of their outdoor enclosures.

The truth is that animal escapes never cease in a zoological collection because no matter how you design the zoo or enclosures, and how much you "know" your animals, people can still make mistakes, and animals are not 100% predictable—especially wild animals. Most escapes, however, result from human error and occasionally cage design.

The "regular" escapes at most zoos, including Lincoln Park, are of the many fast, small creatures, such as small birds, reptiles, and tiny mammals. They are usually caught without much fuss. We design the back areas so they are "doubly secure," so if animals get out, they are usually within an enclosed back area and not in a public space.

But all animal escapes that are the result of human error, regardless of whether they involve large or small or benign or dangerous animals, are dealt with in the same way. The person responsible for inadvertently letting an animal out is subject to disciplinary action, typically an automatic suspension, although the terms vary depending upon the situation.

When designing animal habitats, we spend a great deal of time considering the safety of the animals, the safety of staff members who work with the animals, and, of course, the safety of the visiting public.

It is important to provide the animal with an enclosure that meets its physical and behavioral needs, but it is equally important to keep the animal safe, in terms of potential vandalism. Safety considerations all get factored in, as well as giving visitors the wonderful experience of viewing the animal. It is a complex and challenging issue. We want enclosures to look as natural as possible while, at the same time, meeting the needs of animals, staff, and visitors.

Lincoln Park Zoo has been lucky over the years. Vandalism has never been much of a problem, especially in the years when the zoo had several entrances and no perimeter fence. Other zoos around the United States have had extreme instances of vandalism, including people committing such disturbing acts as breaking the legs of flamingos and leaving the animals, but not killing them.

People occasionally feed animals plastic and other potentially deadly foreign objects, but this is usually the result of thoughtlessness rather than a deliberate attempt to hurt an animal.

Sometimes, however, weird things happen—such as when our cleaning crew arrived one morning many years ago at 7 AM and found a drunk sleeping in the outdoor enclosure that housed our ostrich and rhea.

The man was very much alive but the birds were dead.

That should not have been the case because ostrich and rheas, both large, flightless birds from Africa and South America respectively can, with a single kick of their extremely powerful legs, disembowel a lion or puma. The claw at the end of those feet can be lethal. In this case, perhaps the birds died of shock from seeing a drunken man sleeping off his hangover in their home.

A drunk in a bird enclosure is just one of the weird occurrences that begin to seem routine in the zoo community. We've had people try to swim with the sea lions, stroke the big cats, and get into numerous animal habitats. In most cases we have to worry more about animal's escaping than about people getting into the animal enclosures.

Of course, it is the possibility of our "big kids" getting away from us that worries us the most—big cats, great apes, bears, and elephants. These animals, as well as poisonous reptiles, are the "dangerous" animals that we refer to when we worry about animal escapes.

Reptiles are tricky because they can hide *anywhere*. This was especially true in our old reptile building, which was built in the 1920s, before the Shedd Aquarium, and served as Chicago's first aquarium.

A problem for us was that there were hundreds of drains and pipes that filled the building, and we worried constantly about what strange things might come up through the drains into the exhibits, such as vermin. We also had to be concerned about snakes and other reptiles slipping *down* the drains.

During my years as the zoo vet, I remember one particular morning when a keeper called me early and told me to get to the zoo as quickly as possible. The large, spitting cobras had escaped.

Somehow, overnight, the two snakes had loosened the standpipe in their exhibit and had disappeared—probably into the lower drains and sewers that formed a labyrinth of monumental proportions in the basement of the building.

At that point there were questions, such as how much danger there really was; if the snakes were *only* in the drain system; how we would get them back and do we—or *don't we*—tell the public we have a problem?

I recommended we start by closing the building to the public, then advised the staff to be extremely careful and look everywhere when they arrived in the morning because if the animals had gone down the drain, we had no idea where that old drain led and where they might come up!

We scoured the zoo for architectural blueprints of the old building, but if any ever existed, they were long gone.

The picture that was taking shape was pretty scary because these animals are potentially very dangerous. The spitting cobra has a unique adaptation—it can bite and inject venom the way other cobras and related snakes can, but it can also spit the venom four to five feet and usually tries to hit the faces of its victims.

We searched for the snakes several times each day for several days, all to no avail. After about five days, the keepers decided to put some food—rats and chicks—into the snakes' cage.

Lo and behold, during the night, the snakes returned to their cage for the food, and we found them tightly curled up there the next morning!

We reinstalled the drainpipe and breathed a sigh of relief—for the time being.

Stories about animal escapes at historic Lincoln Park Zoo made for a good laugh after the fact, but I'm sure that at the time they occurred, these situations were just as scary as any I encountered during my zoo career.

In 1878 there was already concern at the zoo that the wooden cage used for the bear might not be strong enough to contain it, so anticipating that more bears would be added to the collection and additional structures would be needed, construction of new bear cages began in November of that year. The original bear and several new additions were moved into their new quarters in the Spring of 1879. Everyone assumed that the bears and the public would now be safe.

But the bears being clever—as well as dangerous—soon learned to climb up the round, rocky sides of their dens. Their almost nightly escapes to roam Lincoln Park became the stuff of legend. I was told that for quite some time, the entire zoo workforce was called into service each morning to corral the bears and return them to their official quarters.

According to published accounts, one enterprising new arrival, a grizzly bear, wandered down Pine Street, adjacent to the zoo, and ultimately took refuge from its pursuers in a tall elm tree several blocks away on Oak Street. It was evening by the time the bear was located, so a policeman was stationed at the base of the tree to keep the bear from coming down until the next morning when it was captured. No information is available as to how the police kept the bear in the tree—or got it down—and back to the zoo. *That* might be quite a story itself.

There is also no record of injury to people or damage to property from these bear escapes, but the midnight foraging came to an abrupt end in 1880 when large, inward curved iron bars were fastened to the top of the bear dens.

For some years in the late 1800s it was also customary to walk Duchess the elephant from her winter quarters in the animal house to her outside summer quarters, and then reverse the trip each fall. The animal was not restrained in any manner— she just walked beside her keeper for the short journey.

But on one occasion in 1891, Duchess decided to go off on her own. Racing in a westerly direction, the elephant soon ran through and over back yards, fences and one small wooden structure. Reports had it that a summer house on North Avenue was carried away on her shoulders, while the gate of a nearby brewery was torn off its hinges.

Duchess remained on her safari, committing several more expensive pranks, finally allowing herself to be caught with a rope, though of course she could have continued if she really had wanted to. She was returned to her quarters and, perhaps needless to say, future walks had her dressed in practical, if not fashionable, leg restraints to limit her potential runs.

Even before Duchess' escapade, a group of sea lions made history—by escaping from the zoo!

Purchased in 1889 from the Pacific coast, the sea lions were placed in a large pit that had been built expressly for them near the center of the zoo. We presume the pit had water in it so the sea lions could swim, though that detail is not included in the reports from the Lincoln Park Commission.

We are told, however, that the iron fence surrounding the pit was not completed when some of the sea lions escaped. Two of them waddled across the park to Clark Street, a busy commercial area in Chicago, where they entered a restaurant, much to the confusion and dismay of the establishment's regular customers.

Another sea lion headed toward Lake Michigan and plunged in. It was last sighted off a beach in Milwaukee and never returned to Lincoln Park Zoo.

# Chasing Sam

There was a time when we could have some fun with a story about an animal escaping from the zoo. These days, in our litigious society, that's not possible, but occasionally great escapes still end in a great story. The media have fun, the publicity helps bring more visitors to the zoo and, as long as nobody gets hurt, it creates excitement, though usually of a kind I could do without.

One such memorable bit of monkey business occurred one summer in the 1970s when a group of subadult chimpanzees were living in the outside cages on the west side of our old Primate House. The building was showing significant signs of its 65-plus years of wear by that time, but we didn't fully appreciate just how rusty the old outside cages had become.

That is, until five chimpanzees living in one of the larger cages broke out. The hinges on the door had apparently become so rusty that when challenged by the chimps, they simply gave way and the animals let themselves out on to the zoo grounds.

When the alarm was given, we quickly marshaled our forces and proceeded to recapture them with nets. They were still young and, although boisterous and hooting and hollering, the nets contained them until we could get them back into an inside, more secure cage. All but one, that is.

While they were swinging through the trees on the zoo grounds some people thought it was actually part of a show, but I knew the potential for serious injury to both the animals and to people. Obviously, I was greatly relieved when most of them were captured quickly.

But then there was Sam, who after touring the zoo from tree to tree, took off toward downtown Chicago, along scenic Lake Shore Drive.

Each time we came close to him, the chimp ran just ahead of me and out of reach. The nets were ineffective as Sam moved more quickly through the trees than we could on foot.

I finally spotted a police car and hopped in, asking the officer to help me. At first he looked a bit startled but we took off in the direction Sam was heading and were soon in the lead, hoping the animal would continue along the route we expected. While the zoo staff was still in pursuit, I jumped out of the police car and waited.

Sam spotted me standing on the sidewalk and ran toward me. Hooting wildly, the animal leapt into my arms, wrapped himself securely around me, and softly began whimpering, clearly as glad to be with me as I was to have him.

With the chimp clutching me in his incredibly strong grip, I climbed back into the squad car, and we returned to the zoo. I've never been sure which of us was more relieved, but Sam definitely seemed happy to be back with the other chimps—in a cage we made certain did not have rusty hinges. With the police involved and the word spreading rapidly, Sam's escape became front-page news (though Park board member Frank Schmick, who loved the chimp and had been with me in West Africa when we collected Sam, was convinced the animal was on his way down Lake Shore Drive to visit him!)

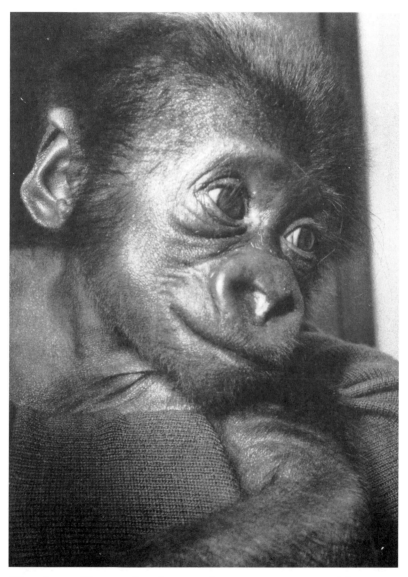

Kivu the gorilla spent her first year in our apartment cared for round the clock by my wife Beth and our daughters Jane and Kate. (ca. 1979) Courtesy, Chicago Tribune

Otto became a star in the film *Otto: Zoo Gorilla* documenting our pioneering and historic move of 25 great apes (including 12 gorillas) to their new home at the zoo in June, 1976.

Heine, the chimp, set a longevity record on his 50th birthday (June 12, 1971). Courtesy, Chicago Park District

June, the chimpanzee, painted her way to fame at the Children's Zoo. (1979) Courtesy, Chicago Park District

Lenore, a wild-caught gorilla from Cameroon, and her first baby, Patty (1977). Courtesy, Chicago Tribune

Kevin Bell, Curator of Birds, holds Mikuluk the first polar bear born at Lincoln Park Zoo. Mikuluk did not survive, despite being hand-raised in a quarantined area of the Bird House. Courtesy, Chicago Park District

*The Ark in the Park* with Ray Rayner and friends. Courtesy, Chicago Tribute

Marlin Perkins joined Ray Drymalski (far left), President of The Lincoln Park Zoo Society, and Barbara Whitney (far right), Executive Director of the Society at the opening of the Regenstein Large Mammal Habitat in 1982. Courtesy, Chicago Park District

The first koala at Lincoln Park Zoo arrived during the 1980s. Courtesy, Lincoln Park Zoological Society

Bozie, an Asian elephant, and gift of the Sri Lankan government, presented her "not-so-best" side to Mayor Michael Bilandic when she arrived at the Zoo (1976).  Courtesy, Chicago Park District

Jane the orangutan and her baby in the old Monkey House. Courtesy, Chicago Park District

Koundu the gorilla was British-born at Howlett's Zoo Park—the offspring of our male, Kisoro, who was shipped to England in 1973 on breeding loan. Courtesy, Lincoln Park Zoological Society

# Escape of a great ape

When a great ape escapes, it is perhaps one of the more memorable events, especially to me, as I may be the only zoo director in the world who had three adult silverback male gorillas get out on his watch—all at different times.

There was the legendary Bushman, but *that* escape shouldn't count against me as it occurred during the time of my predecessor, Marlin Perkins. I was there, however, so if we count Bushman, it's actually *four* escapes, giving me an even more dubious record.

Though it happened decades ago—in the late 1940s actually—I remember as if it were yesterday. Early one morning in the days when I was still the zoo's part-time vet, I received a call at my home in Riverside, just outside Chicago.

"Bushman's out," Marlin said. It was really all he needed to say. At the time, Bushman was one of two of the largest silverback gorillas in the world. The other was Gargantua, owned by the Ringling Brothers' Barnum and Bailey circus. At 550 pounds, Bushman was not only big, he was incredibly strong and he was *the* star attraction at Lincoln Park Zoo.

"Why call me?" I thought, but instead of saying anything I had enough presence of mind to just grab my emergency bag, get in my car, and drive to the zoo. Back then the bag only had the most basic equipment, as this was long before the era of dart guns and other safe capture equipment.

As I drove toward the zoo, the voice coming through the car radio kept issuing bulletins about Bushman's escape and reminding people of the potential danger the animal posed to the Lincoln Park community. Today a great ape on the loose sounds like something that might be a fun story, but in Chicago in the 1940s, it was very serious business. I was extremely anxious about this, and my anxiety went into overdrive when I arrived at the zoo to find police cars ringing the Monkey House and reporters from every newspaper shouting and trying to get the inside story. I had no idea what to expect.

But when I entered the Monkey House, I looked up to see Bushman already back in his cage. The big escape, caused by someone failing to secure the lock on his door, was over.

But as it turned out, his safe return hadn't been easy. Eddie Robinson, his long-time keeper, had tried to talk him back into his cage. As Eddie had cared for Bushman since he was a baby, the ape was very fond of him. But on this occasion, Bushman would not be swayed by Eddie's cajoling. When Eddie tried to take Bushman's arm and tug him back into the cage, the ape gently but firmly bit Eddie's arm.

Finally, someone remembered Bushman disliked snakes. Years earlier some employees had been fooling around with Bushman and had brought some garter snakes from the Reptile House to show him. His reaction to the little, non-venomous reptiles was to become terrified, so when Eddie's efforts to control the animal failed, a staff member quickly located a garter snake, and placed it in front of Bushman, and that was it. He went back into his cage.

For many zoo animals, their cage is their home and as such, represents a place of safety and security. When an animal is reacting badly to a strange environment, returning it to what it knows as a comfortable and secure place, which at the zoo is its cage or exhibit area, has a calming effect. We rely on this psychology for most animals, but particularly the great apes. The advent of capture equipment, however, has provided the most help in safely returning escaped animals to their habitats.

The first big silverback gorilla to get out on my watch was Sinbad, successor to Bushman and just as impressive an animal. The date was August 3, 1964.

I was sitting in my office at the north end of the old Primate House, in the midst of a budget meeting, when a keeper came running quite literally through my office—in one door and out the other—yelling, "Sinbad's out!" The door to the back of the private bathroom attached to my office was also the door that led out to the runway behind the primate cages. It was usually secured and had a sign that read " DANGEROUS ANIMALS! KEEP OUT!" This was probably the only sign of its kind to be hanging on the inside of a bathroom door.

But on this particular day the door was no longer secured— after the keeper came flying through it and left it open.

"Out? Out where?" I shouted at him. But wherever he was I had to act fast.

I closed the bathroom door to the keeper run and secured it, then went outside to the public area of the building and quickly directed everyone outside.

Next, we secured the building and learned from another keeper that Sinbad was in the primate kitchen at the south end of the building—at the opposite end of the building from my office. The ape was roaming around, sampling food and having himself a great time. He was still within the confines of the building, not in a public area, but he was not under the keepers' control and that was a problem for us.

Gene Hartz, my assistant at the time, ran to the hospital to get a capture gun. While Sinbad looked out, we looked in through a screen door and window that the great ape could easily have walked through.

We managed to get off a shot through the screen door, hitting Sinbad in a muscle in his huge shoulder. Although he could have walked right passed us, he obviously thought the screen was a physical barrier, so he remained "secured" inside for us to get to him. He quickly succumbed to the anesthetic and was carried back to his cage.

The ape that escapes and heads for the kitchen to enjoy an unscheduled feast-for-one may not seem like the stories of escaped gorillas terrorizing the town we've seen in the movies. This one makes me smile now to think about it. But if Sinbad *had* made it outside of the zoo, the potential danger to both the animal and the people it came in contact with would have been very real and not very funny.

This story couldn't end without a word about another keeper who was not going to risk being chased through the zoo by an es-caped ape. When Sinbad escaped from his cage, the keeper was in the inside passageway behind the cages. Seeing the ape had gotten out, the terrified keeper knew he couldn't outrun Sinbad, so he used his head instead of his feet and jumped inside an empty cage, where he locked himself in until the animal was safely secured. After giving the situation a few minutes thought, we decided to send someone for the key and, eventually, we let the keeper out!

# Escape of ANOTHER great ape

My second silverback gorilla escape was the most dramatic as it occurred in a public area, with visitors on grounds.

Otto, a big breeding male, was a true Chicago celebrity having been the star of *Otto: Zoo Gorilla*, a PBS documentary about mov-ing the gorillas to their new home at Lincoln Park.

Otto was big, lanky, and in his prime. He lived in the new

Great Ape House, just south of the Monkey House, and had access to a beautiful outdoor yard with an 11-foot wall that was topped by "hot" electric wires to prevent escapes.

On an early June morning, I had just settled in at my desk in the Crown-Field Center, the new administration building north of the Monkey House. My schedule for the day was filled with routine business and no indication whatsoever that anything out of the ordinary might occur. Then the phone rang.

A keeper in the Primate House reported a gorilla was out. Because the call had come from the Primate House and Sinbad was the only gorilla living there, I assumed it was Sinbad. Again. By this time he had become too old and arthritic to be moved to the new Great Ape House with the other gorillas.

He was so old in fact that I remember thinking, "I can run faster than he can," so I raced out of my office, around the side of our round administration building, and came face to face with *Otto!*

I stopped in my tracks.

Upon spotting me, Otto froze as well.

The first thing I said to myself was, "Damn . . . it's Otto." The next thing I thought seemed to sum up the situation pretty well—*He's big, he's young, and he's trouble!*

Then I spotted a zoo docent (one of our volunteer educators) walking between the Reptile House and the Lion House, right where Otto was heading. I called for her to get inside a zoo building immediately because an animal had escaped, but she called back cheerfully, "I'm late for my docent class," and kept right on going.

I yelled something that I think might have caught her attention, but I don't remember because my focus was now completely on Otto, who by this time was on the move again.

My first inclination was to try to contain Otto in the zoo. Then I realized our zoo fencing was about the same height that Otto had just cleared getting out of his outdoor habitat, so that wouldn't do any good. Never mind that the gates were wide open awaiting the arrival of the yellow buses that would deposit thousands of young children from summer day camps, expected at the east entrance in less than an hour.

Fortunately, perhaps, Otto continued cruising away from the zoo entrances, moving along the walkway that ran between the Reptile and Lion Houses. I kept following close behind him, keeping him in sight at all times.

I'm sure it was only a matter of minutes (though of course it seemed like hours) until our zoo veterinarians arrived with their capture guns. The Chicago police had also picked up on the animal escape on their radios, and dozens of uniformed officers arrived with their guns drawn, followed by a heavy weapons unit, including a team of sharpshooters. At that point, my mind was racing and all I could think was, *"Please, don't kill Otto!"*

We climbed into our zoo truck and drove back and forth from the east to the west side of the Lion House, keeping Otto contained in the walkway between the two buildings, where I'd first cornered him on foot.

Finally, Otto stopped moving long enough to look at the lions through the plate glass viewing window at the east side of the Lion House. Those lions were probably surprised when they looked back at *that* zoo visitor!

His stopping gave us the opportunity to drive up alongside him in the truck, close enough so one of the vets could get a clear shot at him with the tranquilizer gun. Otto was now drugged, but not down, and that's when things really got dicey.

He began heading up a nearby ramp to the top of the administration building. With each step he appeared more wobbly, indicating to us that the anesthetic was kicking in.

Unfortunately, as he walked up the ramp, Otto reached the top of the Crown-Field Center, about a one and a half story drop to the ground. He stood at the edge, teetering back and forth as the police officers drew their guns and took aim. It was like a bad old movie scene, but it was all too real.

"Don't shoot! Don't shoot!" I kept shouting as they moved in to kill my beloved Otto. The ape was also so close to falling off the edge of the building I feared he might kill himself!

Suddenly the drug took hold completely, and Otto tumbled backwards into the bushes at the edge of the Center. We moved in quickly. It took five grown men to carry one adult gorilla back to his home in the Great Ape House. If we had needed a hundred men at that point, I would have gladly dispatched them. I was thankful Otto was alive, unhurt and, back under control.

We never learned how Otto got out. We'll never know. What we *do* know is that for temporary management reasons, that morning Otto had been locked in his outdoor enclosure by himself for the first time in his life. Until that time he had always had free access to go in and out as he wished. And, as no one saw him actually leave the enclosure, we never figured out how he vaulted the 11-foot wall and broke the electric hot wires as he went over the top. We only know he did it and, seemingly, did it effortlessly.

In fiction, a plot unfolds and facts of the story are provided, but in real life, sometimes the facts aren't always clear. An escaped great ape can present an enormous danger to a community. If an animal can escape and we don't how, can we ensure that it will never happen again? Most likely, someone made an error—a *very big error*—leaving an access point unlocked or improperly closed. Or Otto had used his fingertips to hold on to the wall and launch himself up and over it. We eventually surmised it was this last scenario that made the most sense, and we raised the height of the wall.

It certainly wasn't the first time in my career that I saw what animals could do under stress. I've seen African antelope clear extremely high fences that in theory they shouldn't be able to jump. Conversely, I've seen timber wolves stay inside a low chain link fence that they could easily climb beyond, had they been motivated to do so. Motivation seems to be the key and perhaps the most important factor in animal escapes.

# Possibly my last story of an escaped gorilla

Sometimes animals escape because they are presented with an opportunity to do so. My third adult male gorilla escape was Freddie, who was so gentle we called him "Uncle Freddie."

Though it was a relatively uneventful escape that led Freddie and his group to explore the inner keeper core of the Great Ape House, it was one of the most problematical, just because they *were* in the inside core. They couldn't get out, and we, in turn, couldn't get in!

Freddie and his entire family left their habitat when a keeper failed to secure a lock. As I later explained to the media, gorillas know when their cages are locked and when they are not locked. They are always testing the locks and literally spend their lives monitoring these things. If a padlock is put on and not properly closed, they will know it. And, in this instance, it wasn't and they did!

Their keeper discovered Freddie, Kisuma, and her baby named Hope, when he entered the central core early in the morning. Startled by the keeper, Freddie bit him, but by distracting Freddie, the keeper then locked the escaped gorillas in the central core of the building. The animals spent the next two hours exploring the building's central core and sampling food that was being prepared in that area. At one point Freddie apparently decided that powdered milk made great talcum powder and applied it to himself liberally. He was the only white gorilla in Chicago during his escape.

The problem was, as I noted, the gorillas were locked *in* the central core, and we were locked *out*! Getting them out was like solving a puzzle. While the apes on-the-run posed no immediate danger to the community, we had to get them back in their habitat for everyone's sake.

Eventually, we went in the upper level of the inside core while Freddie was downstairs and corralled him with fire extinguishers and capture guns. He and his family went back into their cages and we never had to dart any of them with anesthetic, but the ape's "white fur" did startle zoo visitors for several days.

Of all the great apes, orangutans are perhaps the greatest great ape escape artists. They are the most patient and methodical. These traits, coupled with their high intelligence, enable them to endlessly study their enclosure and find the smallest flaws.

Even bolts and other construction materials may be worked on for long periods of time. In fact, orangutans have been known to loosen nuts that were tightened with large lug wrenches. They just work a screw with a fingernail, or work at a nut with their nimble fingers for hours, for days, for weeks, until it is finally loosened. They consider it behavioral enrichment; we consider it difficult to contain them!

When our new Great Ape House was completed in 1976 and the final construction inspectors had released the building with the assurance there were no loose screws, nuts, bolts, or metal rods in the animal enclosures, the orangutans found otherwise. Over the course of a few weeks, they located all the loose parts (and created some on their own) and each day, the animals, in exchange for food, would reluctantly pass the items out through the mesh to their keepers. They thought it was a new game, while the inspectors were just plain embarrassed.

The new buildings with their modern plastic, glass, and mesh materials make animal viewing better for visitors. But new advances in technology and design are not ends in themselves. We need to check the smallest details of construction to be certain the animals living there will not be able to just get up and go whenever they feel like it. Few of us have *that* luxury.

# A bear is loose!

Every animal species has its own unique ingenious ways.

Elephants use their sensitive trunks to find the littlest flaw in a lock, while at the same time they can throw their substantial weight around and bend steel.

Great apes apply their considerable intelligence, as well as their incredible strength, to test every part of their enclosures.

Bears, especially smaller bears such as spectacled bears and sun bears, are terrific climbers and can get their paws into the smallest crack to leverage their way up and out.

Birds, particularly parrots, are excellent locksmiths, using their beaks and feet to manipulate locks and clasps. Snakes can even hold their own when it comes to squeezing through tiny crevices that lead through and out.

It's no wonder we remain challenged every day when it comes to preventing escapes from the zoo.

One routine procedure that has helped prevent escapes caused by human error is our multiple lock system. Instead of just one set of locks on cages for bears, for example, we would often install three sets. This procedure, instituted at many zoos over the past several decades, has helped to cut down on someone forgetting to lock a cage. Even the most preoccupied or absent-minded keeper should find it difficult to forget to close *all three* locks.

The answer to preventing escapes, however, is not just to install locks and more locks. Sometimes Mother Nature plays a role in escapes, as happened in early January of 1976.

Winter that year brought us a lot of snow and very cold weather. Along our Bear Line, the old pipes would freeze so, in order to provide the bears with fresh water, we ran water hoses from the top of the bear areas into their cages. We ran the water 24 hours a day from behind the cages where we had our birds of prey tethered at the top.

The bears enjoyed the running water in good weather, and during the winter, it kept the pipes from freezing so the keepers could wash the debris, animals droppings, and leftover food out of the cages.

Unfortunately, during the winter when the bears retreat to their dens, they also have their babies. And bears like it quiet in their dens. Strange sounds threaten them, and, if they feel insecure, some female bears will eat their cubs.

So during the winter of '76, with babies in the bear dens, we tried to keep it as quiet as possible for them. We ordered no snow plows be allowed to clear the sidewalks in the area, and we asked staff to make as little noise as possible when working the bear line. We simply let the hoses run, even as they created spectacular ice bridges, from the bottom to the top of the polar bear cage.

We knew full well about the ice bridge. We could see it growing daily, but we were more concerned that chopping it down would upset the bears and threaten the cubs. We let it go despite temperatures continuing to drop, and the ice continuing to build up.

I walked over to the zoo on the very cold morning of January 16th and had just entered the West Gate when a keeper came running up to me.

"Doc, we got a polar bear loose," he said.

I have already expressed my feeling that the polar bear is the most dangerous of animals, so he didn't need to say anything else.

I ran to the Lion House and called the Chicago Police and Park District headquarters to alert them. Then I tried to find out who was at work and where they were at the moment. We quickly ascertained that the bear was cruising the ridge area above her cage, where the birds of prey were tethered out. It was Szazka, big Mike the polar bear's diminutive mate, but nevertheless, a polar bear with a classic predator attitude.

She was pacing back and forth, looking at the birds of prey, which were flapping their wings, straining at their tethers, and clearly terrified. She would watch one, take a swat at it, and be startled when it flew up out of her range.

Meanwhile, below on the Bear Line, the police and animal team assembled on foot while traffic helicopters reported the scene from above. As the zoo was scheduled to open when Skazka was found, it was a story in the making for zoo visitors that day.

The police were ready to shoot the bear. They are always there as a precautionary measure, but I pleaded for them to wait until we could dart her with anesthetic using the capture gun. The scene was extremely tense, and a polar bear on the loose was my worst nightmare.

We all held our positions and waited, watching the agitated bear and the terrified birds. Finally, we lined up Skazka in our sights and, happily, with one dart we were able to do what we had to do. She went down quickly and, with the help of many hands—including the policemen—we carried her 600 pounds of dead weight back to her cage on a canvas stretcher.

Meanwhile, we had moved Mike to an adjacent cage to ready her transfer back to her main area.

The *Chicago Tribune* had fun with the story, which appeared under the headline, "She'll have to bear up to unliberated life."

Jon Van and Connie Lauerman wrote:

> *Mike, like many a human male in a similar situation, seemed stunned at the fact that his mate had deserted him. He wandered absently around the enclosure but made no effort to follow Skazka up the ice and out of the cage.*

I was quoted in the story, saying, *"Mike is so heavy that the ice wouldn't have supported him if he'd tried,"*

Later, when I re-read the story, I wondered if I really believed that. I think we were just plain lucky not to have had *two* of the zoo's most dangerous animals on the loose.

We never again let the ice bridges build up—babies or no babies.

And, once again, it was a great escape story, and kept people's interest in the zoo and its animals high through some of the coldest days of the year.

Most importantly, no one was hurt or killed. That had been my real concern during all the years I spent at the zoo.

# Princes, Mayors, Jane, Joy, big stars & other memorable zoo visitors

I looked over at the table our board member Hope McCormick was hosting and —*to my horror*—saw that my wife Wendy was *standing* next to His Royal Highness Prince Philip, Duke of Edinburgh.

I couldn't believe my eyes!

"How could she?" I thought to myself, mortified beyond words. After all the briefing we'd been given about when to stand, when to sit, how to address His Royal Highness, and particularly about the end of his visit, I simply couldn't fathom what she could be thinking. We had been admonished that no one—and I emphasize *no one*—was to stand once the luncheon was over. *His Highness* was to stand and, accompanied only by Secret Service and Scotland Yard personnel, would leave the building. Once he was out of the building and on his way in his motorcade, then we were all free to do as we pleased.

I was in shock. After all, my wife is an *Anglophile*. She was *born* in London, raised with British parents and accustomed to pomp, circumstance, and protocol, particularly as it relates to the British Royal Family. Now, here she was flaunting it all in front of a select group of about 60 guests assembled in our Large Mammal House as guests of Mrs. Brooks McCormick's at her beloved Lincoln Park Zoo.

As I continued trying to restart my heart, Wendy came walking out—with His Royal Highness—breezing passed my table, as if it had been planned that way. When she reached me, she simply leaned down and quietly asked me to accompany Prince Philip with her to the polar bear pool because he hadn't had a chance to see the polar bears.

It had actually been Hope McCormick's suggestion to His Royal Highness and, having checked his watch and realizing he was ahead of schedule, he'd decided to take her up on the invitation to have Wendy show him our new exhibit. My anxiety abated, and I now felt terrible that I had doubted Wendy. With great relief, I tagged along after them.

It had already been a long morning. We had been briefed by five separate groups prior to His Royal Highness's visit. First there was Scotland Yard, then our own Secret Service, a special detail of which had been assigned to accompany the prince on his Chicago visit. There were instructions from the Chicago Police and, finally, His Royal Highness's retinue. Then the British Consul's staff had *really* briefed us in minute detail on protocol.

Prince Philip arrived about 11AM at the zoo, under close guard. We had been told that under no circumstances was he to walk from building to building at the zoo, nor was he to have anything "get" on him when he was taken behind-the-scenes in the Ape House, which was expected to be a highlight of the tour.

This was in 1978 and the Ape House was just two years old. We'd had good luck with breeding since the big apes move to their new quarters, and we were on our way to becoming the "gorilla capital of the world." That is what Prince Philip had come to see.

Well, the inevitable happened next to a chimp cage. A youngster scooped his hand and shoveled off straw, water, and *you-guessed-it* right on top of His Royal Highness and me. Next, as we left the building, Prince Philip asked if we could walk to the next building because it was such a beautiful fall day. I tried to discourage him, but he is a rather forceful individual, clearly used to getting his way, so what could I say?

But as we walked from the south to the north end of the zoo and the new Large Mammal Habitat where lunch was set up in front of the giraffes, I became worried. The reason for all the added security at Lincoln Park Zoo that day was a loud and boisterous protest staged by the Irish Republican Army (IRA).

The security details—Secret Service, Scotland Yard and Chicago's finest—were furious about this change of plans, but I had a great opportunity to talk with Prince Philip, who was not only a very handsome, congenial "man's man," but was incredibly well-informed about our zoo. He was also extremely knowledgeable on conservation issues, both at home and internationally. He had come to Chicago to receive an award from the World Wildlife Fund for his work on behalf of endangered wildlife, and it was clear from his remarks that he deserved it.

Most of us in the United States would probably find meeting a member of the British Royal Family to be a memorable occasion. To do so as a young ape hurls his "business" at us certainly goes even *beyond memorable*. Happily, His Royal Highness took it all in stride.

Both Mayors Daley (father and son) visited Lincoln Park Zoo often. I remember Mayor Richard J. Daley, often described as "the last of the big city bosses," walking the zoo with me many times and always telling me how he felt strongly that it should remain free and accessible.

"This is a place my family could afford to take me when I was growing up," the mayor said. "I will always remember that; I love this place."

The mayor made an annual visit to the zoo, arranged ahead of time, but occasionally he came at other times, always with a very large entourage, so it was obvious by the time he reached the gate that the Mayor of Chicago was on the zoo grounds. Richard J. Daley was a man who wielded immense power—on a *national* level. He enjoyed receiving special treatment so I always made time to walk the zoo with him.

Conversely, Mayor Richard M. Daley, his son, always visited the zoo frequently with his family, and usually unaccompanied by staff. When word arrived that the Mayor was on the grounds, we would be sure to take his children behind-the-scenes as a treat, but Maggie Daley, the Mayor's lovely wife, put a stop to that.

"I don't want them to feel that every time they go somewhere they get to do something special," she told us. "I want them to grow up as normal kids."

I always admired her for that, as well as for serving on our Zoo Society's Women's Board and working hard in support of our programs and plans.

Jane Goodall, the renowned primatologist, visited the zoo to see our chimpanzees and gorillas on several occasions, and stayed with us as a guest in our home. Wendy had a collection of Raggedy Ann dolls, which Jane loved, and she asked if she could have a photo of them, all smiling to greet her at the end of the day. She said it would be a great "pick-me-upper" whenever she felt discouraged.

Unfortunately, when Jane stayed with us, the effects of her many long years in Africa were in evidence, as she frequently suffered from recurrences of malaria, which have continued to trouble her, and many other researchers doing work in tropical climates. It's a secondary hazard that comes with their dedication to saving wildlife.

Joy Adamson, author of the *Born Free* books about Elsa the lion, paid a visit to the zoo. Except for her time spent in our Zoo Nursery playing with some young lion cubs, she walked around crying as she looked at the lions and other animals in captivity. She could not understand that they couldn't just be "free."

In my opinion her interpretation was a disservice with the word "free." In nature, animals are *never* free. "Hunters"—the predators—are confined to a specific territory they cannot leave even if they are starving, and "the hunted" spend their lives trying not to be eaten. None of them are ever "free" in our sense of the word. Clearly, Joy and I never saw eye to eye, despite my having great respect for her and the interest she helped generate in wildlife preservation.

The passing parade of "great and near-great" at the zoo included TV and film actors Hugh O'Brian, Stephanie Powers, and Sigourney Weaver; several Illinois governors, including Otto Kerner, Jim Thompson and Jim Edgar. We were also visited by Jim Fowler, who appeared as co-host on Mutual of Omaha's *Wild Kingdom*, Marlin Perkins's television show; Desmond Morris, author of the book, *The Naked Ape*; and naturalist and author Gerald Durrell and his wife, Lee; and Betty White, the actress and a good friend of ours who has dedicated much of her time and energy to animal causes and issues. These and numerous other prominent people all came to Lincoln Park Zoo for publicity opportunities and to be photographed, but what I especially remember about these folks is their genuine love of animals and wildlife.

Some celebrity and VIP visitors to the zoo were of the four-legged variety, such as the tiger that came from a California studio to film a segment for TV.

Unlike other TV performers, the producers couldn't just "put up" the tiger *anywhere* for the night so, after considerable discussion, I agreed it could come to the zoo. My initial reluctance was more a quarantine issue than anything else, but having a strange animal as dangerous as a tiger for an overnight guest is not my preference.

Once it was on the grounds, the handler asked if he could walk the cat for exercise. Against my better judgment, I agreed and the handler, holding tight to the leash, walked the tiger around the central walkway of the zoo—near our own tigers.

Immediately our Siberian tigers rushed the perimeter of their enclosure and hovered in a pounce position at the edge of their moat. They did not want this particular zoo visitor moving in on their territory.

It was the only time I ever saw our tigers appear to contemplate leaping that moat. I remember hoping at the time that we had built the moat wide enough. Since our tigers stayed put, I guess we did.

It is only at such times when animals are stressed that we find the limits of what they can do in terms of jumping. We know the "normal" leap distance, but just as there are reports of people who lift cars when their adrenaline is flowing, we can't be certain what an animal's maximum leap distance *could* be if the animal really wanted to jump it.

A visitor who *almost* made it to the zoo, but not quite, was the Prince of Nepal, who got as far north in Chicago as The Racquet Club on nearby Dearborn Street.

Once again, it was Chicago's "Grande Dame"—and Lincoln Zoo Board Member—Hope (Mrs. Brooks) McCormick who masterminded this lunch. Hope was an indomitable figure who circulated among the power brokers of the United States, but was so down-to-earth and charming one would never have guessed it. But when she said, "Now, luvvy," I knew she was about to ask a favor I could not refuse.

She charmed her many friends to get huge donations for her Lincoln Park Zoo; she charmed hard-nosed politicians, turning them into puppy dogs—all much the same way she charmed me.

So when she arranged the small, private gathering at The Racquet Club—where we were to meet His Royal Highness, the head of the Prince Mahandra Wildlife Trust and the brother of the King of Nepal—we knew a heavy sampling of her charm was coming up.

Lunch was delightful, and as Wendy I would to be heading to India and Nepal in a few months, we were eager to hear more about the country's wildlife and national parks. The Prince was a knowledgeable biologist and very active in his nation's considerable conservation efforts.

Then, without warning, as dessert and coffee were being served, the Prince stood up to make an announcement. He was giving Lincoln Park Zoo a very special gift—a pair of one-horned, or Indian, rhinos from Nepal. This is the species that Albrecht Durer immortalized in his sketch, and looks like it is wearing plated armor.

He made his speech and I became speechless.

I was taken aback and totally surprised by his announcement— and I didn't know what to do because we had only recently opened our new Large Mammal Habitat and had just committed Lincoln Park's limited resources and space to black rhinos, the highly endangered species from Africa.

Everyone at the lunch awaited my enthusiastic "thank you," including Hope, who was clearly delighted by the Prince's announcement. Everyone, that is, except Wendy, who, when I looked over at her, was as pale as I felt. She knew I simply could not accept the gift.

I finally decided there was nothing to do but talk about it. So I took a deep breath and thanked His Royal Highness profusely. Then I told him there was no gift I would rather accept on behalf of the zoo . . . but I couldn't.

I did my best, thanking him for his great generosity and laboring to explain the reasons why I could not accept his wonderful gift.

There was a stunned silence in the room as I spoke, but once the dust had settled, I think His Royal Highness understood, though he remained looking very unhappy through what remained of lunch. If there was any ill will on his part that day, he didn't let it show.

He also invited us to a reception at his palace when we were in Katmandu some months later, and we accepted. What was interesting about that reception was how we were able to palpably feel the power of life and death he appeared to hold over his subjects. Perhaps, then, it was not so surprising that during a palace coup about ten years later, he was killed, along with several other members of the Royal family. In many respects, humans and animals continue to be not so far apart.

Celebrities—from royalty to politicians to movie and TV stars—are fun to meet, but I must say I find that when it comes right down to it, they are much like the rest of us. This comes from the man who enjoyed his period of celebrity, only to be reminded by those kids in the department store who brought me back to earth with their shouting, *"Hey, look, there's Doctor Whatchamacallit!"*

No wonder my animals never looked impressed.

# The Zoo Society Safari to Stan's Africa

The short, frail woman standing next to Stan Lawrence Brown was clearly agitated, as one could tell from the way she was shaking her finger in his ruddy face. As a wealthy woman from Chicago, unaccustomed to camping in East Africa, she had already put up with a great deal of mud, extremely rudimentary toilet facilities, and two weeks of bouncing around in the converted truck that served as part of our safari convoy. But on this particularly hot, humid morning, as the African sun was already heating up the savannah, she'd clearly had it with Stan.

"It says in our itinerary," she said in clipped tones, "that we go towards Samburu today, yet *you* told us we are going to go in an entirely different direction. I demand to know why we are not following the written itinerary!"

"Because that's not where the game is," Stan bellowed back. "You came to Africa to see big game, and I'm gonna show it to you. But you gotta go where I go, when I go, and do what I say."

Stan turned on his booted heel and walked away.

It was left to me to console the woman and make things right. It always was when we traveled with Stan, which was every time we made the early East Africa circuit through Kenya, Tanzania, and Uganda.

Stan was our guide, a big game hunter-turned-safari leader. In the mid-1960s, all the guides were big game hunters who had turned their talents to the new African sport—photo safaris. They were always accompanied by young Brits or white Kenyans who learned their trade from the "Big Bwana."

Stan was at home in Africa and was, in fact, an actual blood brother of a Masai chief. Tall, lanky, and muscular, he could have been a stand-in for John Wayne, looking as much at home in Africa as Wayne did on a Western movie set. Stan's features were coarse, but ruggedly handsome, and his perpetual leathery tanned skin was proof of 40-odd years spent outside under the Kenyan sun. As the son of a British immigrant to Kenya, Stan looked and acted his part well, and he wore his safari suit as if he'd been born in it. In fact, *he really had been born in it.*

I met Stan in 1964 on my first Lincoln Park Zoo Society trip to Africa. As an urban eagle scout, the closest I'd come to camping was when I had to earn a merit badge by camping overnight in Wisconsin and cooking pancakes over an open fire for our scoutmaster (the first and last cooking I ever attempted). The scoutmaster didn't die and I earned my badge but I never went camping again.

Even my experience on bivouac in the Army provided more comfort than safari travel in the early days, but it was an adventure. I was happy to be following Marlin Perkins into the African wilderness, leading a merry (most of the time) band of stalwart Zoo Society members—who were also expecting the adventure of their lives.

Marlin had started the Lincoln Park Zoo Safari tradition in 1958 with a group of Chicagoans who had a strong interest in wildlife. As zoo director at the time, it was natural that Marlin would lead the tour that went from the western shores of the Congo through some of Central Africa and ended in East Africa in Nairobi, Kenya. The 1958 safari members included Daggett Harvey and his son, Daggett, Jr.; June Fairbank and her daughter, Laurie; Walter Erman; and Marlin. And it was on that trip, around the campfire one night on the Serengeti Plain, that the seeds of our Zoo Society were germinated.

The group discussed the need to assist the Chicago Park District in rebuilding the century-old zoo buildings that were in disrepair and to add significantly to the zoo's animal collections. Although it might now seem to have been a rather grandiose plan for such a small group of private citizens, these were no ordinary Chicagoans. They were among the movers and shakers in the city and knew the people to enlist for help and support.

Returning from Africa, in 1959 the group incorporated as The Lincoln Park Zoological Society with the stated goal of assisting the Chicago Park District to improve Lincoln Park Zoo. As an entity, the zoo was wholly owned and operated by the District. The Society was to be a support organization to raise money and was not to be involved in the management of the Zoo. Under this arrangement, it would not interfere with Marlin Perkins and his staff who were employed by the Park District to run the zoo.

When I became zoo director in 1962, I became aware that the Council on Foreign Relations in Chicago was serving a growing membership by taking charter flights to various parts of the world. Many airlines were inaugurating low-cost charter flights. Soon, it was not only the Council on Foreign Relations that had hooked onto this idea; but some of the other cultural institutions were using the concept to build membership. I believed we should consider a similar program for the Zoo Society's membership, which at that time included mostly personal friends of the founding members. I also thought it was one of the few perks of membership we could offer members. Unlike other museums in town, since the zoo charged no admission, we couldn't offer the usual member perk of "free admission."

I looked into setting up a charter trip program. A person at British Airways suggested I work with a travel agent and recommended a company called Special Tours and Travel owned by Ernest Prossnitz. Ernie was of Czech heritage—my own family background—and he proved to be the perfect partner for this project.

Ernie had started his career in the Congo, which later became Zaire and is now the Democratic Republic of Congo. He worked for Sabena Airlines, which, being Belgian, served the former Belgian Congo. His specialty was working with big game hunters, or those who wished to become big game hunters, and he very much wanted to arrange safaris.

We decided the first trip for the Zoo Society should be to East Africa, to the three countries that made up the East African Confederation: Kenya, Tanzania, and Uganda. With common borders and common currency at that time, it was soon to become a standard tourist circuit to visit all three, going in an approximate circle, typically beginning at Nairobi and ending up in Mombasa.

As the early safari lodges were few and far between, we decided to try something different—our own tented camp safari. Ernie had worked with some of the professional hunters in that area and engaged the services of Stan Lawrence Brown, who with his brother and partner Jeffrey, were well known as safari hunters/operators in East Africa.

And so my association with Stan began.

The early years were interesting, partly because of the incredible logistics involved. Our group size was usually 15–20 people, as the airlines had worked out an incentive system where if 15 or more people traveled as a group, the leader went free. It was certainly the only way I, on my meager zoo director's salary, was going to see the world. But it also was a way for me to share my knowledge and interest in animals with members of the Zoo Society and to, hopefully, build the members' interest in helping the zoo when we returned to Chicago.

Once in Africa, we used customized versions of International Harvester trucks in the early years to get us around. We also had landrovers for game runs. The vehicles would bounce over the open savannah or through the woodlands as fast as they could go, but would occasionally come to an abrupt halt when a wheel would fall into the den of an aardvark or warthog. It was not unusual for some of our brave explorers to be thrown from one of the trucks, but fortunately no one was ever seriously injured, and the safari continued. The absence of paved roads or, in many cases, any roads at all, just added to the spirit of adventure!

Our tented camps were reasonably comfortable (with "reasonably" being the operative word), but our logistics problems extended from the number of people traveling as guests to the number of staff needed to set up camp, feed us, and break up the camp so it could be moved to the next site. There were so many people involved—drivers that took the visitors around during the day, cooks, tent keepers, grounds keepers, repair people for the vehicles, and so on—that we had at least as many staff as guests. Still, every few days we moved the camp, rain or shine.

The fact was we went where the animals went, which accounted for the divergence from the stated itinerary. If Stan felt the animals had gone off in a different direction, we went that way too.

## "Please don't bring your group back!"

Eventually, after we'd gone on safari several times, we developed a system that worked best for us and it became more of a routine, and a little less difficult. We found a good way to move the group was to spend one or two days in camp at a good site, then go to an adjacent area lodge (of which there seemed to be a growing list to choose from), and then go back to a camp. This allowed the staff to break camp while we went off to spend a night in the lodge, then move ahead of us and set up the next camp and await our late afternoon arrival on day three. Through it all, the camp staffs worked terribly hard—sometimes under horrific weather conditions.

For our part, we would head off on a carefree early game drive on the morning camp was to be struck, taking just an overnight bag in our vehicles. As soon as we were gone, the staff would strike the heavy canvas tents that took three men to move, pack up all the gear (including the mess and cook tents, as well as tents the staff slept in and toilet tent), then load up the trucks by late that afternoon.

They would drive all night and most of the next day to the

designated location beyond the lodge where we were staying and set up the camp that night and most of the next day so that when we arrived, we could move into our tents by late afternoon. Then they would repeat the entire process a day or two later, again and again for three weeks. Most of the African staff was given a week off every six months or so in those days.

Spending part of the time in the lodges provided our group with opportunities for decent showers every few days and the chance to sleep in better beds and eat something other than camp food. However, people who have been on safari know that camp food in Africa is usually incredibly good—especially the bread, which appears miraculously at every meal, having been made in an old bread pan that was put into a hole in the ground and covered with tin and hot coals. I have never ceased to marvel at what fabulous meals have come from the most rudimentary camp kitchens! Showers in camp are another miracle.

In East Africa, after a hot long day on a dusty game drive, one has only to ask the tent man for "majimoto" and, within minutes, a bucket of hot water arrives, always at the exactly right temperature for a shower—and they do *not* have thermostats or thermometers to determine the temperature.

Then, standing outside in the privacy of a canvas enclosed shower stall and under a canvas bucket with a shower spicket attached, one can take a leisurely shower under the early evening stars, looking out on a herd of giraffe grazing nearby. There is truly nothing like it.

Of course, it's necessary to first learn to be a bit thrifty with the water or risk running out while still covered with soap. But that's all part of becoming an experienced safari-goer. We can always tell the first-timers as they invariably have to yell out in the midst of their showers, "majimoto" and wait for a second bucket of water to come from the back of the camp!

Going to lodges broke the rhythm of the camp experience, but in rainy, muddy weather, that wasn't all bad. In fact, it was a blessing.

I remember a particularly awful two days in Kenya, when it had rained for days, so we decided to break the monotony of wet game drives with lunch at the Mount Kenya Safari Club. We were not staying overnight at the Club, just taking lunch there.

In the 1960s the Mount Kenya Safari Club was very posh (as it still is more than 40 years later). It was built in the grand manner of British colonial Africa, with a wood-paneled library and drawing room, and red velvet drapes that have absorbed many hunters' cigar smoke and conversations that continued on past midnight over glasses of fine port and brandy. The Club's imposing white columns and adjacent gravel driveway have witnessed the arrival of grand carriages and motor cars coming and going on great adventures through the last century.

As with everything else at the Mount Kenya Safari Club, the dining room is imposing and the food impressive. The luncheon spread is unrivaled, and the dessert buffet unmatched in East Africa.

One is expected to "dress" for meals at such a posh club, although the dress code does tend toward "safari chic" decades before the fashion industry coined that phrase.

Our group, though dressed in safari clothes, hardly could have been called chic. We were, quite honestly, thoroughly bedraggled, but the maitre d' managed a thin smile and escorted us to a table for 16.

We enjoyed a magnificent feast, but it wasn't until we saw the dessert buffet that the full damage we were doing became apparent. Starved for fancy desserts, our group consumed the entire contents of the dessert table, leaving nothing for other guests of the club.

As I sheepishly herded my group out of the dining room, the maitre d' took me aside and said, "Please, do not bring your group back—*ever again.*"

And I don't think we did for many years.

# The chief, Stan and the lady

During one of the earliest safari trips we visited a Masai village, where Stan's blood brother was the Chief. I was invited into the Chief's mud hut where one of his wives welcomed me. It was so dark inside that I couldn't see anything at all, but the Chief invited me to sit down with him on his cowhide bed.

I began to feel itchy almost instantly, and, as I emerged from the hut, I realized I was covered in fleas. I stripped off my clothing as fast as possible and literally danced around covered in bugs. I was the central entertainment for not only my own group but the entire village, as I stripped down to my underwear before getting any relief.

I don't really remember how I "de-bugged" my clothes, but think I took them back to camp for a thorough washing with lye soap. Everyone thought the incident was hysterically funny—everyone except me.

Gradually, the trips became known as "The Les Fisher Safaris," not because we always went to Africa, though we did go there two out of every three trips, mostly because Africa is one of the few places in the world where we could see big game—and lots of it. It is also the place that many people think of first when they imagine safaris and wild creatures.

South America has a far greater diversity of species of birds, mammals, and reptiles, but they are harder to see in their jungle environment of the Amazon basin. On the other hand, Africa's wonderful open, wooded plains and savannahs enable one to see herds of wildebeest, zebra, buffalo, and all kinds of antelope, plus of course, giraffe, elephants, and, with some luck, the big cats—lions, cheetah, and leopards.

In my mind, Africa is a magical place that combines animals, people, and geography that are each in their own way, incredible. I never tire of returning to Africa, even though years ago the East African Confederation split up, and Kenya, Tanzania, and Uganda went their separate ways.

But before that happened, and in the earliest days of our safaris, I wasn't the only person who thought the trips to Africa were magical. Many of the young (and not-so-young) women who joined me on those trips were captivated by Africa. They caught the safari bug and fell in love with the place, the animals and, on occasion, our young, dashing drivers!

It wasn't unheard of on several of my early trips to celebrate not one, but several, "engagement" parties around the campfire before the trip ended. I could see how easily it could happen with handsome young drivers, beautiful starry nights, the occasional full African harvest moon, and the captivating sounds of animals hauntingly calling at night.

The engagement usually ended the minute the trip ended, but it was fun for all while it lasted!

There *was* a poignant ending for one not-so-young married woman who went on safari with me to Africa. She fell in love with Stan, who was himself married, and she left her children and her husband, moved to Kenya and lived with Stan until his death many years later.

She eventually returned to Chicago (though she and her family were never the same). Africa does strange things to people and I have always felt badly that I somehow had a hand in that family's breakup.

# Uganda, Idi Amin, and a very scary safari

For many years I led an annual trip to East Africa, timed for optimal viewing to see the great migration of wildebeests in the Masai Mara in Kenya, and onto the Serengeti plain in Tanzania. The two areas are contiguous, and the animals move in a great circle route between the two countries, timing their migration to the rains, the new grass, and birth of their calves.

But the thousand-year-old cycle was disrupted for tourists in the early 1980s when Tanzania closed its border to Kenya and, for a time, one had to fly either to Addis Ababa, Ethiopia or to The Seychelles, a group of islands off the Indian Ocean to make the transfer, which by car takes less than 20 minutes. Today, the border is again open, and the migration continues as it always has. The animals need no passports.

Uganda, in my opinion perhaps the most beautiful of the three East African countries, was always a favorite of mine when we visited Queen Elizabeth Park and Murchison Falls. I returned to Uganda again for the first time in late December 1992, having left in an extreme hurry in 1971, when the madman dictator Idi Amin came to power.

To lead a safari—much less dozens of them over the years—is a privilege and an enormous responsibility. When all is going as planned, it's wonderful to be able to accompany guests and share my passion for animals. But when things go *wrong*, and there is always something that can—and does—on safari, the responsibility to make certain the guests are safe, comfortable, and happy is awesome.

At no time did I feel more weighted by responsibility—and even more so *after* the incident took place—than when I had a Zoo Society safari in East Africa, in Uganda, at the moment Idi

Amin came into power. Amin became world famous as a despicable despot responsible for great civil strife in his own country, as well as for the murders of thousands and thousands of innocent people.

But even when we were in Uganda, the political undercurrent was moving toward Amin, and there was great concern. I remember coming back from a glorious game run in Murchison Falls, where we had seen hippo wallowing in a hippo pool, a pride of lion lazing in the sun, and stepping out of the Landrover under the warmth of the African sun, to smell the bacon and eggs that would soon be served for the camp breakfast. That was when I received a message on the short-wave radio.

"Hurry, Doctor," the driver said. "There's a very important message for you."

I dropped my camera and binoculars in my tent and hurried over to the main, mess tent. The message came in crackles, but was distinct enough to hear.

"Get your group to Kampala. Stop. Fastest possible. Stop. Get earliest flight out of Uganda. Stop. Amin now in power."

Telling a group of unsuspecting people that they have a few minutes to pack everything and that their safari is over as of right now, is not a pleasant task. But telling them they may also be in grave danger compounds the problem by ten.

But leave we did, as quickly as possible and, upon arriving in Kampala, Uganda's capital, we went straight to the airport. We were able to arrange for a plane to take us to Nairobi and, from there, continued the safari back in Tanzania.

For years after, Uganda became totally off bounds for tourism and it wasn't until late 1992 that I returned to Uganda to Queen Elizabeth Park. We were one of the first tourist groups welcomed back and the Ugandans made a huge effort to be as accommodating as possible.

But what Amin's soldiers had done to Uganda's beautiful game parks was tragic.

Queen Elizabeth Park had served as a military training ground where Amin's men shot the animals for target practice. Only 60 elephants remained in an area of more than 300 square miles, but they were beginning to come back, along with many other species. The park remained in a state of imbalance with huge numbers of warthogs, waterbuck, Ugandan kob (an antelope similar to—but more robust than—impala), hippo, and numerous cape buffalo. With few predators, these species had grown into much larger groups than one typically finds.

Birds were also affected. There was an overabundance of guinea fowl and coucals, while the park was nearly devoid of other, equally typical, species.

I will never forget celebrating New Year's Eve in our camp, pitched on a bluff overlooking the Kazinga Channel, under the steely bright stars of the Ugandan sky. We had enjoyed a wonderful meal, complete with champagne, and had sung *Auld Lang Syne*—to which the camp staff responded by singing *Happy Birthday!* We were all asleep before midnight with the full moon rising and a lion's muffled roar somewhere in the distance.

# A "luxury safari" to Tanzania

During the time that Uganda was off limits in East Africa, Kenya built up its tourist trade enormously, creating paved roads between major key tourist destinations and parks, and adding many fine new lodges. Tanzania hit the skids, however, by turning to a socialist government, which received significant assistance from China. The beautiful lodges built in the early years fell into total disrepair, and, often, upon arriving at a lodge in Tanzania, one would find that food was rationed, there was almost nothing bottled to drink, and there was no running water.

For some trips to Tanzania during that time, we subsisted on half a piece of toast and a boiled egg for breakfast; some kind of inedible meat at lunch and dinner, accompanied by cabbage and kale . . . cabbage and kale . . . cabbage and kale. It was dreadful, but the animal viewing remained superb in the Serengeti and Ngorongoro Crater.

On one safari to the Serengeti in the late 1980s we decided to do a mobile camp—going back to tenting, but staying at one campsite for five nights. This was to give people a luxury tenting experience in the midst of the wildebeest migration route. And, of course, the food would be much better than that served in the lodges, which were still in dire straits.

All went well the first night, except for a lion that had made a kill right behind my tent. That had attracted a group of hyenas that were (literally) cackling and whooping it up all night long. It wasn't so much the sound of hyenas cackling that was so disturbing, but the incessant sound of crunching bones that made sleeping quite difficult. Under the circumstances, however, it must be remembered that we were there for just that—to see and hear the animals in their own world!

Those among us who were a bit panicky about having lions and hyenas so close to their tents spent a nervous night. It is a bit odd to expect people to accept my simply saying that they are safe in flimsy canvas tents when they hear hyenas munching right through big animal bones—the same hyenas that have been known to eat tires off trucks and actually eat into metal refrigerators when they smell food.

Actually food was very central to this camp, because I noticed that with each meal, we saw less and less of it. It wasn't until day three (of five) that we hit an all-time low. For lunch, we were down to a tin of sardines and five crackers for seven people on what was supposed to be a *luxury* safari, for which people had paid a *lot* of money.

I confronted the camp manager, who admitted that, after the first meal, the cook had left and stolen most of the food. A supply truck had also been hijacked on its way to our camp. The manager had been too embarrassed to say anything to us—*like we wouldn't have noticed!*

Tanzanian roads presented their own challenges, particularly the road from Ngorongoro Crater to Lake Manyara, a drive that required a vehicle with good springs, plus stamina on the part of those on safari. The roads were not only used by those of us on safari, they were the main transport roads to Mombasa, so truck traffic was heavy.

The road was dirt so, in heavy rains, it became a virtual mud wallow that left deep, unforgiving ruts when the sun baked the red earth dry again. It was beyond bumpy. It was also dusty and crowded with vehicles, people, and cows being herded to the next pasture. Many times it was simply impassable, and we had to wait hours to get through. It took patience in the extreme to traverse the road.

Once, just outside of Lake Manyara's town, Mosquito Gulch, so nicknamed for the ever-present malaria in the region, we stopped to do some curio shopping. Our vehicle was one of four and, as our group wanted to shop longer, we sent the other vehicles ahead, which is usually not a good idea in case one of the vehicles breaks down. It is far better to travel as a group in the event someone needs help. But off they went, and we followed about an hour later. We were just outside of town on the hot dusty road when the vehicle's fan belt broke.

Our driver explained that we had to repair it ourselves. We didn't dare flag down another local vehicle to help us, he warned, as it was a dangerous road. Tanzania was so poor at the time that anyone we stopped to ask for help would surely rob us.

We stood and waited (and waited) while our driver tried to jury-rig a repair. It took most of the day and the heat was intense. We had one beer and one orange soda, to be shared by eight passengers and the driver, who got most of the liquid as he was the one working on the problem. Every time a truck passed, we were covered in dust. Around 4 PM—some six hours after our roadside ordeal began—we were moving again in a vehicle that limped back to the main town of Arusha about 10 PM as one of our other vehicles was just starting back to look for us. It wasn't very far in terms of miles, but with the bad roads and our band-aid repair, we couldn't go more than 20 miles an hour, so the trip took forever—or seemed to.

Fan belts on cars and trucks break every day—and rarely at a time or place that's convenient for the traveler—but when a group is anticipating the excitement and adventure of a safari, it's not the type of adventure under the hot sun one finds in the brochure.

On another occasion, while going up a narrow, winding part of the road to Ngorongoro Crater in a particularly bad rainstorm, we encountered a road block caused by a semi-trailer truck that had skidded sideways and was hanging by three of its four wheel pairs over the side of the Crater. Most people were standing around discussing what to do when finally, after about three hours and the usual African ingenuity of moving heavy things without the benefit of heavy construction equipment, the road cleared enough to let us slip past the truck on the mountain side of the road.

No visit to Tanzania would be complete without a trip to Ngorongoro Crater, a true natural wonder. It is a huge crater formed when a volcanic mountain taller than Mt. Everest blew its top several thousand years ago. The caldera that is left falls away from the rim some 8,000 feet above sea level, down to the floor of the crater, which is about 4,000 feet above sea level. Around the

Manyara side of the rim is a lush rainforest filled with blue and Colobus monkeys, along with the occasional elephant and an abundance of jungle birds including colorful turacos.

Down inside the crater exists a resident population of zebra, Thompson and Grant gazelle, hartebeest, lion, cheetah, leopard, spotted hyena, elephant bulls and most of the last remaining black rhino in Africa (which now are under a 24-hour armed guard to prevent poaching).

Young male and female elephants with their babies traverse in and out of the crater, but the walls are too steep for the old bulls to climb. The crater is like a big, open, zoo. Its resident population stays in the crater and is accustomed to seeing tourist vehicles, as well as the Masai and their cattle that have grazing rights within the crater. The Masai come down each day with their cattle, going back up to the rim and their bomas at night.

The main lodge at the crater was in very sad shape during the 1980s. On more than one occasion, because there was no place for the lodge staff to sleep, they slept in the lobby each night. In the morning, I had to go outside in the dark before the generator kicked in for the electricity, and rouse the staff so they could bring some hot tea to our guests before they headed out for the day.

As in the Serengeti and elsewhere in Tanzania, food was very hard to come by. The packed lunch they sent with us was typically inedible as there wasn't enough refrigeration to keep the food safe to eat. We stuck to bananas and boiled eggs for years.

We continued to visit Ngorongoro Crater during this tough time in Tanzania because the animals and the people there were the best. Fortunately, the economic situation improved greatly through the years and by 2003 Tanzania—as well as Uganda— were considered among the best countries to visit in East Africa.

# Wendy discovers Africa and things I apparently don't quite know

My safari days took a new turn when I married Wendy in 1981. I had taken many of my early trips alone, although my former wife Beth did accompany me on several. But Beth never enjoyed the rustic experience, and, despite the fact she hand-raised many a gorilla and chimpanzee in our home and was exceedingly good with animals, she preferred the comfort of that home to camping.

I introduced Wendy to Africa in 1982, when we took a small group of Zoo Society members to the new country of Zimbabwe (formerly Southern Rhodesia) and Botswana.

Although I loved East Africa and had spent many wonderful years there, I also wanted to see more of southern and central Africa, which had until then escaped my itinerary.

Wendy was shocked by African camps, as I had told her nothing in advance. Her camping experience to that point included backpacking with the Sierra Club on vigorous hiking trips. She was accustomed to situations where there was no toilet and campers relied on dehydrated food. I'll never forget the expression on her face when we showed up at Savuti, our first camp in Botswana, at teatime. There was a full spread laid out that included a Black Forest cake, cheesecake, and assorted desserts.

As for the toilets, removed from the tents in a thatched-in enclosure, she was aghast. All she could say was, "Flushing toilets! And you call this *camping!*"

Wendy was introduced quickly to the excitement of wildlife in camp by the camp manager warning her to be sure to use her flashlight when returning to her tent because it was so dark outside that she might run into the hippo that tended to graze up on the lawn at night.

The first morning she woke up in camp—the morning after we arrived at Savuti—she heard munching under her cot and felt a large beast pushing against her in bed, separated from her only by a thin sheet of canvas. Every time she moved slightly, it stopped munching and leaned in on her, only to resume eating when she again lay quiet.

After several long minutes, the animal moved away, and Wendy got up nerve to get out of bed and peer out the tent flap on the side. Yes, it *was* the hippo grazing and the best grass was under the tent edges because it was the only grass that captured enough moisture from the dew to stay green during the prolonged drought.

My credibility as a wildlife expert hit the skids with Wendy that very same afternoon. A large bull elephant came ambling up from the river and toward the camp.

"Don't worry," I assured her, "he won't come into camp."

We were in the mess tent, awaiting tea, while the other members of our group were in their tents getting ready to join us for tea, to be followed by the afternoon game run. Geoff, one of our safari gang, however, was sunbathing on a towel outside his tent, looking away from us and watching a hippo grazing down river.

The big bull elephant slowly, but deliberately, made its way up toward the mess tent, clearly on its way through camp. Wendy looked at me as the elephant started coming right for the mess tent. I can admit when I'm wrong, so I quickly appraised the situation and said quietly, "If he comes in that end of the tent, we're going out the other."

At that, he sauntered around the tent and was on his way toward the sunbather.

At the very moment we were going to call out for Geoff to move, he turned away from watching the hippo to see this huge elephant slowly bearing down on him.

I don't recall ever seeing anyone move so fast in my life.

After a quick head-swiveling double take, Geoff picked up his towel and actually dove into his nearby tent, somehow managing to unzip it and zip it back up quickly just before the elephant got to it.

As the elephant wandered through camp going right next to several tents we could hear people unzipping side flaps to look, then zipping them right back up.

For some reason, there seems to be a greater sense of security inside a tent when we can't see what's outside and the flaps are up!

Someone later sputtered, "I looked out and saw gray and realized it was his leg, so I zipped up!"

What the elephant was after was a tree filled with ripe marula fruit, which was right next to one of the tents in the middle of camp. Its branches overhung the tent, so he calmly, but very deliberately, laid his head against the trunk, placing his huge tusks on either side of the tree and shook it until the fruit dropped off, landing on top the tent. Then he reached out his trunk and literally vacuumed off the pods, putting them in his mouth. He repeated the process again and again until all the ripe pods had fallen down. By that time he had become bored and moved on off through camp and beyond.

Sadly, this same elephant (nicknamed "Baby Huey" by the park rangers) was becoming too tame, primarily because unknowing visitors in the nearby public camp were feeding him. As a result he became bolder and bolder and finally became a nuisance. It became necessary for rangers to kill him as he was a menace to campers in the park. His bold behavior when we saw him was what doomed him to an early death.

When we reached Linyanti, the next camp, my wildlife expert status again came under suspicion to Wendy.

We arrived late in the afternoon, in time for a game run to look at birds on the Linyanti River. But first we were shown to our tents to settle in. Ours was the last tent in a semi-circle that followed the curve of the river. The steep riverbank dropped away about two feet from the tent opening and in the river just beyond, one could see a small pod of hippo, mostly submerged.

Wendy asked if the hippo could climb up the bank to our tent—recalling her last encounter with a hippo leaning into her tent.

"Of course not," I insisted, "the bank is too steep."

But when we awoke the next morning and Wendy tried to unzip the front of our tent, she found it encrusted in fresh hippo dung from a hippo that had not only climbed up the steep bank, but decided to mark our tent as his territory!

As if this wasn't bad enough, my credibility was totally lost when we got to Bumi Hills, a magnificent lodge in Zimbabwe overlooking Lake Kariba, formed when the Zambezi River was flooded in the 1950s to provide electricity for most of Zimbabwe.

To get to our room, we left the main lodge and walked along paved paths leading out in fan fashion to rooms that were built on the side of the escarpment facing the lake. As we passed each room, there was a cement archway along the path, which we walked under, then down a few steps to reach our room.

Again Wendy asked, having seen elephants on the road coming up to the lodge, "Now, elephants can't walk under those and down to our room, right?"

I assured her they would not and *could not* pass under the archway. The only thing to worry about was keeping the large picture windows closed and locked to prevent baboons from getting in our room.

Again she believed me, only to find out the next morning I was wrong. Again. When she opened the door to our room there was a large pile of steaming elephant dung, accompanied by a small sea of urine running down the steps and under our doormat. From that time on I think she realized the great Dr. Fisher was just a man— flesh and blood and clearly fallible.

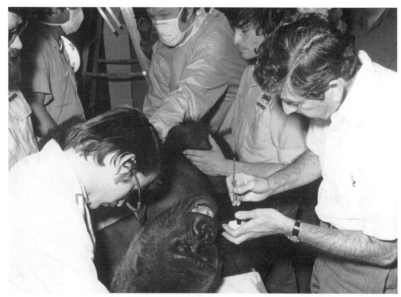

Otto and each of the other 24 great apes received a full physical, including a dental exam, when we moved them to the new Great Ape House in June 1976. Courtesy, Chicago Park District

Rajah the gorilla being sedated for his trip to Europe to breed with a female—but "he" turned out to be a "she"! (1964) Courtesy, Chicago Park District

Patsy, the chimpanzee, not only controlled the excitable Keo, but with him produced many beautiful babies. Courtesy, Chicago Park District

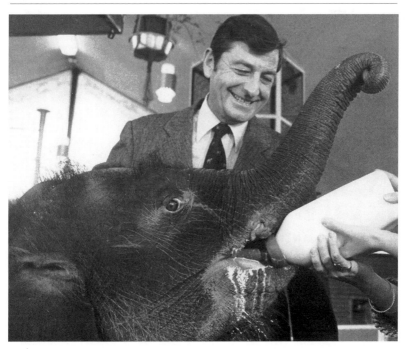

Bozie lands safely in the US from Sri Lanka (1976). Courtesy, Chicago Park District

Bozie (center) celebrates the birth of Shanti, her first baby and the first elephant born in Illinois (October 11, 1990). Courtesy, Chicago Park District

Mike the polar bear and his diminutive mate Szazka. Courtesy,
Chicago Park District

Early live *Zoo Parade* show with Marlin Perkins and Jim Hurlbut. (c. 1950) Courtesy, Chicago Park District

Ray Rayner compares a photo of Sinbad as a baby with the "real deal" in his outside cage some 30 years later. (1971) Courtesy, Chicago Tribune

With my clown friends Cookie (l) and Bozo (center). (1980s)

Joan Crawford makes friends with a lion cub on the Lee Phillip Show (May 1965). Courtesy, Chicago Park District

A chimp joins in the April Fool's Day shenanigans at the zoo's reception desk. Courtesy, Chicago Park District

Joe Regenstein (l) generous supporter the "new" Lincoln Park Zoo, including the Bird of Prey Habitat, at the dedication with Hope Mc-Cormick, Bill Bennett, President of The Lincoln Park Zoo Society, and Chicago Park District President Bill Bartholomay (1989). Courtesy Chicago Park District

Mayor Richard M. Daley and his wife Maggie at the 1990 Zoo Halloween Party.

Returning Sinbad, the gorilla, to his cage after his 1964 "Great Escape" was a relief to Gene Hartz, assistant director, and me. Courtesy, Chicago Park District

Freddie, the gorilla, looked the part of King Kong but was so gentle with his family that we called him "Uncle Freddie." Courtesy, Chicago Park District

# The elephants are kindly, but they're dumb . . . or are they?

In Paul Simon's song *At the Zoo*, there's a line that goes "The elephants are kindly, but they're dumb." I've been asked on occasion if that was true. Elephants are fabulous, intelligent animals and we have had the privilege of seeing many of them many times in Africa—in the wild, sometimes so close we could touch their legs and hear them as they sucked water into their mouths, while we viewed them at a watering hole from an underground hide in Hwange Park, Zimbabwe.

We have watched elephants swimming the Chobe River in Botswana, completely submerged except for their trunks, which they would poke up out of the water like a periscope, to breathe.

We have been among huge breeding herds in Chobe and Hwange as the females shepherded their small babies along so they were almost invisible as the herd quietly moved past. To use the word "quietly" when referring to the movement of a herd of elephants might seem odd, but the fact is an entire herd *can* pass by virtually without making a sound.

We have been trapped for hours in a viewing hide up a marula tree, while five elephants came for the tasty pods, surrounding the tree (and our hide), and shaking it to get the fruit.

We have been charged by a huge matriarch in the Lake Kariba area. She stopped her charge just short of the vehicle as we sped away, leaving her tiny baby in a cloud of dust with its ears flapping like Dumbo.

In the same park, we watched a baby elephant, just a few days old, trying to learn to use its trunk to suck up water and unsuccessfully aiming it at its mouth, and squirting the water all over itself.

We saw a group of young elephants wallowing in mud like large pigs. A little one got stuck in the mud and started squealing and we watched while two old females worked to extricate him by putting their tusks under him on each side to leverage him out, eventually popping him out like a cork when the suction of the mud was broken.

We have seen a bull trying to mate a cow elephant as she fled screeching across the road at 20 miles per hour, with him in hot pursuit bellowing after her, finally catching her and, amid great crashing sounds, succeeding in mounting her.

We watched baby elephants sleeping in the only shade under their mothers on a sweltering afternoon at Mana Pools, Zimbabwe. The temperature easily reached 126 degrees in the sun.

We witnessed the destruction caused by elephants when there were too many of them to live in the space allotted them, and we listened to the ongoing debate about what do to when elephants are eating themselves out of their habitat and destroying it for every other creature. There is no easy answer.

And we have seen two old bulls on their last legs, thin and gaunt, waiting to die in Tarangire, Tanzania. They clearly had lost their last set of teeth and, unable to eat any longer, waited together for the inevitable.

One experience, however, changed the way Wendy and I will forever think of them, but it will nevertheless not diminish our respect and love for these wonderful creatures.

We were in the Serengeti to see the wildebeest migration. On our last day in Tanzania we went out for a morning game run in our Landrover with a pop-top that was open for better game viewing. Near Ndutu Lodge we came across a mature bull elephant with huge tusks of a kind rarely seen because most of the "big tuskers" have been poached out during the last hundred years. As a result, big tusk elephants have not been able to pass on their genes to other generations of elephants. This bull was clearly walking from the waterhole to a forest area. Our driver carefully positioned our vehicle off to the side so we could observe him walk by.

As he came abreast of our vehicle, he stopped and looked at us, but instead of going on his way, he changed direction and walked purposefully toward our vehicle. We didn't think much about it, but he got closer and closer.

We had been standing but thought it would be prudent to sit down. So did so.

He got so close that we were concerned he would put his trunk into the top of the car, but instead he approached us and laid his head against the vehicle. Then he backed off and put his tusks firmly up against the metal top of the vehicle, just above the glass windows. He then very deliberately started to rock the car back and forth for a full 40 seconds, though it seemed like hours. We sat very still and remained quiet in our Landrover.

I remember thinking, "*Well, I've heard about an elephant turning over a vehicle, and I guess this is it.*"

I thought this was the moment it would happen.

But it didn't.

The elephant stopped rocking the vehicle just as suddenly as it had started. Then, without a sound, it turned and walked back in the direction it had been going when this whole bizarre experience began. Even our driver thought it was a close call, and safari drivers specialize in having tall tales to tell.

What had we done to provoke such a response from an elephant on the road? We've wondered about it.

# Lions and car trouble in Africa

Lions are among those fabulous African animals that, quite frankly, one doesn't want to get too close to. It's hard to believe lions would—or could—do *anything* when someone would drive up in a safari vehicle and get within a few feet of them. They are usually sleeping off the meal from the night before and are sometimes so lazy they can barely lift their heads to acknowledge a visitor's presence.

Even when we would see lions on a kill, they appeared docile; although occasionally a big male would give us that long cold stare that made the hair on our neck stand straight up. We observed that unforgettable stare as a male was eating—actually finishing off, a giraffe that he and his three brothers had managed to take down in a dry sand riverbed. There was something about seeing that stare from a lion only a few feet away—especially from an open vehicle—that made us understand why the lion is called the king of the beasts.

We had lions walk through camp in the middle of the night on many occasions, once killing its prey right outside our camp, which created a cacophony of sounds from other lions, hyenas, and jackals for the remainder of the dark hours.

Through all our safari adventures, we have only had two truly heart-pounding experiences with lions. Both took place in 2002.

The first incident was at the end of our migration safari to Kenya and Tanzania to see the big herds of wildebeests. It preceded the incident of the elephant trying to overturn our truck by about 15 hours and occurred in the same area, same camp.

We had set out on a late afternoon game run, just three of us and two guides—the second had come along just for the ride.

Driving around a lake with dozens of wildebeest skeletons strewn around the shoreline, we remarked to one another about what might have caused such a situation. Our guide explained that this particular lake had "ozuma"—quicksand—so when animals came to drink from it, they would become stuck and then would be easy prey for the big cats.

Since we had seen five female lions not ten minutes earlier, lying on the road between the lake and Ndutu Lodge in the Serengeti, we knew there were plenty of lions inhabiting the area. In fact, the lions we had seen were clearly there for the night, their bellies overly full and not anxious to move anywhere until morning.

As we rounded the edge of the lake, our guides decided to take a shortcut rather than make a wide circle to rejoin the road on the other side. After a bit of lively discussion in Swahili about the best way to go through the mud and grass at the end of the lake, Winston, our Masai guide and driver, gunned the engine of the vehicle and we flew out across the terrain, about 10 feet, before coming to an abrupt halt against a large hummock of grass and mud.

After a few feeble attempts at rocking the vehicle—and after looking around to see if there were any other lions or more formidable creatures such as cape buffalo in the immediate area, we piled out to assess the situation.

For a full 45 minutes, our two guides tried valiantly to jack up the rear wheels, but as one corner of the vehicle lifted up, the other sank even further into the spongy mud. Even standing on it, we could feel ourselves beginning to sink in. This was the "ozuma" the guides had described—and we were in it.

Finally, after an hour or so, Winston declared we needed to start walking.

Walking, however, is not something one usually does in the African bush, unless accompanied by a ranger or two (armed with high-powered elephant guns that can take down *anything*). Rather, a person stays with the vehicle and waits for assistance. But in this particular area there was little traffic and not much chance of being rescued. We were told also that the hyenas were so aggressive that it was not safe to remain with the disabled vehicle.

Reluctantly, we began to walk, taking Winston with us, along with his Masai blanket. Our other guide stayed with the vehicle and waited for us to get help and return for him.

It was late afternoon, and the sun was beastly hot as we made our long way back to Ndutu Lodge for help. There were also some logistical problems to cope with, the first being that we had only one small bottle of water for four people, and the temperature was at least 105 degrees in the sun.

Further, Winston said we needed to reach the lodge by dark. We reminded him that the sun would set in less than 30 minutes and the lodge was more than an hour away. That we would be walking in the dark—without any light whatsoever to guide us. He did not respond.

We also addressed the fact that there were still those five lions, lying in the road en route to Ndutu. Winston assured us that he could wave off any lions with his red blanket and added that we were safe because he was Masai.

But when we asked about cape buffalo, he quietly replied that would be a different matter. They were a serious problem as we were walking around the lake's edge, and the tall grass beyond could easily conceal a big bull. If one were to charge us, we should immediately hit the ground and lie as flat and still as possible. With their poor eyesight, Winston felt we would be able to escape being hurt.

Wendy and I kept our thoughts to ourselves. We were with Jim Heck, our tour escort, who had more than 20 years of safari experience. Fortunately, we did not have clients with us. It was only us and we just kept walking and hoping.

As the sun was setting, a small landrover appeared. We waved furiously, and, mercifully, it stopped on the road on the other side of the wide swath of tall grass that separated the lake edge from the road. In Africa they call this type of grass "adrenaline grass" and for good reason. Before starting into it, we called loudly and clapped our hands to scare up anything we couldn't see.

"What if they don't have room for us?" I asked Winston.

Before he could answer, Wendy said, "I don't care if they have to lash us to the roof of the car—we're getting on that vehicle!"

A delightful Swiss couple welcomed us aboard, and, rather than taking us to Ndutu Lodge, they took us back to our own mobile tented camp about a half-mile out of their way. We invited them in for a drink to thank them, and when we all got out of their vehicle, Frank, our mess tent man appeared with a look of horror on his face.

He ran at me quickly and asked, "Where is your vehicle?"

We told him our other guide and the vehicle were safely back at the lake, stuck in the mud. Immediately, two trucks with four men and a lot of chain went to the rescue, but when they reached the vehicle, they found our guide on its roof.

He had been charged by a hippo while we were gone!

# Facing down the lions . . . sort of

Our other incident involving a lion occurred less than eight months after the first at Singita Lodge, near Kruger National Park in South Africa. We were on the last stop on our Fall 2002 Luxury Safari to Botswana and South Africa, and we liked that we could take walks with our armed ranger—something we could not do in East Africa—unless, of course, our truck broke down and we were left to stroll merrily through dangerous terrain!

The one to two-hour guided walks were basically nature walks. Animals know that someone approaching on foot is usually not friendly. They have learned through thousands of years about hunters, so the walks are mainly to show visitors insects, animal tracks, and plants of the region. Suffice it to say, they were very interesting, if not exciting, experiences. And it's always a welcome experience to have a chance to get out of a vehicle and stretch one's legs.

On this particular walk, both our ranger and spotter came along as the African spotter was learning how to be a ranger. They both carried rifles, a requirement for walking in South Africa. Having taken many such walks over the years, I came to believe the guns were merely decorative.

Wendy and I never got very close to anything that could be considered dangerous (except for an encounter with Jeff Stutchberry and his rhino years ago, but that's for later). We'd been briefed about talking as little as possible and keeping our voices low—no louder than a whisper—and, if we did have a problem, to never—*never*—run.

We started out in single file with our ranger and spotter at the front of the line. One of our clients was at the back. We did actually encounter a herd of female elephants on the road, but we gave them a necessary wide berth, and they quickly seemed to melt into the shrubbery the minute they smelled and saw us. There was no further sign of major wildlife, though we stopped periodically to look at animal tracks in the road, discussed the insects we saw, and listened to our African spotter discuss various medications made from different kinds of plants that were used by his people.

We stayed on the road and came up over a small rise, with nothing in sight. Suddenly, our client at the back of the line walked quickly up and in a breathless whisper said forcefully, "Lion. *Lion!*"

On cue from our ranger, we all stopped and stared. Sure enough, not 40 feet away was a huge male lion that had obviously been sleeping and now, though still lying down, was fully awake and growling at us.

Immediately, a second large male lion head popped up about ten feet behind the first. He too was growling.

It is one thing to see sleeping lions while seated in the safety of your vehicle, but quite another to see them at eye level, growling and only one short pounce away. We were frozen in place, not sure what to do, but we *did* remember not to run. Our ranger spoke to us in a low voice, explaining these were the two dominant male lions in the area. We had heard they had eight prides of female lions that they shared. They were brothers and they were magnificent— and *enormous.*

Though they were still growling and our feet were rooted into the earth, we did manage—with our ranger's permission—to get a picture of the lions. As we turned slightly, much to our horror, we noticed another group of walkers from our lodge coming up the hill, directly into the path of the lions.

Shawn, our ranger, dispatched our spotter with his gun to head off the other group as quickly as possible. That left us with two big male lions, eight people, and one loaded rifle.

We were told to first walk backwards very slowly, down and away from the lions, then turn slowly and continue walking slowly in single file down the road. Shawn said he would be at our backs with his rifle.

We did as we were told and walked down the road and back to our vehicle. That was the end of our nature walk. The scenery was beautiful, the air clean and the hike *memorable.*

Later, Shawn said he thought we had been in only moderate danger, though he did allow that, had the lions charged, he would have had to shoot to kill. He would allow an animal to get to within 10 meters, then fire. These lions we encountered were only 10 feet beyond that point.

In all my years of traveling to Africa, this was a first for me. It made a good story and an even better photo, as Wendy, who was standing directly behind the ranger, managed to capture the lion's head with the ranger's head and gun in the foreground. No fancy camera available at that moment, she had only her little "point and shoot" camera, which was good enough!

## Accommodations in Africa, a close call, and Jeff

Africa is a continent rich with great animal adventures and stories and sometimes they involve people as well. One such story involved the Mikumi Lodge, in Western Tanzania.

We had just arrived in Africa and, rather than rest a night before setting out into the bush, we left directly on the long road trip to Mikumi Lodge. By the time we arrived there and had dinner, our entire group was exhausted and ready for sleep. The generators shut down at 10 PM and there would be no electricity until 6:00 the next morning, so we hurriedly went to bed.

Suddenly we heard a loud and constant banging next door. I decided the lodge must be doing construction, but couldn't understand why they would be working at this late hour. I got up, dressed, and stormed out to the lobby to find the manager—but I never made it that far.

Next door to us were our friends standing in the hall, while the staff valiantly tried to remove the doorframe to their room. Not the *door*, which was already off, but the entire doorframe.

It seems our friends had left their door open and gone across the hall to visit with their adult children who were accompanying them on the trip. Their kids had called to tell their parents to come see an elephant that was munching branches under their window. No sooner had Al and Lenore left their room (with their key inside on the table), than the wind blew the door shut.

A locked door in Tanzania presented serious problems, as

there were no spare keys. Each room had *one* key and, on several occasions through the years, we have checked out of lodges in Tanzania, and been driving away as a staff person would appear behind us, running frantically down the road. Someone had forgotten to turn in a key!

On this occasion, the problem required removing the doorframe, hence all the noise. But after an hour that was accomplished, and everything returned to normal—until the next morning.

Al came to breakfast with a worried look on his face. He said something was wrong, but he didn't know quite what it was. His hair had become sticky overnight. We all took a turn feeling the top of his head. It was definitely sticky, but we told him not to worry about it.

But the next morning he was even more worried. The problem was getting worse, but no one still had any idea what was wrong.

On the third day, however, Al himself figured it out. When he woke up each morning it was still dark and there were no lights, as the generator was not on. As he would move to slick back his hair with his daily application of Brillcream, he had been using his toothpaste instead!

Returning from an exciting African safari adventure, this would be yet another moment one would prefer not to have recorded in the travel journal. The rest of us, however, thought it was very funny.

On the same trip we moved onto Ruaha, a remote and beautiful region farther west in Tanzania. The road to Ruaha is magnificent and along the way we could see thousands of baobob trees—Africa's upside down tree—so-called because when it is not in leaf, its tree limbs look like roots and the Africans have a fable that *God got angry one day and stuck the tree in upside down.*

Although beautiful, the road to Ruaha was very rough for traveling and poorly marked. Eventually our drivers, who had never been there before, got lost along the way. We arrived at camp well after dark and could see nothing. Our group was more than a little concerned about the accommodations and the wild animals in the area.

We assigned everyone to the nearest cabins on the hill surrounding the main lodge, but that left Wendy and me, as trip leaders, to take the cabin that was farthest from the main lodge and quite remote. The toilet area was quite far from this cabin and we were told not to walk there at night, to just use the bush out back and stay very close to the cabin due to the large number of elephants that regularly came around the lodge area.

We were too lazy to look for our flashlights, so we simply felt our way to our bed and crawled into it. During the night, however, Wendy had to use the washroom, or bush.

She didn't want to wake me and planned to walk outside to the front of the cabin, where she thought she would simply step off to make her stop. But I awoke when I heard her footfall and decided to accompany her. I suggested, instead of the front, she go out the side door where we'd entered, and that's what we did. We could hear the rushing Ruaha River nearby but thought nothing of it.

When we awakened at dawn we looked out the front of our cabin. We saw that the little balcony Wendy nearly stepped off during the night overhung the raging Ruaha River, filled with a torrent of water from the recent rains, and rushing downstream amid boulders at a furious rate.

Had she stepped off the balcony the night before, she would have been swept downstream instantly and probably drowned. *That* was one close call we talked about for quite some time!

Still on the personal side, while camping on houseboats in Lake Kariba, we always knew when someone had used the bathroom because there was more than the sound of a flushing toilet. The water camp was the idea of Jeff Stutchberry, a hunter and character who looked like a thin, lanky version of Ernest Hemingway. Jeff ran the water camp while his tall, drop-dead gorgeous blond wife Veronica ran the Bumi Hills Lodge—both located on Lake Kariba in Zimbabwe.

I always thought they liked it that way. Veronica was very refined and her lodge was luxurious, impeccably tasteful, and smoothly run. Jeff was rough and ready, swore at the top of his lungs, and lived in cut-off jeans that had seen better days and a loose white shirt open to the navel revealing his blond, hairy chest. His look was topped off with a tattered wide-brimmed leather Aussie-type hat that had clearly seen a lot of warm weather.

We spent three nights and four days with Jeff on Lake Kariba in his water wilderness camp, which consisted of a central mother ship that served as the kitchen and dining room and had an after deck and upper deck for lounging and viewing animals. There was a small bedroom at the back, where Jeff lived.

Guests were assigned smaller houseboats, anchored around the mother ship in a side lagoon off the main lake. Each houseboat had two bedrooms with a common bathroom between. Every morning we were brought over to the mother ship for breakfast and the day's activities, and in the evening we returned to our houseboats.

But there was this one problem with the houseboats. The entry to the bathroom from each of the bedrooms was about a foot lower than the main doorway. So virtually *every* time someone went into the bathroom, he or she would invariably forget to duck, so—night or day (particularly as sound travels across the water when it is calm)—we would hear a loud thump, followed by the words "oh, shit" and, a few minutes later, the sound of a toilet flushing. It was a predictable ritual that became the joke of the camp.

Jeff exposed us to a variety of water activities and game runs on Lake Kariba. He showed us the sights and gave us an opportunity to try our hand catching tiger fish, aptly named for their sharp teeth—and for putting up a terrific fight.

Jeff's safari walks were by far the most exciting. We would head off with Jeff in the lead, carrying his elephant gun and quietly walk single file until Jeff motioned for us to stop. Then he would pontificate about a plant or animal track that we were looking at. One day, while pursuing a black rhino on foot, we could hear the animal snorting and breathing in the dense brush surrounding us. At times we could even smell it. Finally, we came across a pile of steaming dung. The rhino was very close.

When we asked what to do if a rhino charged us, Jeff said simply, "Climb a tree."

But there *were* no trees in the immediate area, just shrubs and dense bush. When this was brought to Jeff's attention, he simply shrugged, as if to say, "dumb people."

Fortunately, we never did see the rhino, and it never charged us. But that walk did get our adrenaline going.

Another memorable moment from that trip involved a middle-aged woman in our group that Jeff simply could not abide. First, she brought luggage enough aboard the houseboat for a trip around the world. Additionally, it was hard-sided luggage, which

Jeff pointed out was totally unsuitable for a safari. Then, one day at lunch she showed up in white pants. Jeff threw a fit!

"Where do you think you are—on a cruise?" he bellowed. Then he went on to chew her out for wearing the white pants. He was truly insufferable, and the poor woman sat stoically as he ranted on.

But that was Jeff Stutchberry. Like the safari guide Stan Lawrence Brown, everyone did *what* he wanted, *when* he wanted, regardless of what the itinerary showed or what we thought should happen.

As with Stan, we saw marvelous animal sights with Jeff and were exposed to the real Africa where time stands still.

We almost grew fond of him by the end of our four days with him, but we did understand why Veronica spent most of her time in her tidy lodge while Jeff lived on his houseboat away from civilization.

## Rain, roads, and lost in the jungle

Taking people to Africa and introducing them to the sights, sounds, places, and things I loved was rewarding to me on many levels. One person could not get over the fabulous sights and adventures he was experiencing. Every time we would see a giraffe or come around a bend that revealed a scenic view, Sy would burst forth with, "Oh my God!"

Soon the safari became known as the "Oh my God!" safari. In fact, when Sy didn't use that expression and the rest of us thought the scene warranted it, we would ask him, "Doesn't this rate an 'oh my God'?"

His enthusiasm for Africa was unbounded, and he was such a joy to travel with.

Sometimes, however, difficult moments are just that—difficult—and not everyone can go with the flow when situations go awry.

On one trip, for example, we had one of our board members who was a rough and ready oil executive. He had been raised in an oil town in Pennsylvania, was well-traveled, but totally down to earth. It was one of the rare times I traveled with someone on our board and I particularly wanted him to have a good time and be treated well.

Everything was going along as it was supposed to until we

were at Ngorongoro Crater, loading up the vehicles one morning to go down into the crater for the day.

All the passengers were loaded into our three vehicles, except John, Wendy, and me. Wendy and I typically split up to travel in different vehicles with different people, shifting around each day during the safari. I climbed into the next-to-last vehicle, and Wendy waited for John to get into the last vehicle. She would take the seat that was left.

John started to climb aboard, then abruptly got back out and began swearing. I was already seated in the vehicle behind the one John was in, and Wendy was standing next to him when he began ranting at the driver.

"*Damn it!*" John shouted, "This is the third pair of pants I've ripped on this same exposed screw. Why the hell don't you fix it?"

His face was red as he continued to yell, meanwhile everyone else was sitting and waiting, not knowing what to do. Then I heard Wendy's voice.

"Goddamit, John, get in the vehicle right now, sit down and shut up!" she shouted.

He promptly got in the vehicle and sat down quietly. Wendy got in behind John, and the driver started off.

Hearing this, I was dumbstruck. I couldn't believe Wendy had just spoken to one of my board members that way. What was she thinking? What would John say to me?

As it turned out, I needn't have worried. It seems that John's wife had told Wendy when she climbed in after her husband that day, "That was very good, Wendy. Nice going." And nothing further was said.

John regained his composure after that and we all remained good friends. Sometimes a little straightforward common sense works—sometimes it doesn't.

While touring Zambia and the Luanga Valley, we arrived by bus to transfer to our waiting vehicles for a four-hour ride to camp. It was already 3:00 PM and, as we began moving to the vehicles, it started to rain. There was one open vehicle, and the rest, much smaller, were closed.

We could not get to any of our raincoats and concluded quickly that it was going to be a long, miserable ride. Wendy picked the people in our group she thought could take a ride like that in the rain. Meanwhile, I piled everyone else into the closed vehicles. We started off, but not all in the same direction, as we were taking a game run approach to getting to camp.

Wendy sat up front with the young driver and left with her group huddled under one or two tattered wet blankets in the open vehicle. Their story was recorded as another example of things one does not think of when one thinks of going on safari.

After an hour the rain slowed, but by that time everyone was already wet and cold. They sang camp songs and pretended to be having a great time, but the humor was wearing thin. The driver, in an effort to get to camp faster, decided to take a short cut cross-country—they were, after all, in a landrover.

After another hour, with darkness setting in, the driver came to an abrupt halt in the middle of a herd of about 200 cape buffalo. When he put his head down on the steering wheel, Wendy asked him what was wrong. His quiet reply caused her to shudder.

"I'm lost," he said. "I have no idea where I am."

It was now dark as the young driver explained that this was his first day out of bed after having had malaria. He was unfamiliar with this route and had no idea how to get back to the main road.

Wendy decided not to share this information with the group of wet passengers who hadn't heard the driver and were staring off into the dark at the huge herd of buffalo surrounding the vehicle. Each seemed to be lost in thought at the moment. She encouraged the driver to relax and think slowly about where he might be. She had visions of sleeping in the vehicle, wet and cold, but was even more concerned that no one could even get out of the truck to use a bush with all the buffalo around them. As an afterthought, she remembered they were also completely unarmed, in the dark, in an open vehicle.

After what seemed like an eternity, but probably no more than 10 minutes, the young man turned to her and said quietly, "I think I might know where I can pick up the road about a mile or two from here."

Wendy encouraged him to try.

They started off and did indeed pick up the road that led into camp, where they arrived some three hours later. Soaked to the skin and chilled to the bone, the passengers in the open vehicle went straight to the huge bonfire that had been built to welcome them—and each of them threw down a straight triple scotch to warm up. Convinced they had to be the last ones to arrive in camp, to their amazement they saw that was not the case. None of the other vehicles had yet arrived.

"Where in the world are they?" the group's members wondered aloud.

I can answer that. I was with the other vehicles.

Our group had taken a slower route on roads that were extremely bumpy and now also very muddy from the rain, so progress was very slow.

At one point the road dipped, and we crossed a shallow stream. At the moment of crossing, a woman in the back of the vehicle cried out that she hit her head and was injured, causing us to stop and evaluate the situation. By the time we arrived at our camp, the woman's husband was irate, demanding that his wife see a doctor.

Of course the camp *had* no doctor. I had examined his wife and determined that no major injury had occurred. But he was insistent. The camp manager's wife was a registered nurse and examined her as well, concluding that she had no major injury but might have a mild concussion.

Nothing would placate her husband who said that she had chronic neck and back pain and this was sure to exacerbate it.

It might be noted here that this couple had been generous to the zoo through the years and the parting words of our development director as we were leaving on this trip were, "Be particularly nice to them as I think they might be interested in making a larger gift in the future."

Once Wendy and I were reunited in our assigned cabin, we heard a knock at the door. It was the husband who announced to us both, "The first thing I'm going to do when I get home is have my wife see her doctor. The second thing I am going to do is hold you personally—and the Zoo Society—accountable!"

He then turned on his heel and left. Wendy looked at me sheepishly.

"When your development director said be nice to them, I don't think this is *exactly* what she had in mind!" she said.

Happily for all concerned, nothing serious was wrong with our passenger, and she and her husband became good friends of ours after that experience. Nothing further was said.

# The amazing strong woman of the jungle

On the same trip where members of our group got lost, wet, and experienced other assorted mishaps, there was still another significant event—this one on Wendy's watch.

On a night game drive, where we used a bright spotlight to hunt for animals, locating them by the shine from their eyes, the open vehicle Wendy was in was traveling at about 30 miles an hour, over open terrain—until it hit an aardvark hole and stopped suddenly.

A woman passenger seated on the third tier top seats was thrown out of the vehicle and hit the ground—*head first*—while another woman in the middle seat was thrown out, except for her leg which had become entangled and was keeping her dangling outside the landrover.

Without thinking, Wendy leaped the more than 20 feet to the ground, neatly clearing the woman lying on the ground and went to lift up the woman dangling by her leg, in an attempt to take pressure off the woman's leg.

The driver quickly jumped out to help, and the woman was extricated. Fortunately, the woman who'd landed on the ground had sustained no serious injuries, and the woman who had been hanging by her leg recovered from her injury.

What was so amazing to many of us—including the driver—was Wendy's leap from the truck, which she couldn't have repeated again, *ever*. It was clearly the result of an adrenaline rush in a moment of crisis.

On another night drive on the same trip, one of our male passengers suddenly and unexpectedly called out in the pitch darkness, then crumpled to the floor of the vehicle. Beside him was a flailing Egyptian goose that had apparently been on the ground, became frightened by the vehicle as it sped by, and flew directly up and into the man's head. Goose and man were fine, and, when his headache subsided, everyone had a good laugh back around the campfire!

# Mountains, mist and those legendary gorillas

Africa is a big continent and our travels through the years were not limited to just East or Southern Africa. I recall three trips to Rwanda to climb and see the mountain gorillas, but the first trip up was probably the most memorable for me.

The year was 1985 and we had brought a group to visit Rwanda's Akagera National Park and Parc de Volcans—the first to see the beautiful park, the second to see the mountain gorillas. We also drove from Rwanda to Zaire up to the Ituri Forest to see pygmies living much the way they have for centuries.

We stayed in Kigali, the capital of Rwanda, at the Milles Collines Hotel, then drove to Gisenyi, the town from which we would drive each day to the Parc de Volcans to see the gorillas. The Meridian Hotel in Gisenyi was beautiful, set on the edge of Lake Victoria. The sunsets were marvelous, as were the accommodations. We enjoyed looking out across the lake to see fisherman in dugout canoes casting their nets in its rich fishing areas. It was an idyllic scene.

We had enough permits for each person to climb for two days to see the gorillas. The drill was to leave the Meridian very early each morning and drive for about an hour and a half to the ranger station outside the park. Along the way, we traversed the most beautiful country, rolling volcanic mountains that were covered in small subsistence farms that formed rolling patchwork patterns in every conceivable variation of green. Rwanda has been called the "Switzerland of Africa," and the name is appropriate.

On the roads, we passed women in colorful kangas of red, blue, orange, purple, and green, walking with their babies slung across their backs. They usually were carrying baskets of produce—bananas, plantains, or potatoes—on their heads. The men walked as well, but just as often they were wheeling bicycles up and down the hills. Rain or shine, people in Africa walk. It is the main form of transportation in rural areas, with the occasional donkey used for pulling small carts.

Arriving at the ranger station about 8 AM, we were briefed as to what we could expect and were given instructions about making certain none of us had a cold or cough or would leave anything in the park during our visit. We would then receive our official permits and were assigned one ranger and two porters to carry food and coolers. Our permits were good for that day only, allowing us to climb up and see the gorillas, spending a total of one hour with the habituated apes.

At the ranger's check-in area, we divided the group into three, based on where the different groups of gorillas had been the day before and how long each ranger thought it would take to find them again.

I took those people who were older or whom I thought would only be able to handle the shortest walk (or climb). Jim Heck, our tour escort and agent, and Wendy decided who could climb the farthest and led the groups that would have to walk perhaps four hours or more to get to where the gorillas were.

We started off across the farm fields that encircle the bottom of the mountain on which the gorillas live. As we walked through the fields of the subsistance farms, we attracted children like the pied piper and soon were walking single file with our porters behind us carrying cool boxes and lunches, followed by at least a dozen children.

It was cold and rainy, yet these children were barely clothed in thin, tattered, well-used clothes. They all had colds, and many had dreadful coughs, a result of being constantly undernourished, as well as wet and cold. Tuberculosis was making a real comeback in the region, and one could see why. Child mortality was extremely high—as much as 50% for children less than five years old.

As we walked slowly up the mountain, the air grew thinner. We climbed to 8,000 feet, then 9,000 feet. Soon we passed through the park gate and stepped over the grass and mud stile that stood as the official barrier between farmlands and the gorillas home.

Beyond the gate was a vast jungle of wet, thick vegetation. At the lower altitudes bamboo grew in thick, almost impenetrable stands, but broke away farther up the mountain yielding to eight-foot-high stinging nettles and dense underbrush. Our ranger was at the head of the line, hacking through the jungle with his machete and looking for signs of the gorillas.

Each day, people walked to where the gorillas were seen the day before in their mid-day resting place and then followed in the direction it was thought they went in hopes of finding them at rest around mid-day again.

The ranger pointed out "signs"—broken branches, trampled underbrush—indicating which way the gorillas went and we followed, climbing higher and higher, wearing stout gloves to pull ourselves up on the nettles or brush them out of our faces. The ground was slippery, muddy, hard going, and the trip was very tiring.

There was no guarantee of finding the gorillas, but on each occasion that we made the climb, we had good luck, and all managed to see them. Only once did we have a woman who had to turn back before seeing the gorillas. The climb had simply proved to be too physically taxing for her.

On this first trip we had one gentleman who was clearly having trouble keeping up with the group. I hung back and asked him what was wrong. We knew everyone was in good health, as we required a doctor's written approval before people were allowed to sign on for the trip. Still, halfway up the mountain, Jack was gasping for breath.

"If I had two lungs, I'd be okay," he said meekly, "but I only have one lung and am not supposed to be doing this."

I was stunned and appalled as I looked at Jack, seeing his color go from robust pink to pale gray. I could not believe his doctor had signed his permission form. Jack was insistent that he wanted to make this trip, so he had apparently applied pressure on his doctor. Whatever had transpired back home, Jack was now with me on the mountain, and I was responsible for his safety and well being.

I looked at Jack, who looked at me pleadingly. Finally, I told him I would go back down with him, but he was adamant, stubbornly insisting that we forge ahead. I was beginning to get a sense of how that conversation with his doctor had gone. He was a grown man, and I was in a situation that afforded me few options.

"Okay," I said to him after a moment, "but don't you dare die on me up here!"

We moved slowly on.

Jack did see the gorillas that day, and we made it back down alive, but I was not happy about the fright he put up. As someone who loves animals, travel, and adventure as much as I do, I could certainly understand how others would feel that way. Yet, it still mystifies me how intelligent adults will make decisions such as this that endanger their own lives, not to mention putting other people in the difficult situation of being responsible for their survival under trying circumstances.

We returned to Rwanda to see the mountain gorillas on several subsequent occasions through the years, and each time the experiences were rich and wonderful as we viewed different groups of gorillas and their youngsters.

It is awesome to be less than a foot from a huge silverback who has the power to crush a person with a single swipe of his arm, yet simply accepts that visitor as part of its extended family.

On one visit, Wendy actually had a huge female walk up next to her as she sat watching the rest of the gorilla's troop. After appearing to carefully study everything Wendy was wearing—never touching Wendy, but bringing her face only an inch from hers—the animal then grunted contently and lay down for a nap at Wendy's feet.

Wendy claimed the sound of her own heart beating was deafening and only hoped that the gorilla couldn't detect it. Apparently, as the gorilla snoozed on, there was no danger of that.

I am not a religious person, but some people—and I include myself in this—have described encounters with wild gorillas in their bucolic setting as a deeply moving, sort of "religious" experience. I have to admit, it's true.

On each visit, while I sat perfectly quietly with these magnificent, gentle giants and observed the interactions among mothers and infants or other family members, there was a point when we and they would seem to transcend the moment.

It's a feeling of being suspended in time, in a primordial forest setting, across the millions of evolutionary years where humans and the gorillas become one again—just primates, separated by nothing but a few slender strands of DNA. It is easy to forget the world beyond until I looked at the silverback next to me in Group 9. He had no forearm due to having it caught in a poacher's snare. Although he survived, the snare cost him his arm and I am reminded that these wonderful animals' future is far from certain.

I will never forget my time spent with the mountain gorillas, a few hours that are among my most memorable spent in Africa.

Recounting that first trip to see the mountain gorillas in Rwanda, after two days with them we moved on through beautiful Akagera National Park, a place filled with zebra and gazelles, topi, and other types of antelope.

We stayed at a wonderful private home, run by an eccentric French woman, and took extensive photographs of zebras chest-high in yellow flowers brought forth in the rainy season. Sadly, these pictures that were at first snapshots of a wonderful time in a beautiful place, became tragic remembrances of a park and all its animals that were completely wiped out by the subsequent war in Rwanda several years later.

# The sadly indescribable roads of Zaire

We drove across the border into Zaire, to Goma, a forgotten little colonial town consisting of a small main street, where once-proud Belgian government buildings stood decaying next to African shacks constructed after the Belgians left "their" Congo and turned it over to what became Africa's new nation of Zaire.

Older children in the unpaved dirt streets were wheeling homemade scooters ingeniously carved from wood, while younger boys played with charming little toys made of wire with wheels that could be rolled along. We bought one of those toys from a boy about six years old, who beamed proudly. We also acquired some wooden sculptures and a lovely ceramic mask that was a contemporary rendition of the traditional mask made in wood. It came from a tiny art gallery that was wedged in between two rather imposing old buildings.

Years later, when we saw news photos showing more than a million refugees pouring into Goma from Rwanda during the war, it was impossible to imagine this little town or how all those people could even fit into such a small space, much less think of the lack of sanitary conditions that prevailed.

Even later, when we saw how lava from the volcanic eruption had oozed through the center of Goma, down its main street, it was equally hard to believe we had once stood right in the middle of that street, next to the bank building that was ultimately en-gulfed in the lava flow.

We left Goma around lunchtime and started our two-day trek into Zaire on roads that can generously be described as atrocious.

Warned in Rwanda about "the Zaire roads," we had to ex-perience them to appreciate what in the world the Rwandan guides meant.

When the Belgians pulled out of Zaire, they left no infrastruc-ture behind, so what passed for roads were merely glorified dirt byways that crisscrossed the country in a haphazard manner. The problem, as if that description wasn't *problem* enough, was the roads had to accommodate not just local vehicular traffic, but the many heavy trucks that had to get across Zaire on a transcontinental route.

The ruts created by this heavy traffic were deep—more like gorges than ruts—so when it rained, whole vehicles could be, quite literally, lost in them—but more about that later.

We had to allow two days to get from Rwanda into Zaire to reach our remote mountain lodge near Mt. Hoyo in the Ituri Forest. It was only about 90 miles, but after driving along for a few hours, we would be stopped for a few hours more at the next impasse, usually created when rain turned the road into a swamp, causing multiple vehicles to become stuck and create an extremely effective roadblock. Nothing could move.

So we pressed on and, after day one—and being stuck several times but managing to extricate ourselves—we spent the night in a charming auberge outside a small, unremarkable town.

Going through the town as the sun was settling in the west, we couldn't imagine where we might stay, but of course our tour guide knew we were in for a treat. On the other side of the town we turned down a little unmarked dirt road, which led to a flowering oasis with an absolutely gorgeous European inn. It was a classic colonial home that had been turned into an inn run by a French woman. This little auberge was a true respite from the red earth we had "eaten" and been coated with all day. The white stucco building with the thatched roof and beautiful walled garden full of flowers could not have looked more out of place.

It was warm, friendly, comfortable, and provided us with such delicious food, we thought we had temporarily been transported to Provence for the evening. As we sat on the veranda after dinner in the semi-darkness sipping liqueurs, we watched thousands of fruit bats—a virtual black cloud of them—heading out to feast on the banana fields of the nearby village.

A full moon appeared shortly thereafter, and I remember how much it seemed we were again in another place and time, all of it magical.

The next morning, however, when we were back on the African roads in the dust and ruts, we knew that our respite to a magical place had been merely temporary.

After taking one of these rough roads that climbed through a gorgeous green patchwork of mountains, dotted with subsistence farms and crossing the mountain passes at the top, we descended into a more dense forest region that marked the beginning of the Ituri Forest, home to the pygmies.

We were making good time and looked forward to an early afternoon arrival at the mountain lodge. But then, as a friend of ours says about safaris, TAB reared its head. TAB stands for "That's Africa Baby!" It means that anything that *can* happen, will. And, of course, it did.

We encountered a bad stretch of muddy road that brought more than a dozen cars, carts, and trucks together in a huge roadblock. We sat for several hours waiting while a secondary road was built around the vehicle that had created the initial problem, then simply cooled our heels in the truck, remembering this was part of the overall experience.

By mid-afternoon, a pygmy woman, wearing nothing but a thin G-string walked passed our open mini-bus where we sat glumly inside. She walked with her head down, picking her way carefully through the deep muddy ruts of the road, but as she approached our open door, she demurely looked up and, offering a faint smile, said, "Bonjour" and walked on.

It seemed incongruous, but was actually totally in keeping. We were on the edge of the Ituri Forest, where the pygmies live, and the official languages in Zaire are Swahili and French. Seeing that we were not African, the pygmy woman had courteously chosen the logical language to greet us. I will never forget this wonderful naked little lady speaking to us in perfect French. This to me was all part of the experience of Africa.

# A place to stay, naked pygmies, and butterflies

The mountain lodge was so remote that it was truly on the road less traveled. To get there, we had to cross a rattling, wooden one-lane bridge stretched over a steep gorge. To cross the bridge, however, our driver had to get out of the vehicle, assess the logs that made up the bridge, align them just "so," then climb back into the vehicle and *gun* the engine so we got across quickly. The driver of the vehicle behind had to go through the same process, as *our* vehicle had scattered the logs as we drove across.

We all held our breath while crossing the precarious wooden structure, headed for the lodge. The trip was even more perilous as, by the time we reached the bridge, we had to cross it in almost total darkness, and the logs were slippery because of the heavy rains that had fallen.

En route to the lodge we stopped several times to buy fruit, vegetables, and other items that we planned to eat at the lodge. We thought we would simply be supplementing the food supply, but discovered upon our arrival that the lodge had no food—other than what we were prepared to provide for ourselves. The lodge did, however, have a reasonably well-stocked bar.

We discovered we were the first visitors of the year (this was *May*) and that the last visitors had come and gone more than six months before. Clearly, business was not so good, but it didn't matter. It was a place to sleep after a very tiring two-day drive on impossible roads.

The bar was quite an interesting set up. Wendy and I visited it after settling in and discovered they did have scotch, so that was what we requested. Apparently, we were the only people in the bar—*and* in the large, attached dining room. The others in our group were still in their cabins, as we had agreed to meet around 7:30 and it was only 7 o'clock.

As we waited, our eyes began to grow accustomed to the dark that was only alleviated by the presence of one candle in the entire bar area. While we'd thought we were alone, we could now see that inside the dining area and bar were about 10 or 11 African men, lounging on the furniture and watching us. If that wasn't unnerving enough, as our vision improved, we saw even more people who were apparently sleeping or relaxing at the lodge.

It was an eerie experience for us, but turned out that these folks were just as interested in us as we were curious about them. They were definitely not pygmies, and we never did find out where they came from and what they did.

The next morning at dawn, Wendy and I heard low singing sounds coming from in front of the lodge. We peered out of our rather grimy bedroom window, then dressed and wandered onto the lawn area of the lodge, which we could now see for the first time.

There was a chill in the air as the early morning mountain fog settled over the lodge like a light blanket, covered its few lawn chairs, then skipped over to the old, abandoned tennis courts.

Oblivious to the damp fog—and seeming to have appeared from nowhere—were dozens of almost totally naked pygmy men, women, and children forming a large circle around the lodge's gravel driveway. They stood proudly behind small clothes and animal skins that had been carefully laid down on the ground upon which they had put their wares to sell.

How did they even know we were there? Clearly, they knew, and they were ready to sell things to the tourists.

Their wares included simple, handmade, and used objects. Traded shell necklaces strung with alternating seeds from forest trees, some leather pouches, wristbands of seeds and leather woven together, and practical items, such as leather wrist-guards for bow and arrow shooting.

Although diminutive in size, with warm smiles that spread from ear to ear on their round, wizened faces, the pygmies were tough bargainers. Although their economy is based on the barter system and they were willing to trade, hard currency was really what they wanted.

Most of the women had babies in their arms or on their backs, tucked into hammock-type back slings. Later, when the men and women danced for us, both sexes adoringly carried their babies at all times and constantly cooed to them lovingly.

Leaves were the method of choice for covering private parts of the pygmy anatomy, but modesty was not something they seemed to be concerned about. They were who they were and they, quite simply, liked being who they were. The expression that came along later, to be "comfortable in their own skin," fit them perfectly—and quite literally.

We gathered the members of our group for a rather spartan cold breakfast. Afterward, the market portion of the pygmies' visit escalated into some serious bartering and bargaining. Eventually, we were shopped out, and the pygmies then gathered for what appeared to be (though I couldn't be sure) a spontaneous dance.

Their dance consisted of soft chanting and singing while slowly walking in a circle around a small bonfire they had built. Everyone participated. Those too young to walk were carried and lovingly passed from one family member to another. The babies were doted on and appeared totally content as the dance progressed, even though it didn't seem to have a middle or an end. The fog lifted when the dancing came to an abrupt end, seemingly in as impromptu a way as it had started.

By early afternoon, we were reassembled for a walk to enjoy the forest plant and animal life. We headed into the woods single file, with a pygmy man at the head of the line, and one bringing up the rear. Each was eager to point out different plants and animals, which were invisible, except for a breathtakingly beautiful array of colorful butterflies.

On our way to the lodge, we had noticed clouds of yellow and white butterflies gathering around pools of water in the road, greedily sucking up the liquid, and then flying off as our vehicle approached. But here in the forest the yellow and white butterflies became a rainbow of colorful varieties, most of which we had never seen before.

Wendy was in her element. She had been an amateur lepidopterist as a child and could broadly classify many of the butterflies, but specific identification of species eluded her. As she stayed back with the pygmy man at the end of the line, he eagerly pointed out fluttering specimens or ones that hastily alighted, always eluding her camera shutter. The butterflies simply did not remain in one place long enough to be photographed.

Wendy found that her pygmy guide knew something about collecting butterflies and had actually been trained in how to preserve dead specimens for collection purposes. At the end of the walk, he proudly presented her with dozens of small folded white triangular packets, each the size of a toast point that would accompany an order of caviar. Each one held a brilliantly colored exotic specimen. It was too tempting for an old butterfly collector to pass up. She bought many of them and still has them to this day.

# The shortcut and the art of the deal—the African way

We returned to the lodge that evening, and the pygmies vanished into the forests as quietly as they had first appeared. When we departed early the next morning, there was no evidence they had ever been there. In the chilled morning fog there was no market assembled, no soft singing, no warm smiles. We left the mountain reluctantly and began our long journey home.

Using a short wave radio at the lodge, tour guide Jim Heck had arranged to make our return journey a bit shorter. In an effort to cut a full day out of the long ride back, he arranged a charter flight at a midpoint in the trip. The charter was to take us back to Goma, where we would transfer back into Rwanda, then to Kigali, back to Europe, and home. The thought of having one less day of traveling on those incredible Zaire roads sounded too good to be true.

The trick was to leave the mountain lodge very early in the morning and catch the 4 PM charter flight. We were warned that because we were not the only passengers on the charter flight, we simply could not be late as they would not wait for us.

Our first three hours on the road were slow, but uneventful, then once again, TAB intervened. We came to the mother of all roadblocks. It was in a small village on the edge of the Ituri Forest, not far from where our naked French-speaking pygmy lady had said hello to us.

We arrived in the town and came to an abrupt halt behind a line of some 20 cars and trucks that were up to their axels in mud and, apparently, had been for two full days. An equally long line of cars and trucks was stuck facing in the opposite direction. Nothing was moving.

We got out and assessed the situation, learning that an entire oil tanker had "disappeared" in a rut in the road. All that was sticking out from the mud hole was the top of the oil tanker section and the top of the truck's cab. When I said the road ruts in Zaire were deep, I was not exaggerating. I wondered what was potentially more dangerous, wondering what might be the next move of an aggressive giant mountain gorilla, a nearby African pride of lions or a Zaire road?

It was clear that there was no way we were going to catch the charter aircraft in time without some serious intervention. So Jim Heck, the never daunted tour guide, launched into action.

First, he bribed our way to the front of the line of cars and trucks waiting to pass. Next, he negotiated with the tribal elders of the village to build a secondary road around the oil tanker that was stuck in the main road.

He agreed to purchase some of the forest trees in order to

construct a second road. Then he hired laborers from the village to cut the timber and actually build the road.

Through it all, Jim was courteous while the villagers argued about the best way to build the road. Finally, protocol demanded that he thank them all for their efforts when everything was completed and we could once again be on our way.

Because Jim is fluent in both Swahili and French and has lived in Africa, he knows how things work and was able to make all this possible.

Six hours later, we were on our way again, in a mad dash to catch the charter flight.

Just before we pulled into a small town, Jim stopped our two vehicles to remind all the women in our group it was time to change clothes. We had been warned that because we were taking the charter flight from a Muslim village, the women in our party could not be wearing pants, even if we were only transferring from our vehicles to the plane.

We had just spent four days sloshing through mud, so everyone was in pants and hiking boots of various kinds, all coated in mud. But this matter was non-negotiable, so the women quickly found skirts in their luggage and deftly slipped into them—*over their pants and hiking boots*. I was able to take a great photo of Wendy boarding the plane as she was dressed in what can only be described as "safari chick," as opposed to *safari chic!*

The plane was a marvel. An old C47 transport, it had been stripped of seats, except for the "first class" section, and planks had been placed alongside both sides inside the main fuselage. We boarded and sat in a row on the planks. In the center, between the planks, were crates of live chickens.

We were grateful that the chickens were lashed down and wished we could say the same for the passengers. There were no seatbelts, so as we took off we all slid to the back of the plane and into each other, whereupon we quickly needed to use the supplied food bags for airsick bags. It was so rough that everyone on board immediately became sick.

Well, not everyone. Wendy had managed to secure a first class seat next to an African man dressed in an ill-fitting, very well worn suit. Our assigned seats on the flight were determined based on the flight crew's assessment of our weight, so it was not a matter of choice, rank, first come-first served, or who belonged to the frequent flyers' club. Although seemingly in a much better situation than the rest of us, Wendy later reported she practically gagged when the man sat down next to her as he either hadn't had a bath for several years or had used his suit pants as an outhouse. She never determined which—and hoped to go to her grave never knowing the answer. Without a doubt, it was a three-hour flight neither of us would ever forget, but it *did* save us a day over the dreaded Zaire roads!

# Great places, simple pleasures, and an elephant ride I will never forget

Though we went to Africa more than most other places, as it is conceded to be *the* place to see big herds of fabulous mammals, we have also taken groups to many other great places in search of exotic animals.

Several trips to Papua New Guinea stand out as particularly interesting and exciting, along with a wonderful trip to India and Nepal. We visited Australia several times, as well as Chile, Argentina, Easter Island, the Galapagos, and to our own Alaska.

Papua New Guinea brings up wonderful recollections of watching as the people of this small nation were catapulted from the Stone Age into the twentieth century.

On our first visit there in 1983, we encountered mostly people in native dress in the highland region where the famed Wigmen live. Less than 18 months later, fewer than half the locals were in native dress, and, two years after that only, a handful of older men could be seen wearing their incredibly decorated and colorful wigs and loin cloths. A photo of Wendy's, taken in the village outside of Tari Lodge, speaks volumes about this transition. A wigman in full regalia, with leaves front and back covering his private parts, stands next to huge Kawasaki motorcycle and behind them both is a large "Takeaway" food sign.

I'll long remember PNG for its barter system with a first, second, and occasionally, a third price for artworks, including many amazing wood sculptures, masks, pottery, and baskets. On a remote part of the Black River, a tributary off the Sepik River, there were few tourists in the mid-1980s. We met a man who couldn't wait to move the process along. Following the first price and before we could counter with a polite "And what is the second price?" he pre-empted us with: "First price is 50 Kina, and second price is 30 Kina." Of course we asked for—and usually *bought*—things at the third price, the kina, at that time, being roughly equivalent to the U.S. dollar.

Unfortunately, little wildlife remains to be seen in PNG, especially in the Sepik River region where crocodiles have been hunted almost to extinction. In the Highlands, we did find different species of birds of paradise, with each species occupying a distinct niche depending upon the altitude of the region.

We had a stunningly beautiful visit to a little village at dawn to see the male Raggiana bird of paradise. The birds were plentiful in the village as the tribal chief had made killing a bird tantamount to murder. Anyone found guilty of killing a bird would, in turn, be killed. As the philosophy of many tribes in PNG, particularly in the Highlands, is retribution—an eye for an eye—this was considered very reasonable. The birds in turn were good business as to see the males displaying and calling at dawn, we each had to pay a village entry fee.

Intertribal warfare and retribution is still very much alive in Papua New Guinea, particularly in the Highlands, which were explored first by Europeans only about 70 years earlier. The warfare is normally not considered a threat to tourists.

While traveling in the Highlands on our first trip in 1983, we found ourselves in the middle of a tribal war. However, when the men saw our minibus coming down the road, they obligingly halted their war and waited until our bus had passed before going back to shooting arrows and wielding their machetes, which are truly lethal weapons, at each other.

Probably the most "native" experience we ever had in PNG was staying at a lodge run by a village of wigmen in the Highlands. They were true entrepreneurs, staging a dance for us, showing us their village—*including their ancestors' skulls*—and providing overnight accommodations for us, with breakfast the following morning.

The accommodations were rustic, at best, with one being a little two-room building with two beds to each room. The two couples that slept there said the next morning they could hear each other breathing, as the straw walls were so thin. The rest of us made do with several army cots that had pillows, but no blankets or sheets. There were no towels to wash with, and the outside lavatory was about a block away. In the interests of etiquette, there was one for women and one for men. Etiquette notwithstanding, it rained that night and I managed to have a case of *the trots*, so I found myself becoming very familiar with the route . . . in the pouring rain . . . from my uncomfortable cot . . . to the equally bad toilet . . . and back again . . . about once every hour.

In the morning we assembled for our hosts' idea of a European breakfast: hot coffee, sliced cold bread, peanut butter, and marmalade. Breakfast was served in a four-sided cement room with open windows. Actually, there were *no windows*, just wooden frames set into squares in the cement where windows might have been, should it have occurred to someone to install them.

Our waiters were wigmen in their local dress, who kept wandering in and out of the room to look at us. This story is offered for the benefit of those people who believe there's little adventure left in travel.

One more thought on Papua New Guinea and food. On our first trip to Papua New Guinea, following an international conference in Australia, we led a merry group that consisted of other zoo directors and some of their wives. What had originally been scheduled as a post-conference trip had been cancelled for lack of interest. Wendy and I decided to go anyway, but in the weeks before we were to leave for Australia, some of my colleagues called to ask if they could join us. So it became known as "the Fisher Trip"—especially as things began going awry.

Most of my colleagues had led their own safaris on behalf of their respective institutions. Dr. Ken Searle, a Brit who had decided at the last minute to join our group, had his medical practice in Hong Kong, where he was also the Director of the Hong Kong Zoo. As we were leaving Papua New Guinea and waiting for our flight at the Port Moresby Airport, Ken asked Wendy if she would like a cup of coffee. Moments later, as they were sipping their coffee and talking, I went behind the counter, to the preparation area, and was appalled at what I saw.

The cups and dishes were not being washed, but were simply being reused as needed. The waiter would take a cup, dip it into a vat of coffee (using his *hand*), give the outside of the cup a quick wipe, and set it down for the next customer to take. To describe the preparation area as dirty would be generous. I immediately became concerned, thinking of the many exotic bugs Wendy and Ken were ingesting at that moment. Wigmen, other locals and tourists were all drinking the coffee. I had visions of our 48-hour trip that would take us from Papua New Guinea to Australia, the Philippines to Japan. Over the Pacific to Los Angeles, then home to Chicago with Wendy being deathly ill the whole time. Fortunately, Wendy rarely becomes ill, and neither she nor Ken seemed to suffer any ill effects of the coffee. Still, I decided not to tell them what they had been drinking until we were all safely back home.

On another trip to Papua New Guinea—this one with a Lincoln Park Zoo group—we were coming home through Manila. We arrived there shortly after President Marcos had been deposed, and the country was still in the immediate aftermath of the coup. On every floor of the hotel, militiamen with machine guns stood guard at the elevators and entrances to each hall. I spent a very uncomfortable night, lying awake, concerned about the safety of our group and dealing with a terrible case of dysentery. The flight out of Manila to Japan could not come soon enough.

In Nepal, I had one of my more personally uncomfortable safari experiences.

We began a rafting trip down the Karnali River by arriving at the entry point of the trip later than we had planned. Instead of finding a little camp by the river, as we'd been led to expect, we had to first rappel down a steep cliff to reach the camp. This came after the four-hour ride in broken down buses from the town of Nepulgunge (a town, as it turns out, quite aptly named)—*at night*.

It was certainly interesting getting 16 adults—many of them over 60—down the side of a cliff with ropes in total darkness. Little did I know, however, that our fun was just beginning.

We subsequently rafted down the Karnali River in what was to be a float trip, but turned into three days of "shooting the rapids," as the river was low and turbulent and had apparently not been recently visited by the local tourism board.

Along the way, we caught our own jungle fowl for dinner and used pup tents to camp at the edge of the river each night. At the raft trip's end, we stayed at a permanent tented camp that had been set up very much like the tented safari camps in Africa. We had American fare at breakfast each day, a Nepalese lunch, and a brilliantly created continental dinner with excellent wines every night. We had magnificent birding opportunities—and we actually got a glimpse of a tiger in the early sun one day, as it walked along the banks of the river at dawn.

On the last afternoon of the trip, we were afforded an opportunity to ride the elephants at a nearby elephant camp. But when we arrived, we learned that we would be riding our elephants without the traditional *houdas* or elephant seats. Instead, two of us piled onto each elephant, behind the mahout, who sat astride the elephant's neck, right behind its ears.

By the time I climbed on and took my place—third person back—I was at the point where the elephant's back begins to widen *substantially*. My legs stuck out at an awkward angle, much as if I were doing "the splits." I'm sure I could have handled such an arrangement easily if the elephant ride were a few minutes long, but instead, two hours passed with me stuck in that position.

By the time we returned from our little amble through the forest, I was in agony. Efforts to get me down from the elephant only made it worse. I had visions of a split pelvis, never being able to have sex or to go the bathroom again or perhaps worse.

The elephant dutifully followed the mahout's command to lie down on its haunches. When it did so, I was still a full eight feet off the ground. All the members of our party were convulsed in hysterical fits of laughter at the sight of me. I literally had to be pulled off the elephant and doubted that I would ever walk properly again.

Sometimes when I lie awake at night I can still picture Wendy with an 18-foot python wrapped around her at the snake farm near Bangkok, Thailand, or I see her inside a compound at the Pretoria Zoo with the zoo director—and five adult male cheetahs sniffing her and growling. I would not have done either of those things.

Or I see the image of a friend of ours, wallowing in mud up to her crotch, after she'd stepped off a plank on her way through the mud to a remote village on the Sepik River in Papua New Guinea. We all stood laughing hysterically, as she kept shouting, for help until we realized the shouts were real and she truly needed help!

I can still feel the bugs of every size and description, crawling all over my body in the dark, in Zaire at a lodge that had seen better days. It was an etymologist's delight, but definitely not *my* idea of the way to a good night's sleep.

Or I can feel my knee twisting in directions it was never meant to go, as we traversed the canopy top of the jungle bushes in Nyungwe Forest in Rwanda, trying to follow a group of Colobus monkeys brachiating effortlessly through the trees above, as we struggled mightily to keep upright below.

# Losing people—living a safari leader's worst nightmare

Very honestly, I love the life I have been leading. My animal adventures have taken me through the range of emotions with experiences that were interesting, fascinating, touching, strange, sad, exciting, frightening, and simply fun.

Two of my most memorable—and *worst*—experiences were not among those described so far, nor when we lost luggage (which can actually be a *very* big problem at the time). My worst experiences occurred when I actually *lost* people on safari. Fortunately for all concerned, they were not lost permanently.

The first instance was in 1979, while on a safari in India. I was going through a divorce at the time. Kevin Bell, then the zoo's curator of birds, accompanied me on what we would come to describe as "the trip from hell." It started badly and got worse as the days went along.

Our arrival in Bombay was delayed, and it was the middle of the night when we finally reached the city, so there was no one on hand to meet us. After eight hours—during which one member of our group kept railing at me to "do something"—I commandeered an old school bus to get us to Kanha, the main national park. Because we arrived so late and it was dark, the park ranger would not let us in.

"There are wild animals in the park!" he kept repeating.

"That's why we're here!" I kept telling him.

But the ranger had the key to the park, and he refused to unlock the gate. We spent the night in the bus.

Our itinerary next included an enjoyable visit to the holy city of Veranasi, where we strolled the narrow streets, and a local resident emptied a chamber pot onto the heads of our group, as we passed beneath his window.

The trip had been planned around our seeing the total eclipse of the sun. That the overnight ride on the train to Hyderbad proved so harrowing was *not* part of the plan. After dinner, when

I walked the railroad cars to check on the members of our group, I came upon the stewards. They were using an old dirty rag and a slop bucket to wash dishes—*in the same area where they had cooked our meal*—on a platform, outside, between the cars. As we had already eaten, there was no point in saying anything. At that moment I just prayed no one would become ill. (No one did and I have no idea *why*.)

It was a few days later that I lost one of my clients.

The woman was small, frail, elderly and had not traveled much. She was easily confused; such as if the group were starting off in one direction, she'd go in another. She also never seemed to understand the briefings on the day's activities and constantly re-peated her questions. Then there was the fact that she was a heavy smoker with a persistent hacking cough that annoyed most everyone and would be visited upon us at the most inopportune times. One would think that such a person would be gladly missed, but my responsibility to the group did not allow for that.

We were in New Delhi, on our way to the Taj Mahal. I was concerned about this particular member of the group as, in addi-tion to being elderly and having a smoker's cough, she had also caught a cold. After consulting a doctor, it was decided that she should stay behind, in the care of the hotel manager, and rest for a few days.

On our first day out, I thought it wise to call the hotel and check on her. Making phone calls in India in those days was a challenge in itself, but after several attempts, I eventually reached the hotel manger, who told me very matter-of-factly, "She's gone."

"What do you mean?" I asked, feeling a sinking feeling taking hold of me. "How could she be gone?"

"She left this afternoon," the manager said. "You owe me 4,000 rupees."

"Never mind the rupees!" I shouted. "Where did she go? She's a frail old woman in India! How could she just be gone?"

But the conversation went nowhere as he only kept repeating the words "gone" and "4,000 rupees" over and over. He did sug-gest that she might be trying to catch up with our group, but he couldn't know for sure.

To reach the Taj Mahal, as with traveling in India generally, is not simply a matter of going from point A to point B. Travel was complicated, and whatever could go wrong usually did. I was frantic.

But, sure enough, later that evening the woman turned up in the lobby of our hotel in the city of Agra. Though she looked a bit worse for wear, she was all right. She couldn't tell me how she made her way there, but it didn't matter. She *was* there, and that was all I needed at the moment.

I had a stiff drink and went to bed, vowing I would never again lose a client on safari as long as I lived. And I didn't.

No, I didn't lose a client. But in Africa in 1993, I did something worse. For two full days, *I lost my wife.*

We had just ended a wonderful week in Uganda, as one of the first tour groups to visit that country after Idi Amin's tyrannical rule had ended. We'd spent our second week in Tanzania. From there our plan was to fly from Arusha, Tanzania up to Cairo, then down to Aswan for our final week and a Nile River cruise. The week in Egypt had been Wendy's idea. It was a country she had longed to visit.

Our international flight on Air Ethiopia included a stop in Addis Ababa, Ethiopia. The plan was to be up at 4 AM Sunday morning, getting everyone a light breakfast, and be at the airport by 6:00 AM. Our group seemed understandably tired and cranky, but was very happy with what they'd seen on safari. We were ready for a luxurious, relaxing final week on the Nile.

Our boarding passes in hand, we made our way to the gate, only to find it crammed with other passengers awaiting this same flight. In some situations, manners need to be left at the gate, so we urged everyone to move toward the front of the line and push. We divided our people into pairs. One person from each pair boarded the plane and found seats quickly, while the other went to identify their luggage on the tarmac before boarding.

The mass of bodies surged forward. I led the group members who were boarding the plane, and Wendy was positioned at the back of the group with those members who were going out to identify their luggage.

I didn't suspect any problems until Wendy came barreling down the aisle of the plane to find me in the very last row. I couldn't see any of my clients, but the plane was full and I assumed they were all seated.

"Quick—give me my passport!" Wendy said breathlessly. As

managing groups in foreign airports frequently has a strong component of chaos, I still did not suspect anything was wrong.

We landed in Addis Ababa and disembarked for the three-hour layover. It was then I learned—to my horror—*Wendy was not with us.*

And *no one* seemed to know where she was.

I raced to the Air Ethiopia agent and demanded she tell me what had happened to my wife. She allowed as how too many people had attempted to board the flight, and there was simply not enough room. The others would be on the next flight, and Wendy, would catch up with us in Addis Ababa.

When she did not arrive on the next flight—or any incoming flight—and we were ready with our plan to go on to Cairo, I was assured she would join us there.

The next leg of the trip was a long four hours to Cairo, and I was not really worried. When our plane landed, things seemed to take a turn for the worse. We had no luggage. *None* of our luggage had made it onto the flight. People in our group who had been asked to identify our luggage on the tarmac acknowledged they had not done so, but had just boarded the plane hurriedly—the last to board—thanks to Wendy's insistence with the airline agent.

None of the airline people in Cairo had any idea as to the whereabouts of Wendy—*or* our group's luggage.

The plan called for us to spend the night in Cairo at the same hotel where we stayed upon our arrival in Africa. Everyone in the group was tired, sweaty, and not in a good mood. The weather in Tanzania had been warm, but it was quite cool in Cairo, and no one had a change of clothes, or even their jackets. They asked me if the airline would pay for replacement clothes, and I tried not to laugh as I explained that I doubted Air Ethiopia was among the airlines that compensated passengers for lost luggage, but I dutifully inquired anyway.

As soon as we arrived at the hotel I called Jim Heck, our tour agent. He knew nothing of what was happening, but he became concerned and said he would get on the matter immediately.

As each minute passed without a word or sign of Wendy, I became more frantic. I knew her to be intelligent and resourceful, but still . . . where *was* she?

Later that night, there was a knock at my door. A couple from our group had just received a phone call from Wendy. She told them she was in Tanzania's coastal capitol city, Dar es Salaam—a very long way from where I had last seen her (and a long way from where I was). By the way, she said she had all the luggage.

She planned to connect up through Cairo in the next two days and join the group somewhere en route along the Nile. She wasn't sure exactly where.

I was greatly relieved to know she was safe. Still, I had no idea how or when we would reconnect. Or when our people would next see their luggage. I wished I could have spoken with her myself, but apparently when she called, this particular couple were the only ones who had been in their room. Everyone else had been at dinner or off somewhere.

It was a very long night. I kept going over what had happened—*wondering* what had happened. Would she be okay? When would I see her again? The questions kept running through my mind, but no answers followed. Eventually, exhausted, I fell asleep at some point.

When morning came there was nothing to do but press on with the planned itinerary of the trip. To remain at the hotel and continue worrying did not seem like a good use of anyone's time.

We left the hotel and boarded an Air Egypt flight to Aswan, arriving mid-morning and taking the planned tour of the city and the dam. Throughout the day the group kept up its steady stream of complaints about its missing luggage, lack of fresh clothes, etc. Their welfare was my responsibility. I was sympathetic to their problem, but much more concerned with the fact that my wife was out there somewhere alone!

The group boarded the cruise ship and settled in quickly—*what with not having any luggage to unpack!* Everyone made their way to the upper deck to watch the casting off. The leisurely luxury cruise down the Nile had begun on schedule.

We were to head for Essen, tie up there for the night, and continue on in the morning. Night came quickly, as it does near the equator. As the ship moved out through the black, still water my thoughts remained with Wendy. I became more and more worried as the night wore on.

Around 11 PM the ship slid alongside the quay at Essen, and I received word from the Captain that someone wanted to see me.

In the pitch black of night, out of a tiny, dingy shack about 30 feet from the end of the gangplank came Wendy, followed by five, large Arab porters carrying the now famous luggage.

Our group assembled quickly when word was sent to them, but they were all so concerned for the return of their luggage that no one thought to ask where Wendy had been for the past two days. One of them was even quite put out, growling, "It's about time you got here! We've been without our luggage for two days!"

We did find a funny moment.

I had arranged with the kitchen to get something for Wendy to eat. Afterwards, it being a beautiful moonlit night—*we were, after all, on the Nile*—and we wanted to walk along the quay for a block or two, in full view of the guard at the gangway. As we started to walk off the gangway, his response was a quick, "You can't walk along there."

I explained to him that we were only going for a short walk along the quay, where it was well lit, and he could watch us the whole time.

"Sir," he responded in his best *British* English, "It is very dangerous out there for you—and especially for the lady."

Wendy allowed herself a small, bemused smile.

"I have been out there by myself for two days—with 18 pieces of luggage," she said quietly. "I think we'll be okay."

As we took out short stroll, Wendy began telling me the long, very interesting story of her two days away from the group. That story is almost a book in itself, but I will tell how she contacted us in Cairo.

As I had all the paperwork for the trip with me, Wendy had no itinerary or contact lists of any kind. But Wendy is a shopper and, though I constantly tease her about it, in this instance her shopping experience proved invaluable. It seems that when we came through Cairo on our way to Africa, she saw a piece of jewelry she liked in the hotel shop. She decided to think about it for a while and took the shop's business card with her. Using that card, she had been able to call the shop, which was able to give her the number of the hotel, which was how she was able to call us late that night from Dar es Salaam. I have to admit this was one time I was really happy she had gone shopping.

In life, obviously not all types of losses are comparable. That particular trip to Uganda, Tanzania and Egypt was perfect in so many ways, despite "losing" Wendy and other silliness; but it ended in great sadness for me. When I walked into our apartment I learned my elderly Mother had died suddenly the night before, while we were on the long flight home. As she was always so interested in my travels, I had especially wanted to share with her the wonderful story about our returning to Uganda exactly 22 years to the month after Idi Amin's coup in January 1971. Timing, as I have learned, is everything.

Jane Goodall visits Lincoln Park Zoo's chimps at the new Great Ape House (May, 1986). Courtesy, Chicago Tribune

Jane the orangutan cuddles her baby before being sent to the San Francisco Zoo. Courtesy, Chicago Park District

HRH Prince Philip pays a visit to Lincoln Park Zoo and the Great
Ape House (Fall 1982). Courtesy, Lincoln Park Zoological Society

Returning from East Africa in 1984—my shaver had broken on safari. Courtesy, Chicago Park District

A Highlands warrior, Papua New Guinea, 1990.

With the Mud Men of Goroka, who coat themselves and their masks with gray clay to perform their spirit dance in the Highlands of Papua New Guinea. (1986).

The few remaining rare black rhinos aren't shy—they're protected from poachers round-the-clock by armed guards (Ngorongoro Crater, Tanzania 1993).

A big male guarding his giraffe kill is all business, as evidence by his cold stare. (South Africa, 1994)

Elephants in camp are a common sight on safari, but this large bull tried to walk through the mess tent—at which point we departed quickly! (Botswana, 1982)

Pygmies of the Ituri Forest welcomed me to their gathering at
Mount Hoyo (Zaire, 1985).

Trekking to see mountain gorillas with Wendy in Rwanda, 1985.

Camping on the Bheri River where we dried our groups' underwear by the fire after their raft capsized and listened to the U.S. Presidential election returns via shortwave radio (Nepal, 1988)

Children dressed for the sing sing at Lakwanda Lodge were as interested in me as I was in them. (Papua New Guinea, 1990).

Astride an elephant with Al Shapiro but without the comfortable houdah (1988, Karnali, Nepal).

# Epilogue

From my apartment in Chicago, I look out across Lake Michigan, and I think about the oceans and rivers I've crossed. My path from the Lincoln Park Zoo has taken me where the animals are—from the Monkey House, the Lion House, and "the Farm in the Zoo" to Africa, India, pools of quicksand, and misty mountaintops.

I remember walking the narrow streets of Bahktapor, Nepal, watching the city come awake, and seeing the people do everything humans can do, right in the street.

I recall watching Wendy, padding barefoot around a mosque in Calcutta, amidst a colony of lepers, and saying, "Mother wouldn't like this—she always told me to wear slippers in hotel rooms, because you couldn't be sure who had walked there."

I think of our ambling among the fearless blue-footed boobies in the Galapagos and the walks we almost couldn't take standing up in Chile, at the incredibly beautiful Torres del Paine National Park, where the wind averaged 40 miles per hour, so we walked hunched over, or not at all and the time I crushed my ankle and had to be airlifted out of Denali (Mt. McKinley) National Park in Alaska.

Today these seem like only blips on the "Fisher Safari" radar screen.

Going on safari took me into a world of wondrous events, crazy experiences, and moments that are now often fun to look back on, but were not always such fun when they were happening. Some were sad, and others were terrifying.

All things considered, I have loved the experiences—*most* of them anyway.

My love of animals has taken me far and away. And I look forward to each new day and to what the next chapter may bring.

# Index

590

**BASEMENT**